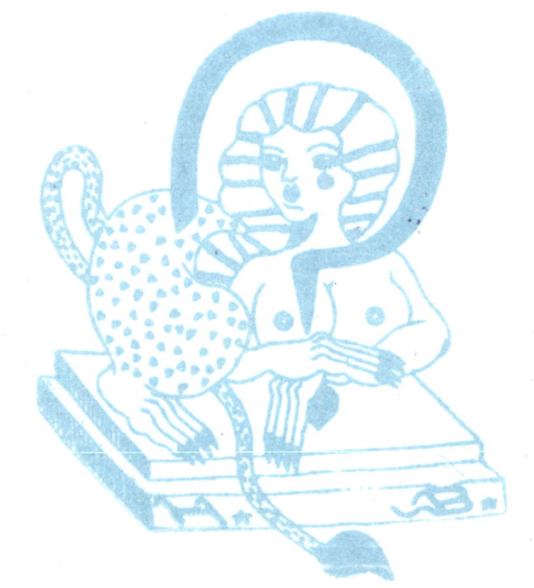

"CAVEGIRL MONOLOGUE"

ISBN: 978-0-9996099-1-0
PUBLISHED BY SACRED BONES BOOKS
FIRST EDITION
1 2 3 4 5 6 7 8 9 10

ALL REQUESTS + CORRESPONDENCE
CAN BE ADDRESSED TO:

SACRED BONES BOOKS
144 N. 7TH STREET #413
BROOKLYN, NY
11249

There are many countless and numbing catastrophes that encase gender disparity, but perhaps the most primitive one is what happens to us as our sexuality blossoms as children. Girls most often begin puberty before boys, leaving us in a physical and mental space where we understand that we can create our own pleasure but that this is a taboo. Our bodies change and this attracts a new kind of gaze, making our stomachs fold whenever we catch men's eyes on the street. We have a vague understanding of what it means, and this is when the word "cringe" makes an emotional and mental equation in its truest form. This will never leave us.

The sexuality of an eleven year old is terrifying, and I have never personally masturbated as much as I did at that age. I'm going to guess roughly that from the age of three we are taught to be scared of our bodies in a way which makes us precautious, that an anonymous fear will transmit our entire being for as long as we live and our erogenous zones will eventually harm us — not because we have done anything wrong, but because others cannot control themselves around us.

This banal but painful reality creates a hysteria where our ability to orgasm must be kept secret—especially from other girls our age, who are disgusted by anyone other than eligible men touching our labia, but not necessarily being aware that a clitoris exists. Wanking, as British people like to call it, or Masturbation, Jerking Off, Fingering etc. is deemed an unsavory and dirty activity for the feminine until we reach the end of our adolescence, where sexual exploration is deemed cool. The vagina will never cease to terrify.

Hormones are real, and as a twelve year old my fingers regularly resembled wet apricots as I made any excuse at school in any lesson which involved numbers to go make myself cum in the bathroom. A new form of humanity evolves from learning how to orgasm, a feral freedom from control and scheduled activity. A female orgasm cannot be tamed, because a female orgasm is pure independence from the rules we did not choose to obey, but rather have to, so that we can remain safe.

Of course, once we start fucking other people, letting others touch our cunts, our emotional well-being becomes compromised. The romantic and the intellectual battle one another, and we begin to undress from notions of saving our shame. All too often the emotional and the carnal explode into a chasm of ego destruction as our expectations for men shrivel before they can ever bloom. We are born sensual but taught to accept the penis's commands as the Holy Grail.

Female sexuality is of course still neglected—still a playground for men to explore with their rigid movements and adoration of the "soft, female form." Our only way of visualizing our desires is still constructed by the shallow pokes of male fingers and mechanical thrusts that limit the potential of the almighty wave.

Heather Benjamin's work encapsulates all of the power of female ecstasy—a pleasure which rejects the expected and lavishes in the many contradictions of our naked potential. Her depictions of sex organs are not pre-pubescent and tidy, but instead capable of a phantasmagoric potential we are tricked into thinking doesn't exist.

Luckily, DIY culture, underground comics, and punk have been fertile environments for the uncomfortable to emerge, and Benjamin's work takes center stage in the progression of this essential art form. Her vision transports us through the endless style of punk women and their attitude from the tough chic of the Hernandez Brother's *Love and Rockets* women and the unapologetic depiction of vulvas in Melinda Gebbie's underrepresented work, to the sternness of Russ Meyer's women, showing it is not just graphic art of which Benjamin's work carries the bastion.

There is no progression without discomfort, and Benjamin's vision of untamed femininity reverberates into a part of our psyche we are conditioned into quieting. Sexual freedom is a concept sold to us and then experienced without the electrifying purity it really should shoot through us. Her figures of unrestrained desire show us females who have not been tamed into acceptable yet futile expressions of lust, and with that her work frees us. The most important culture creates evolutionary possibility to inspire greater human potential, and this is exactly what Benjamin's work does: it takes the prickly subject of the very process that quite literally creates us—female sexuality—and then discards it from the sterile pleasantries that so often cocoon its representation and makes it wet, hard, wild, and liberatingly unrestrained.

by Reba Maybury

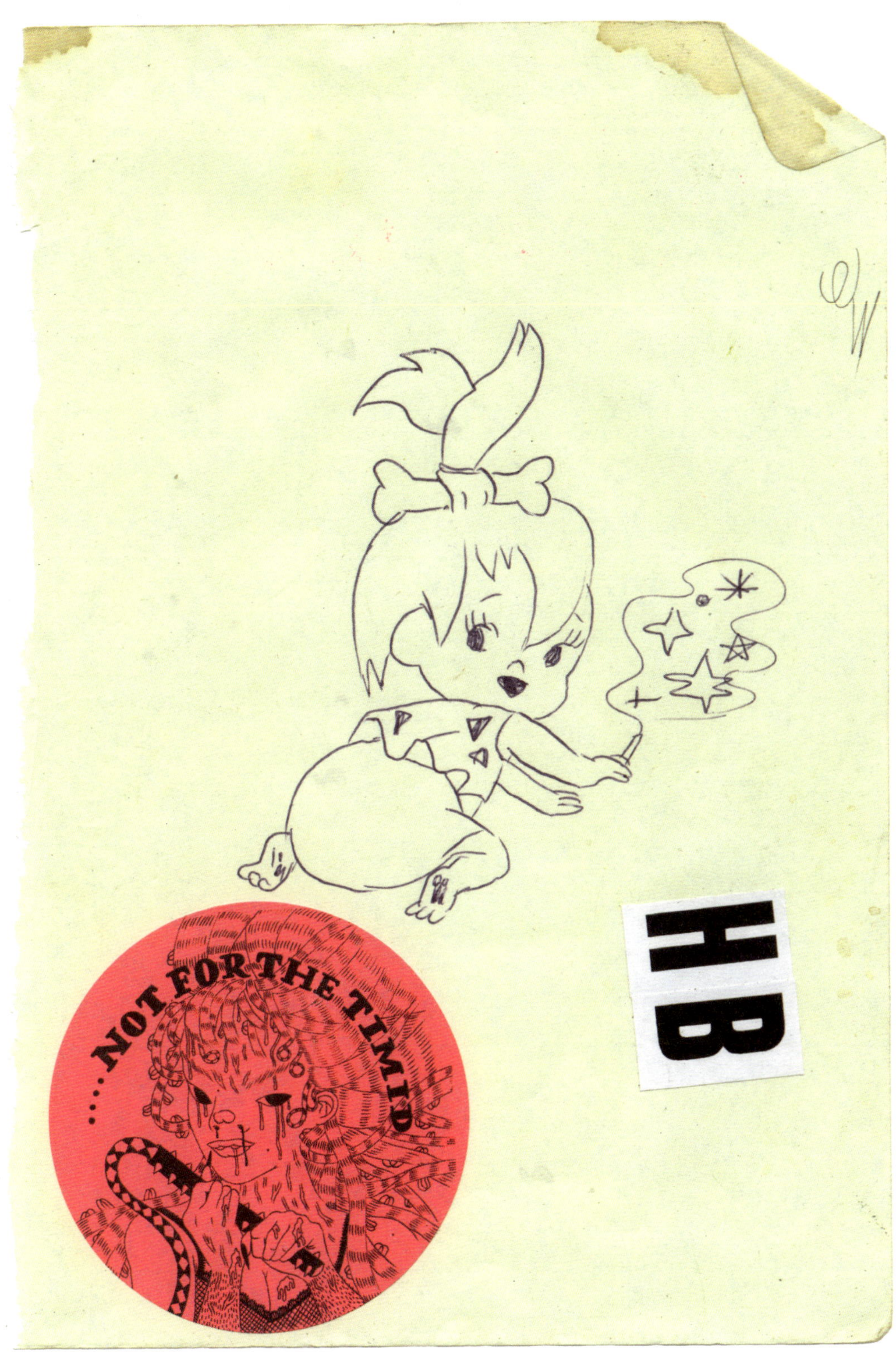

....NOT FOR THE TIMID
HB

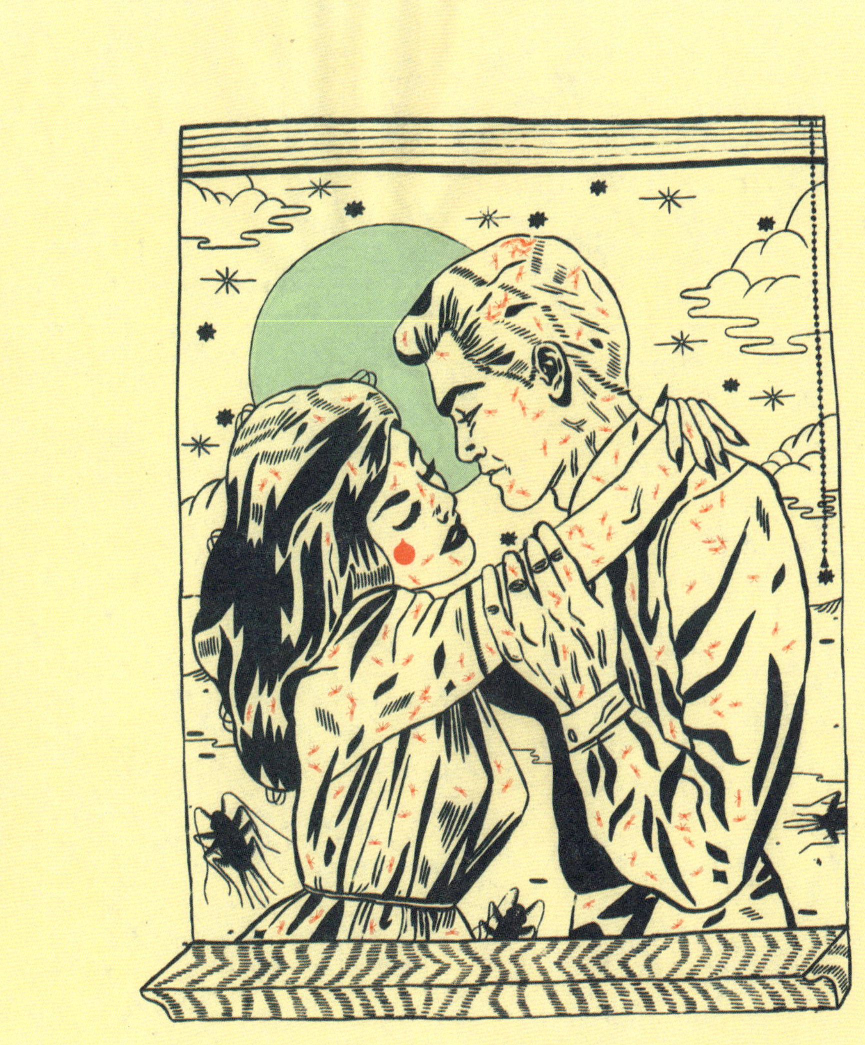

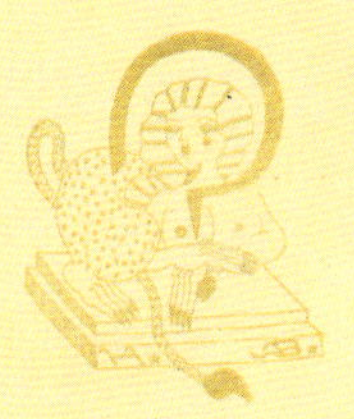

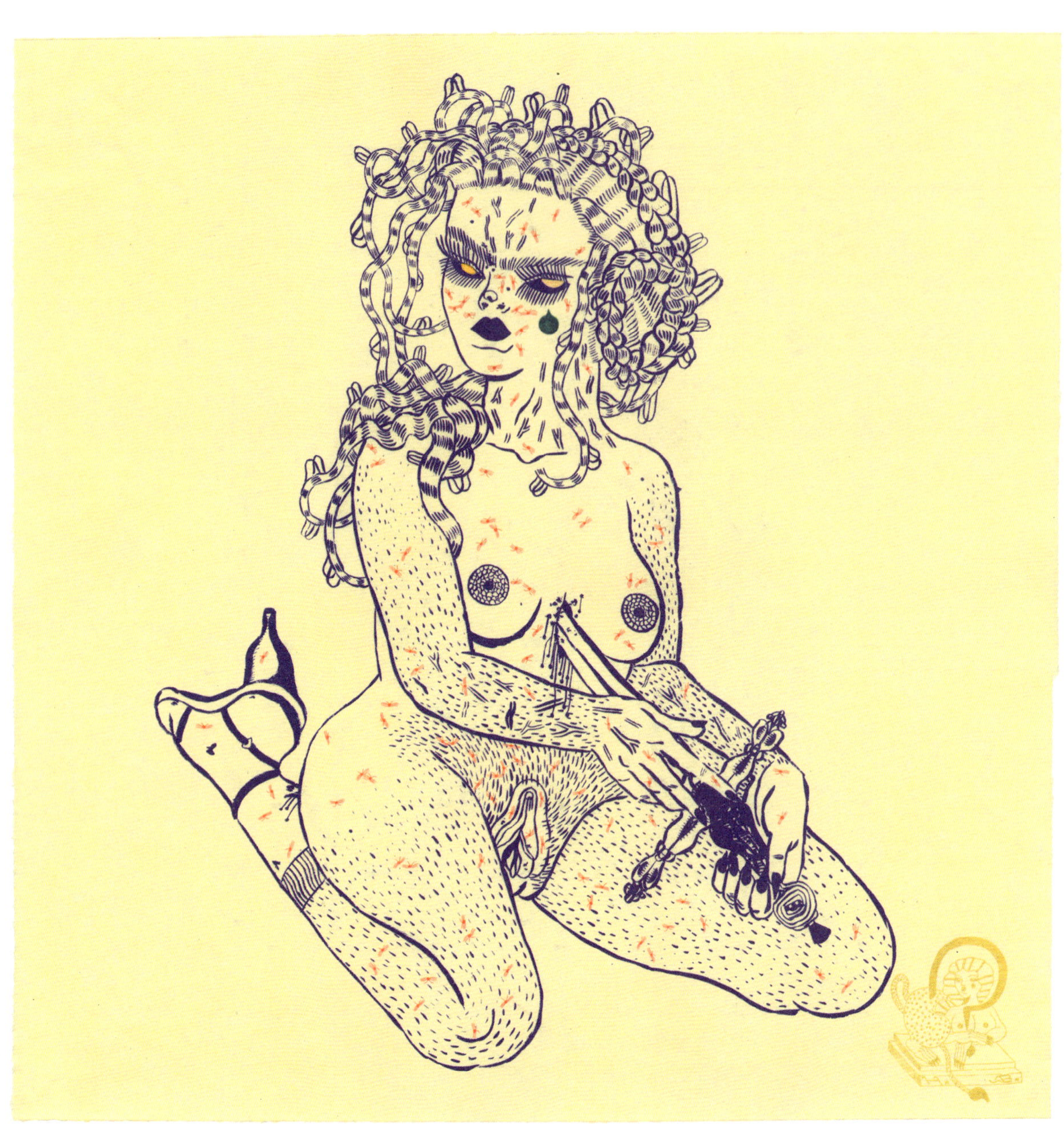

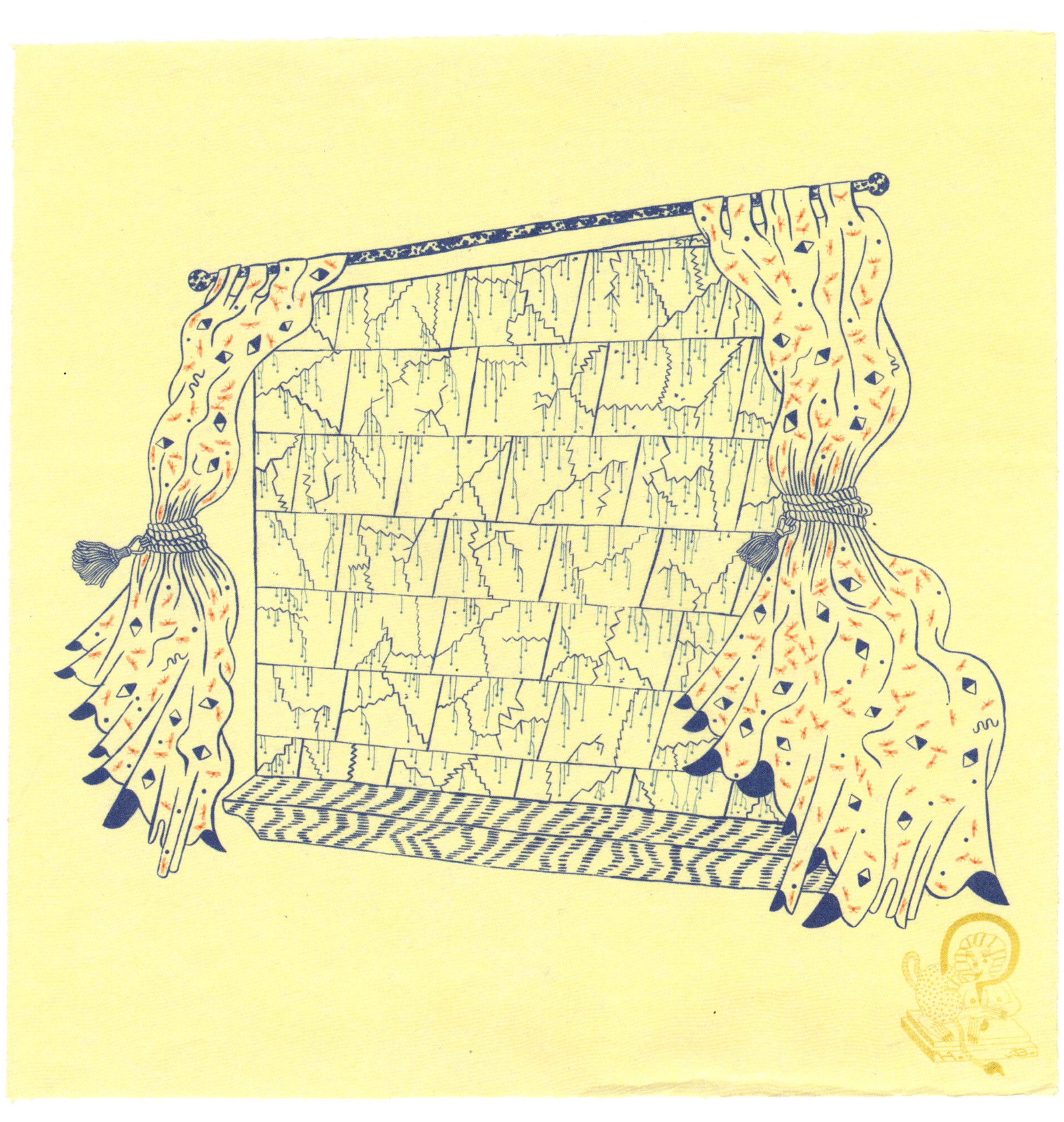

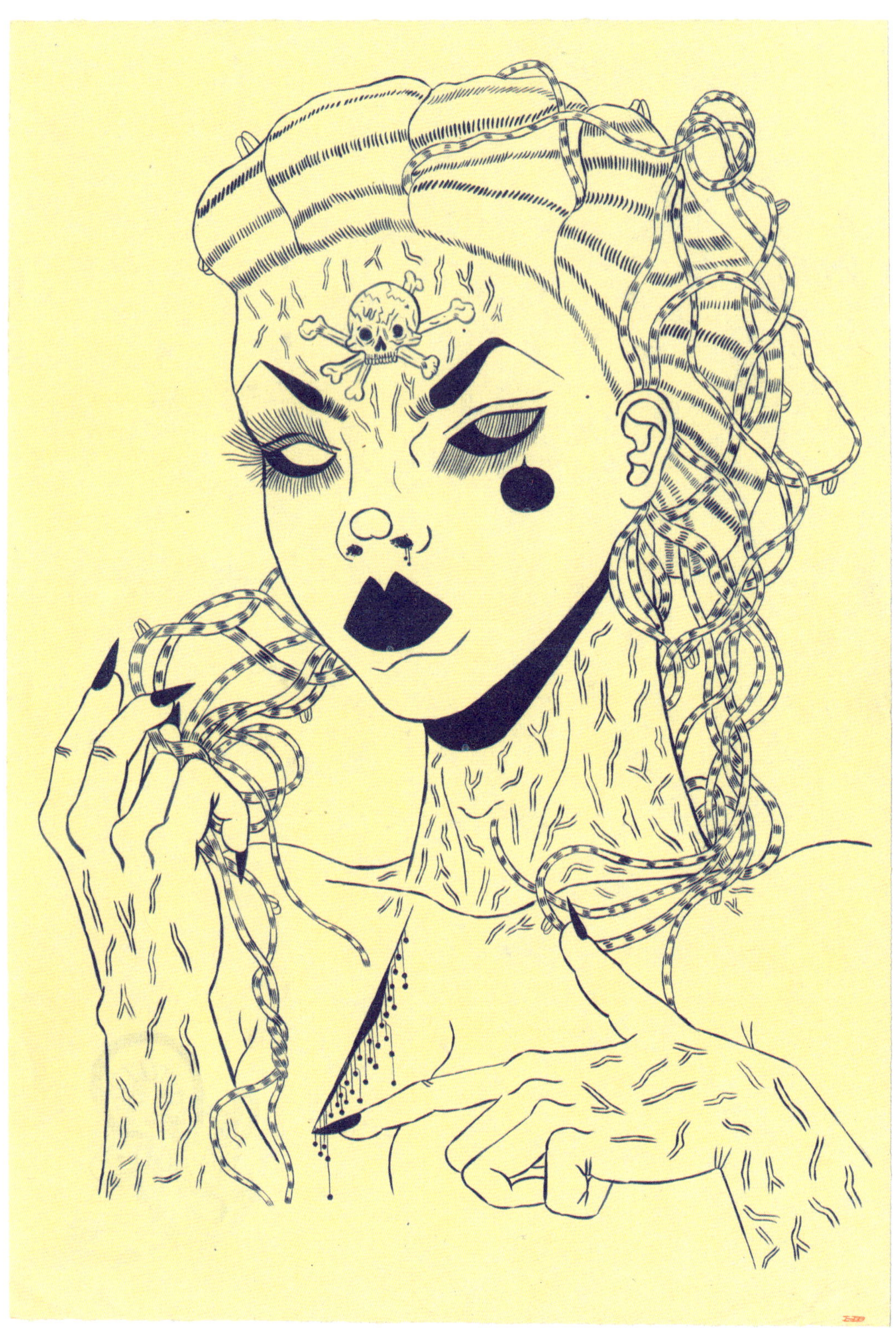

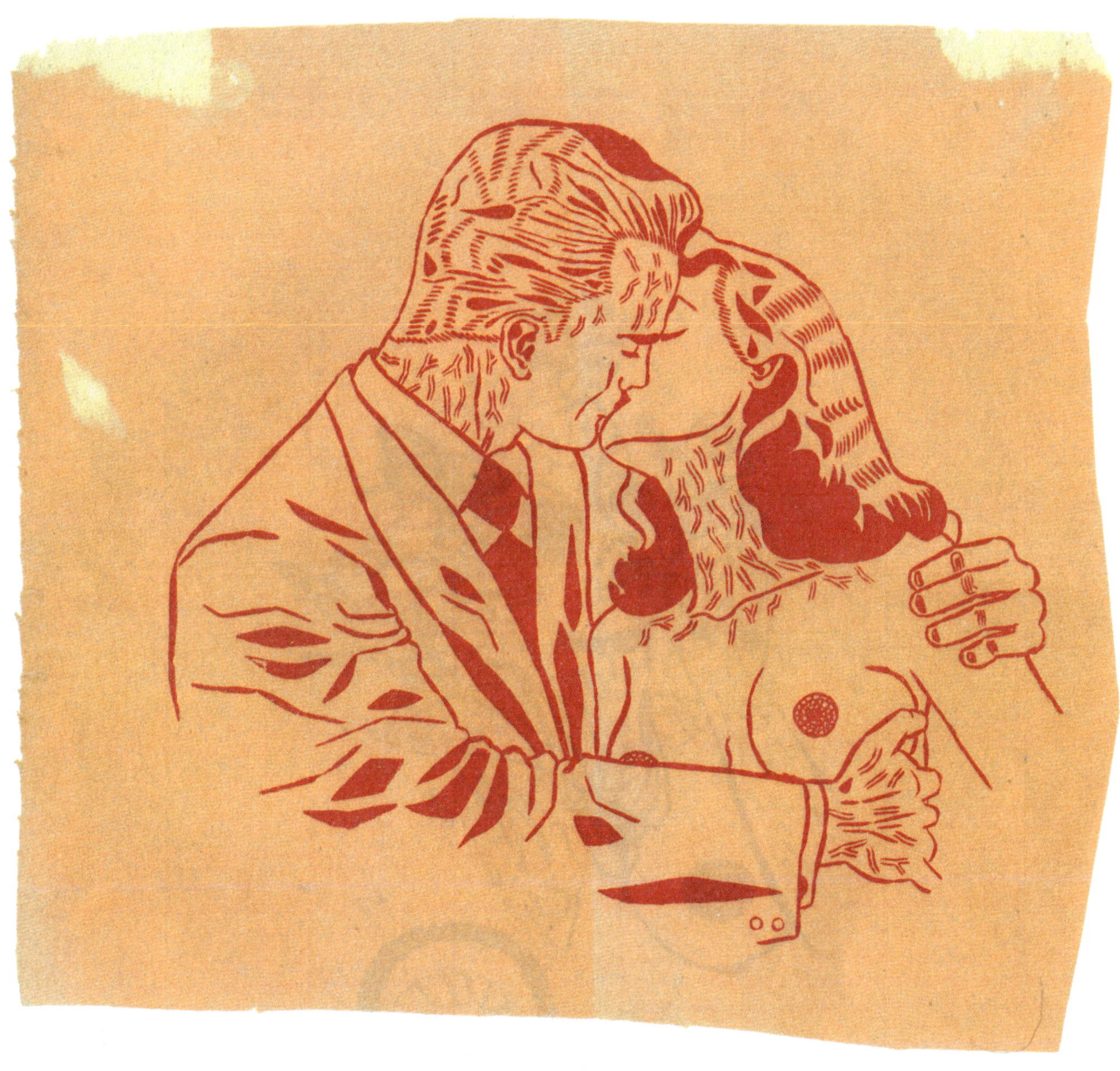

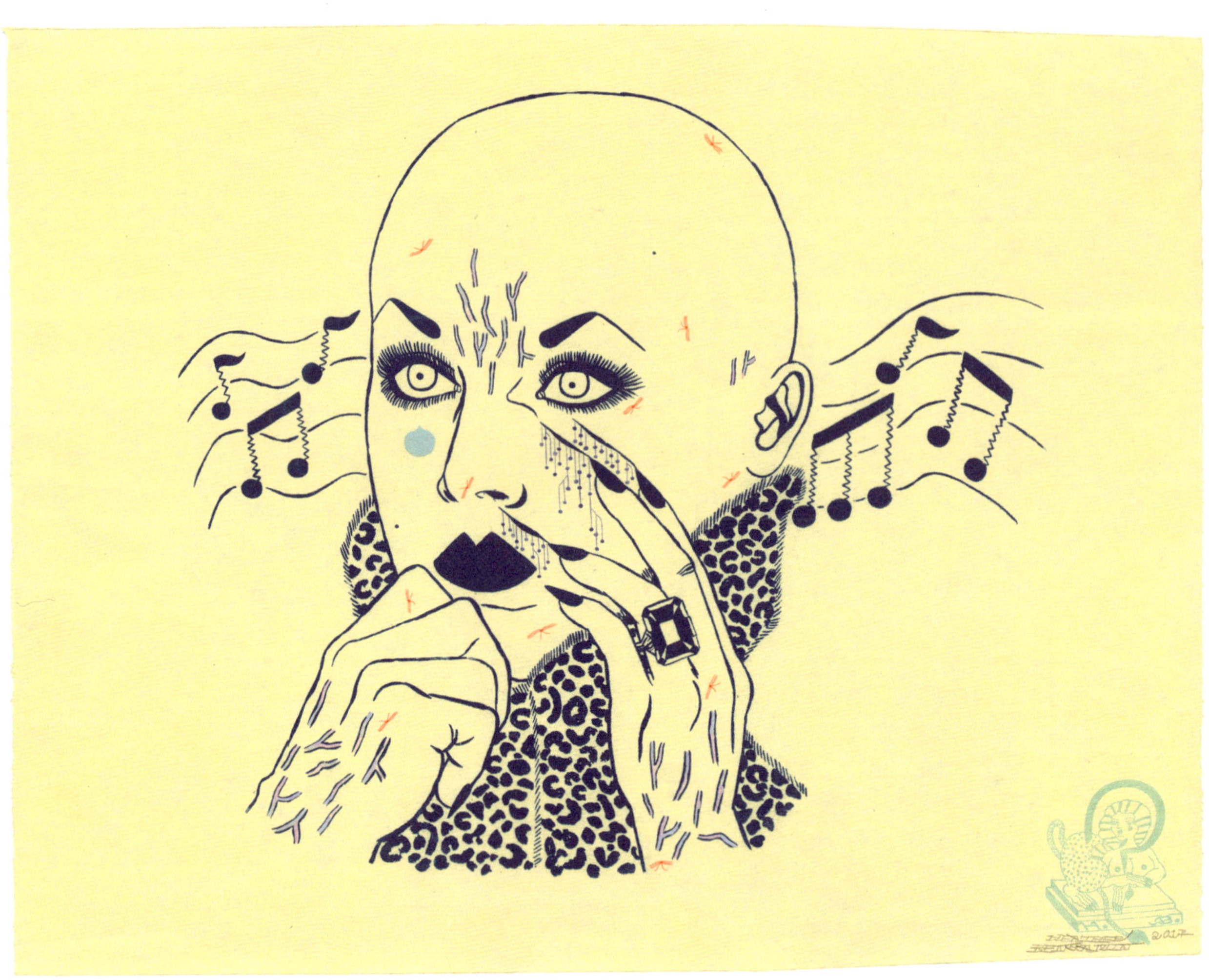

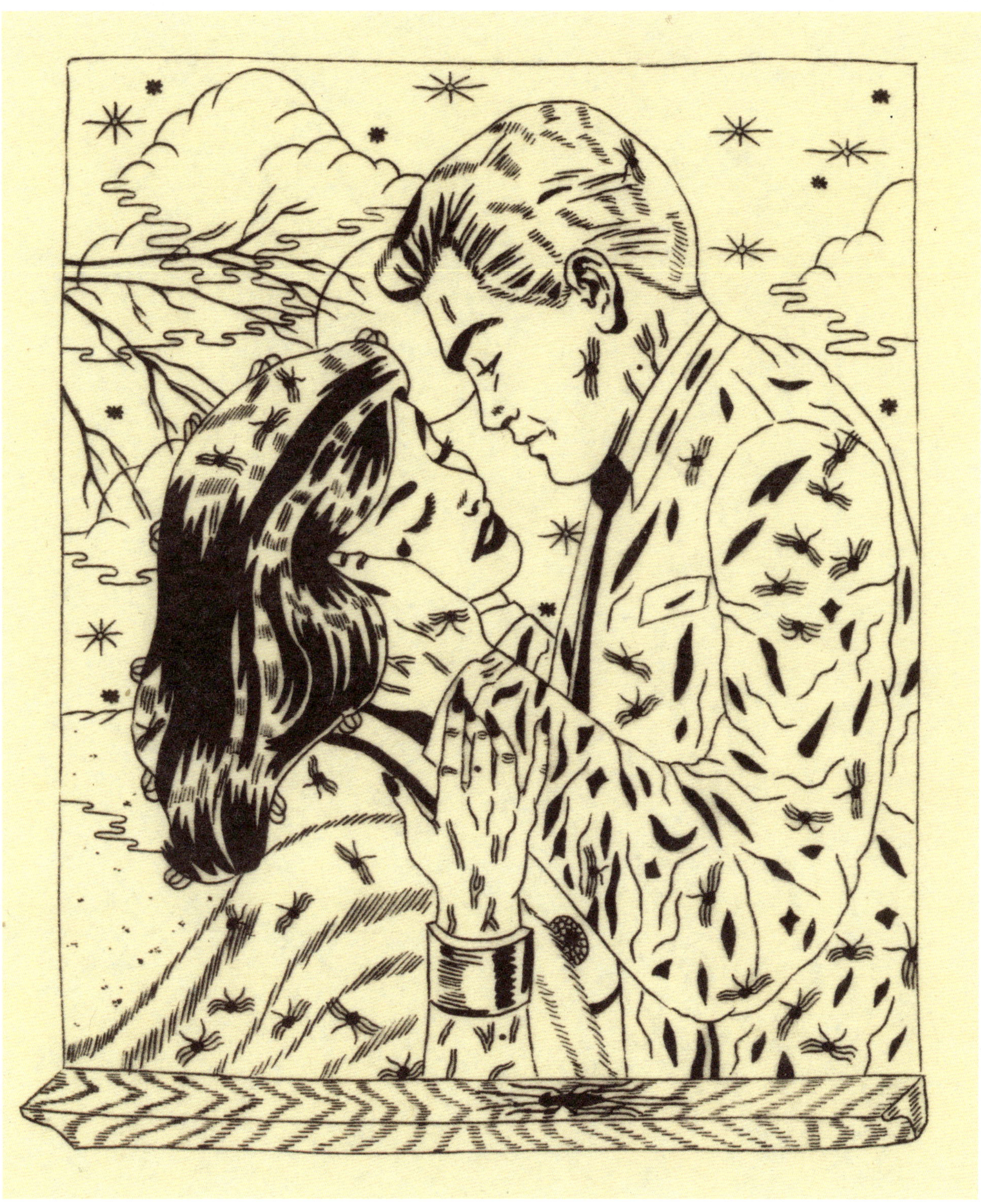

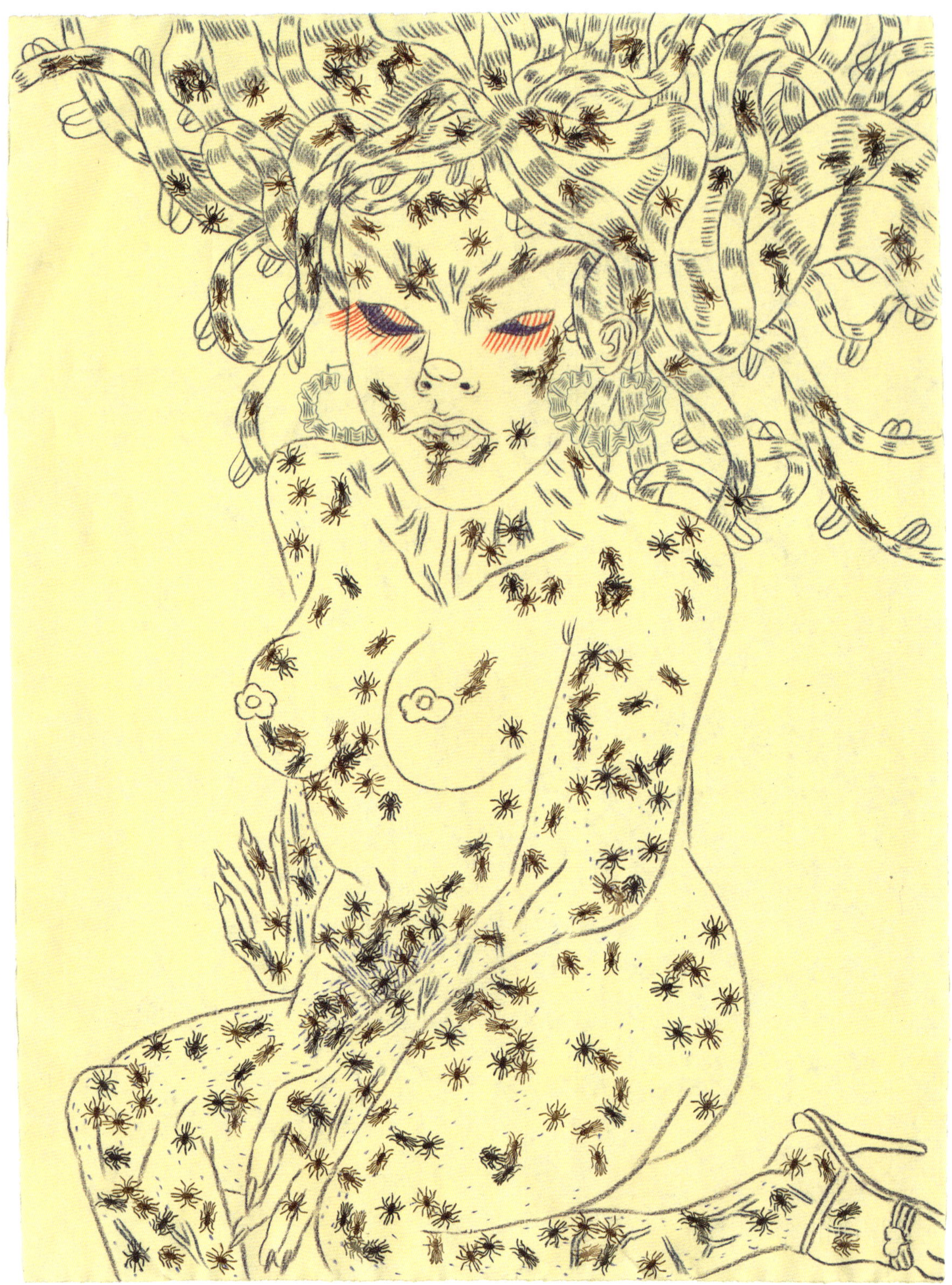

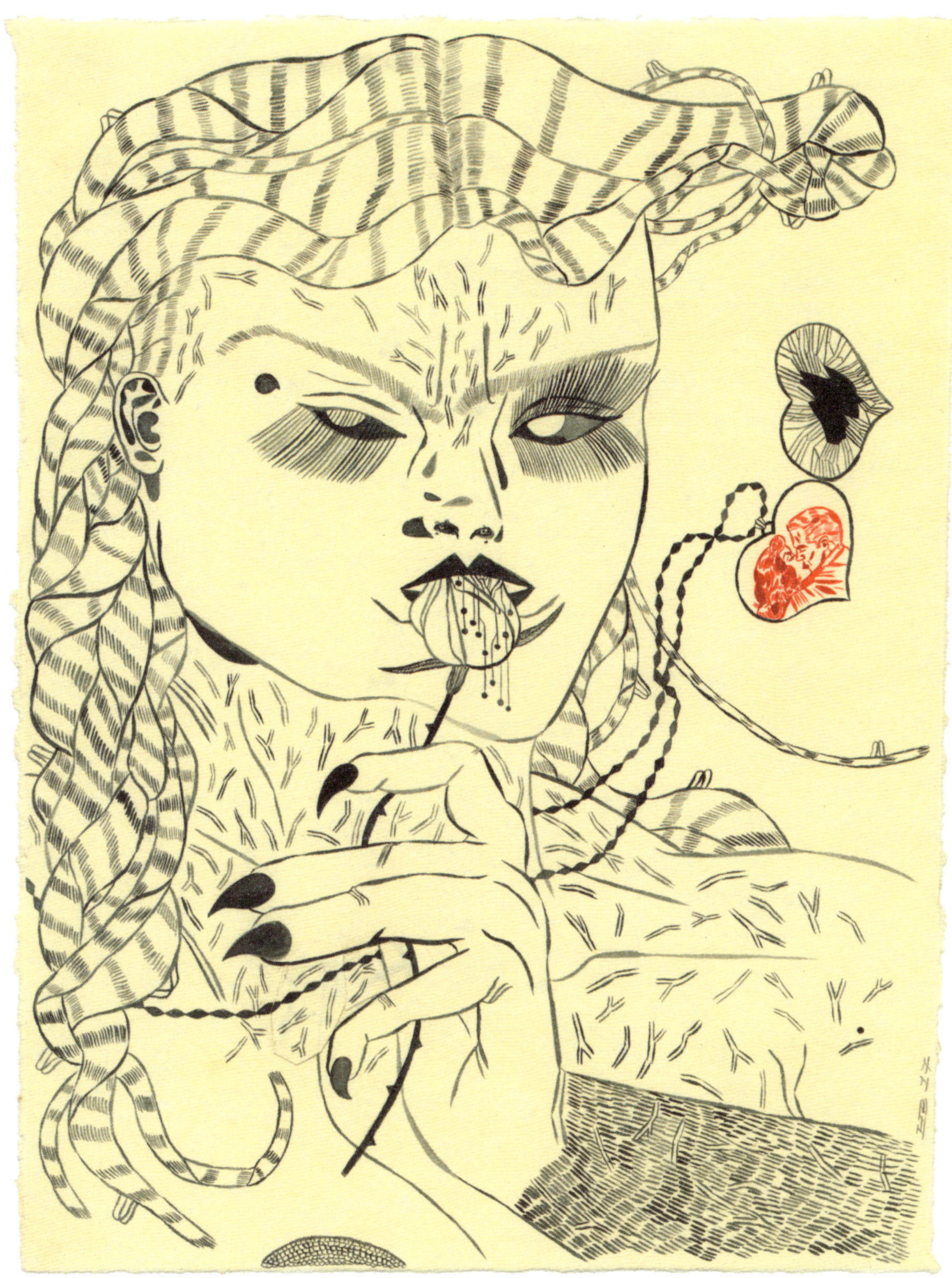

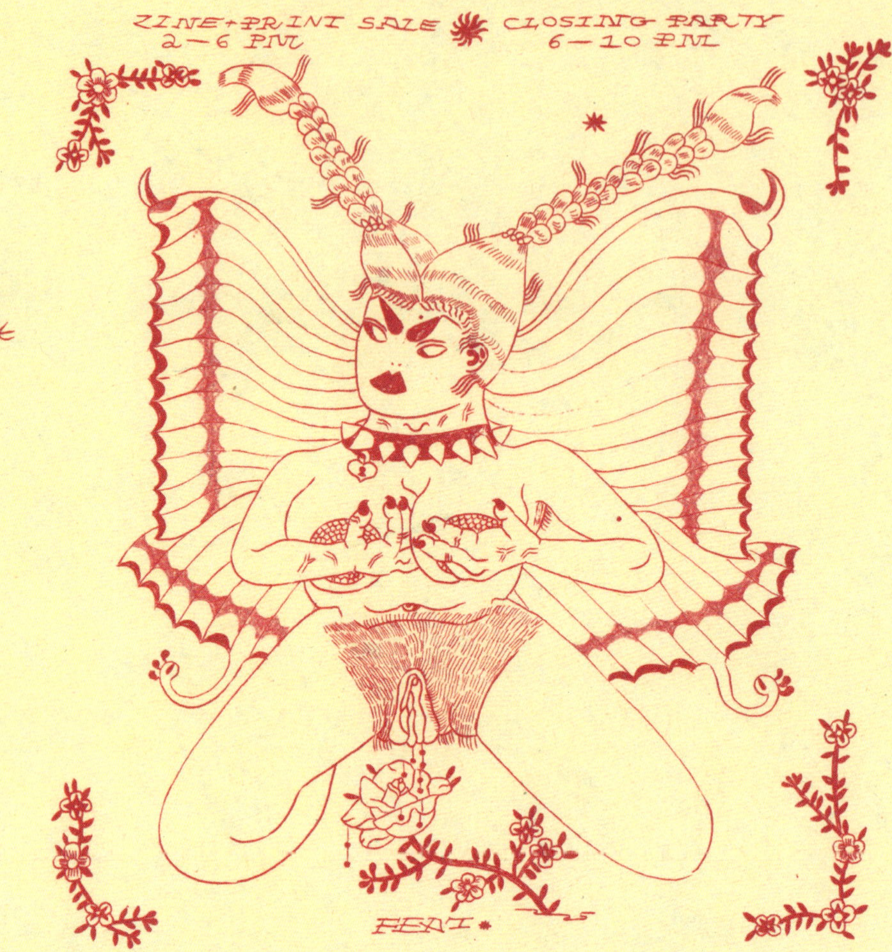
"DEATH OF A TAIL"
NEW WORK BY HEATHER BENJAMIN
THURSDAY 1/18/18
ZINE + PRINT SALE   CLOSING PARTY
2 — 6 PM   6 — 10 PM
FENI
MELODIES BY   NATURAL WINES   FLOWERS
DJ TAEER   BY RACHEL A.   BY SARA
ABRUNA
DRESS SHOP GALLERY
322 TROUTMAN ST.

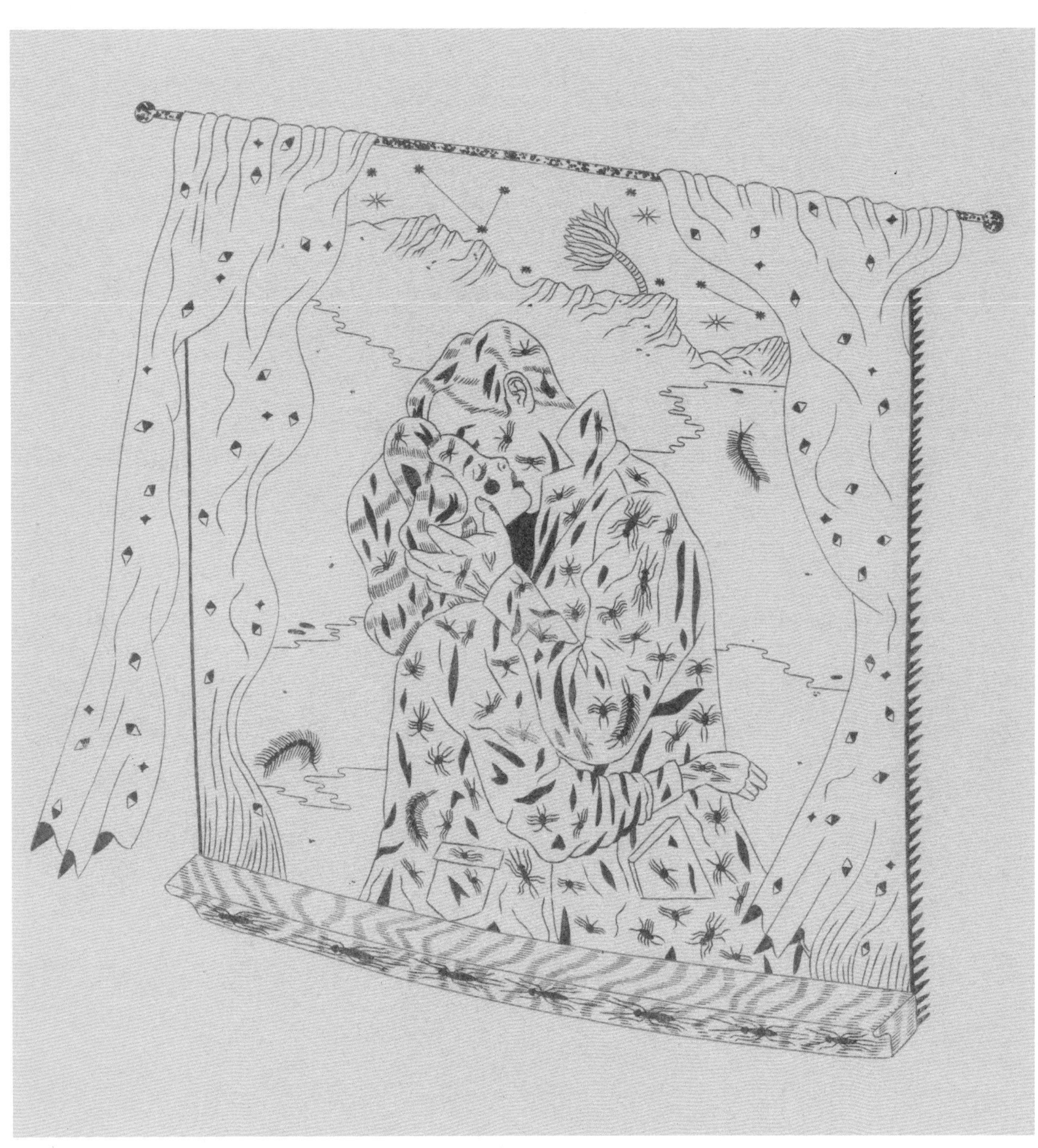

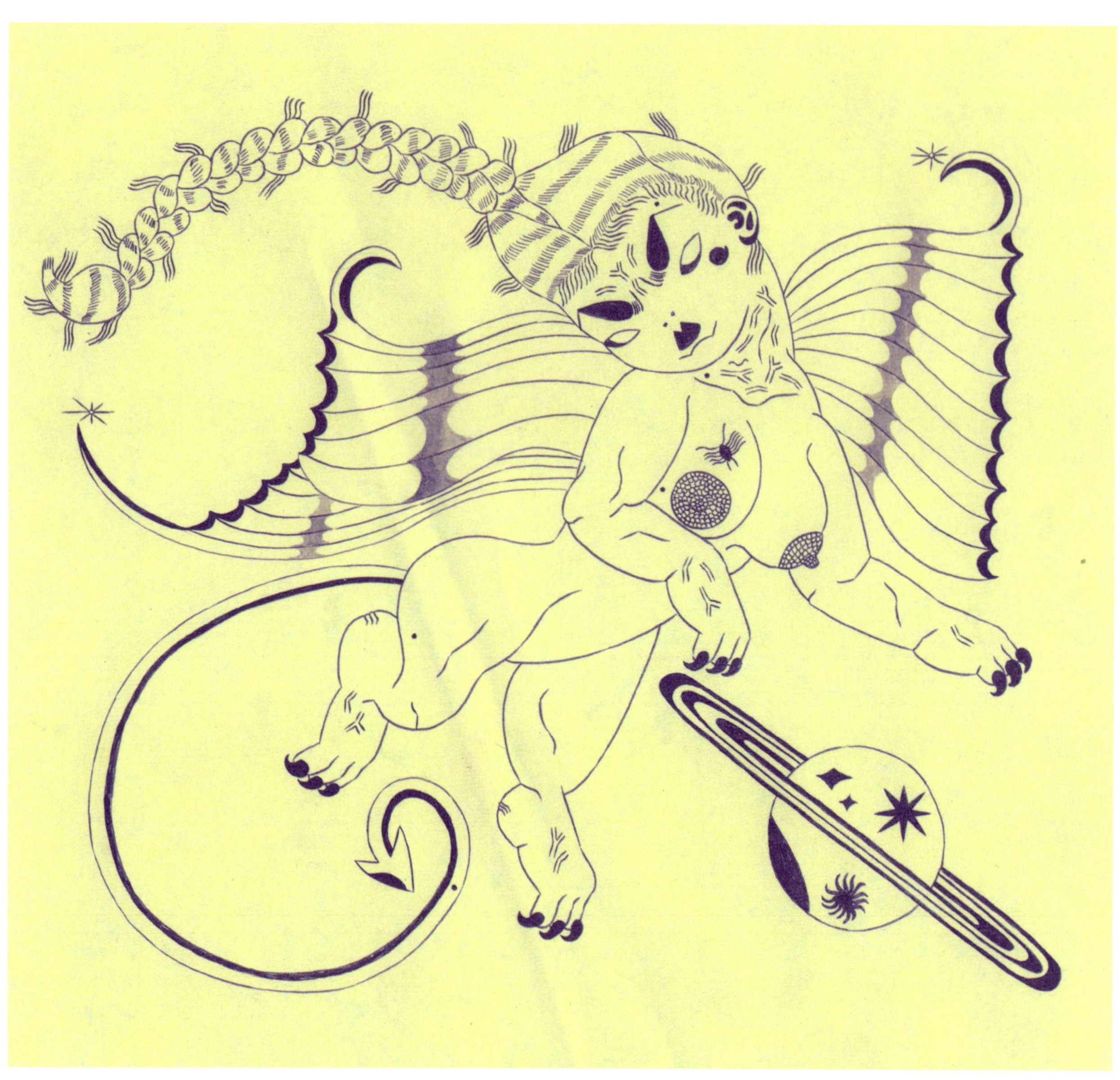

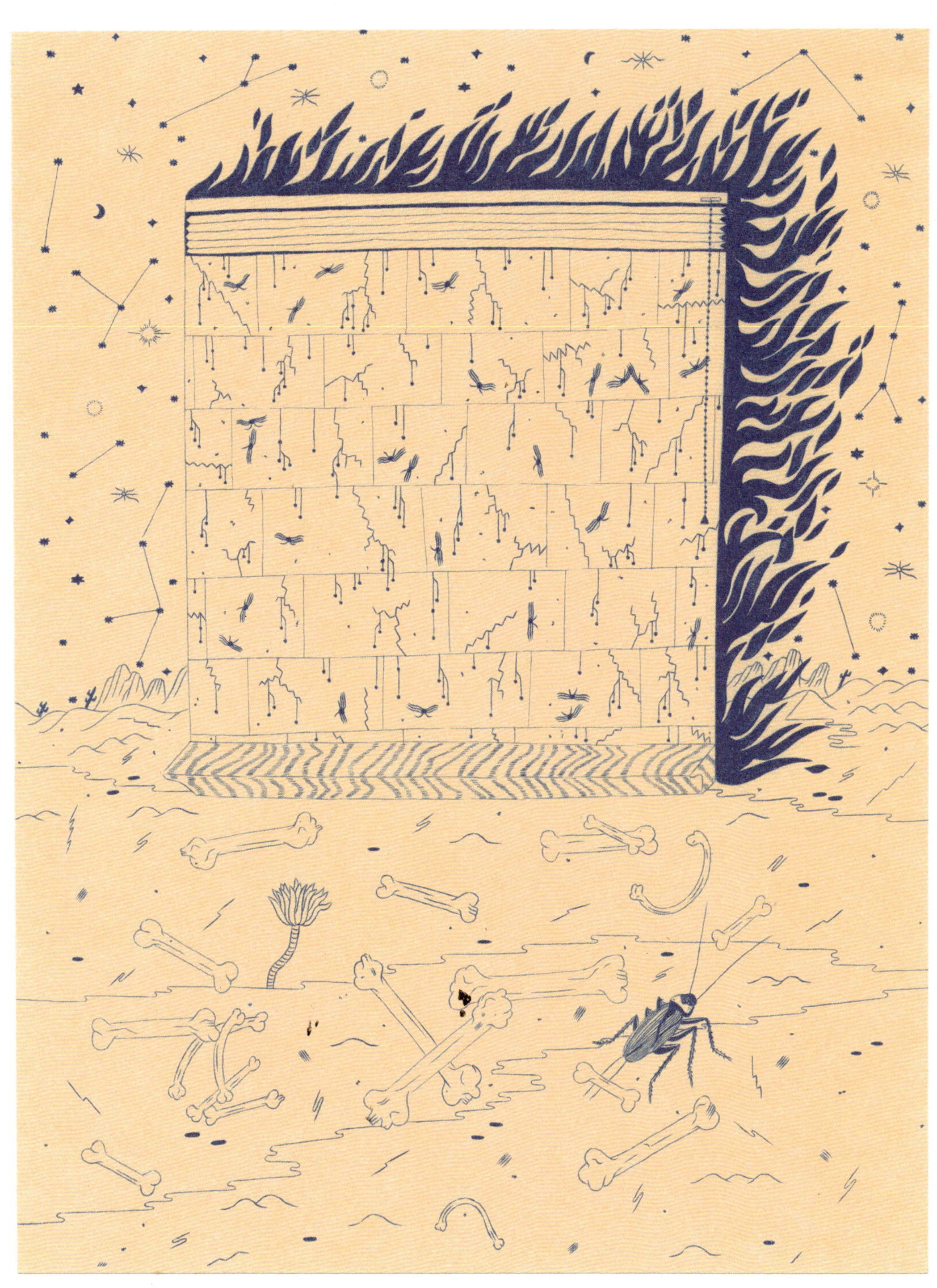

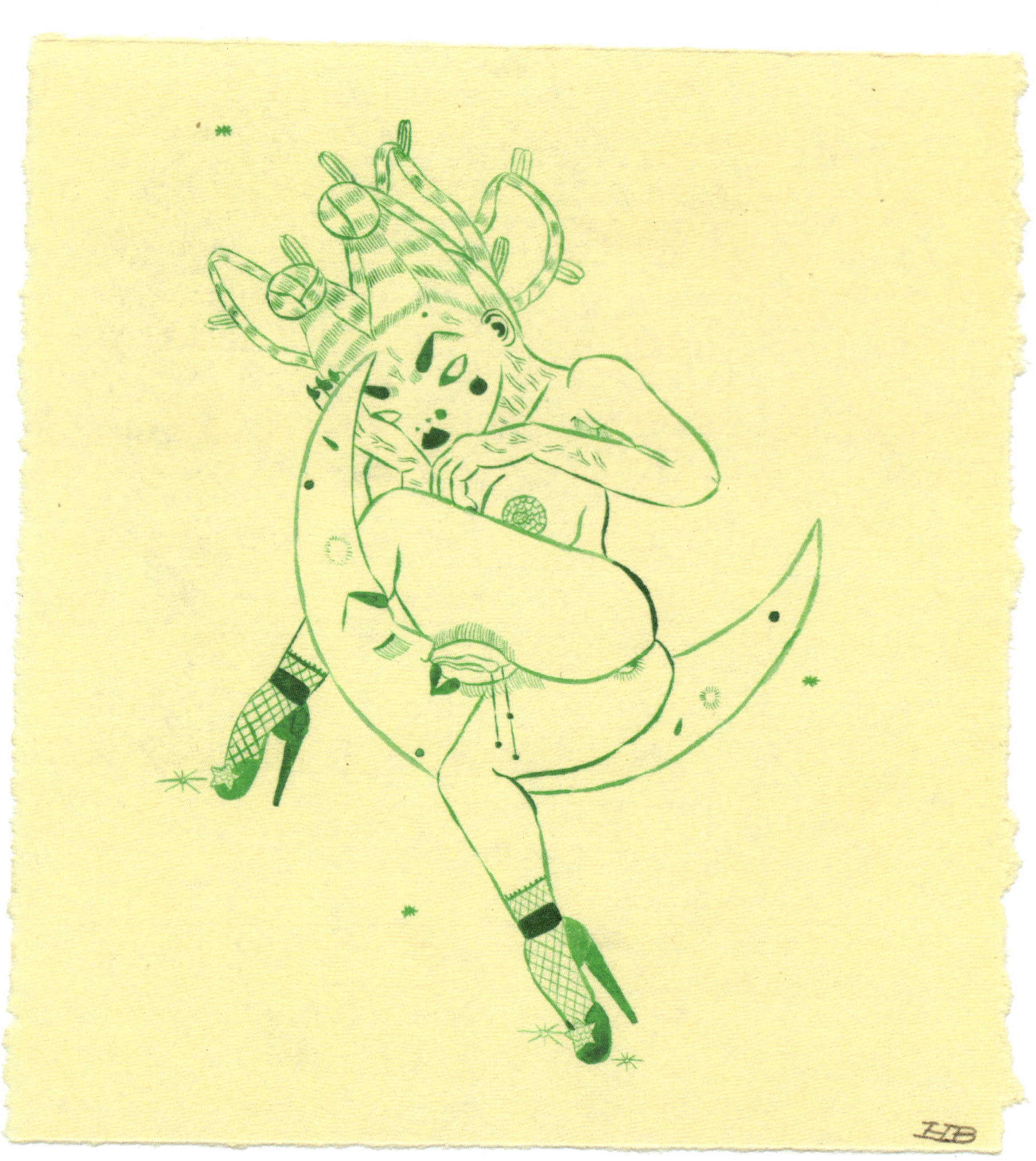

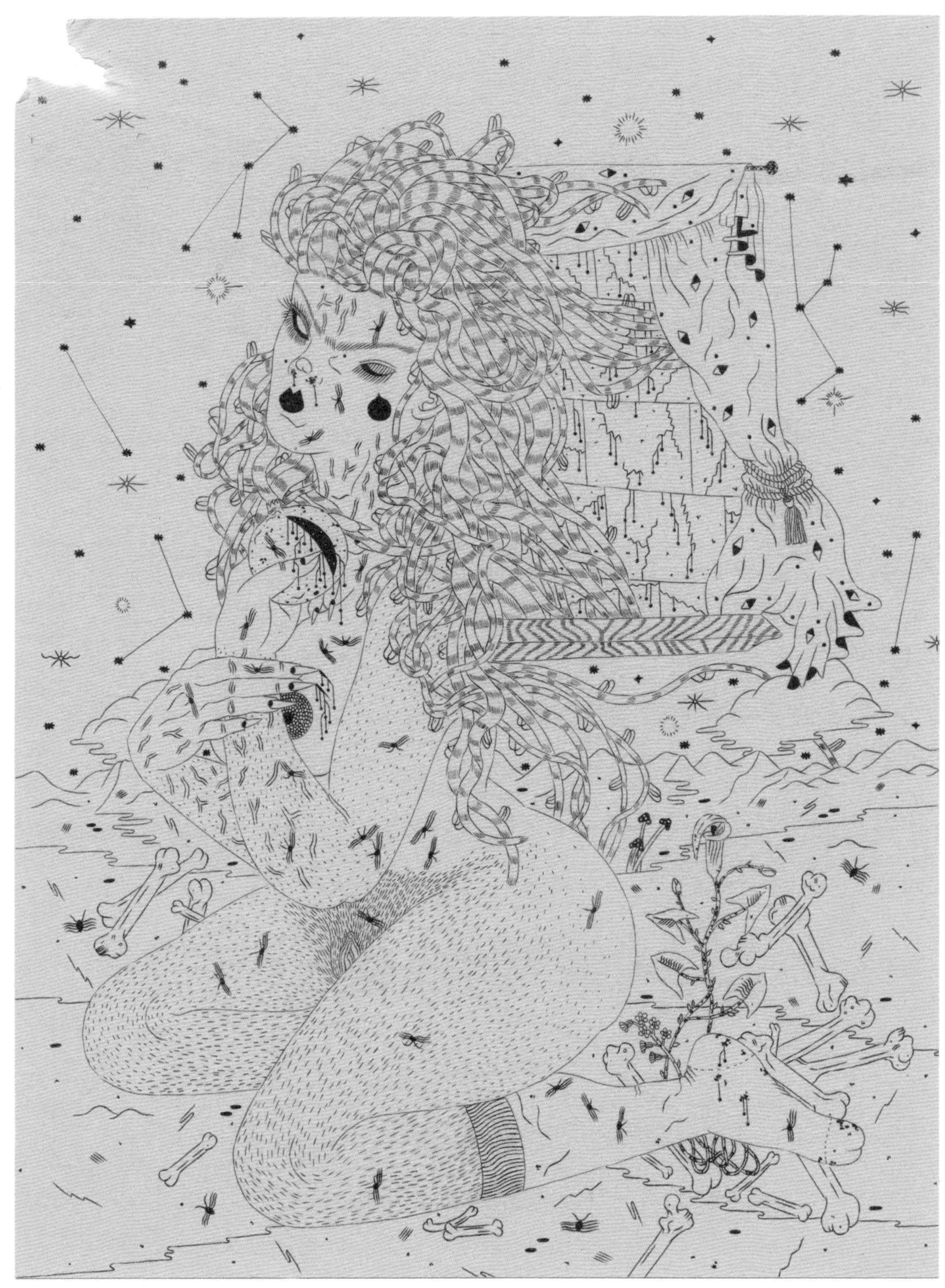

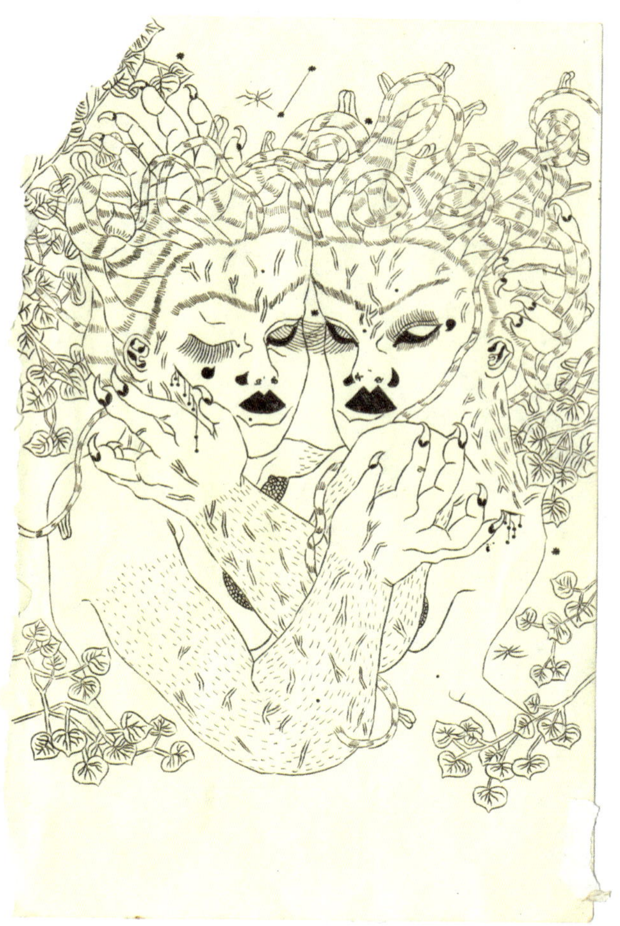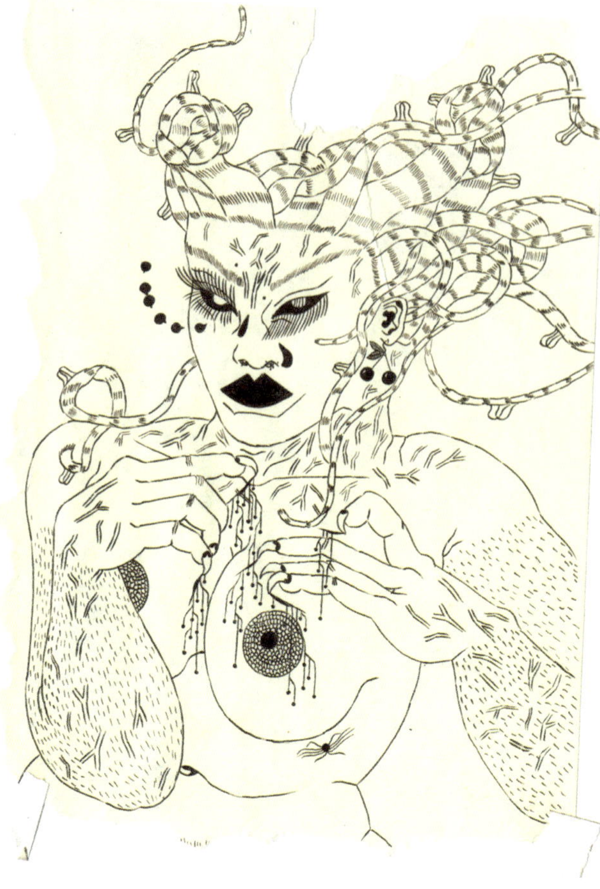

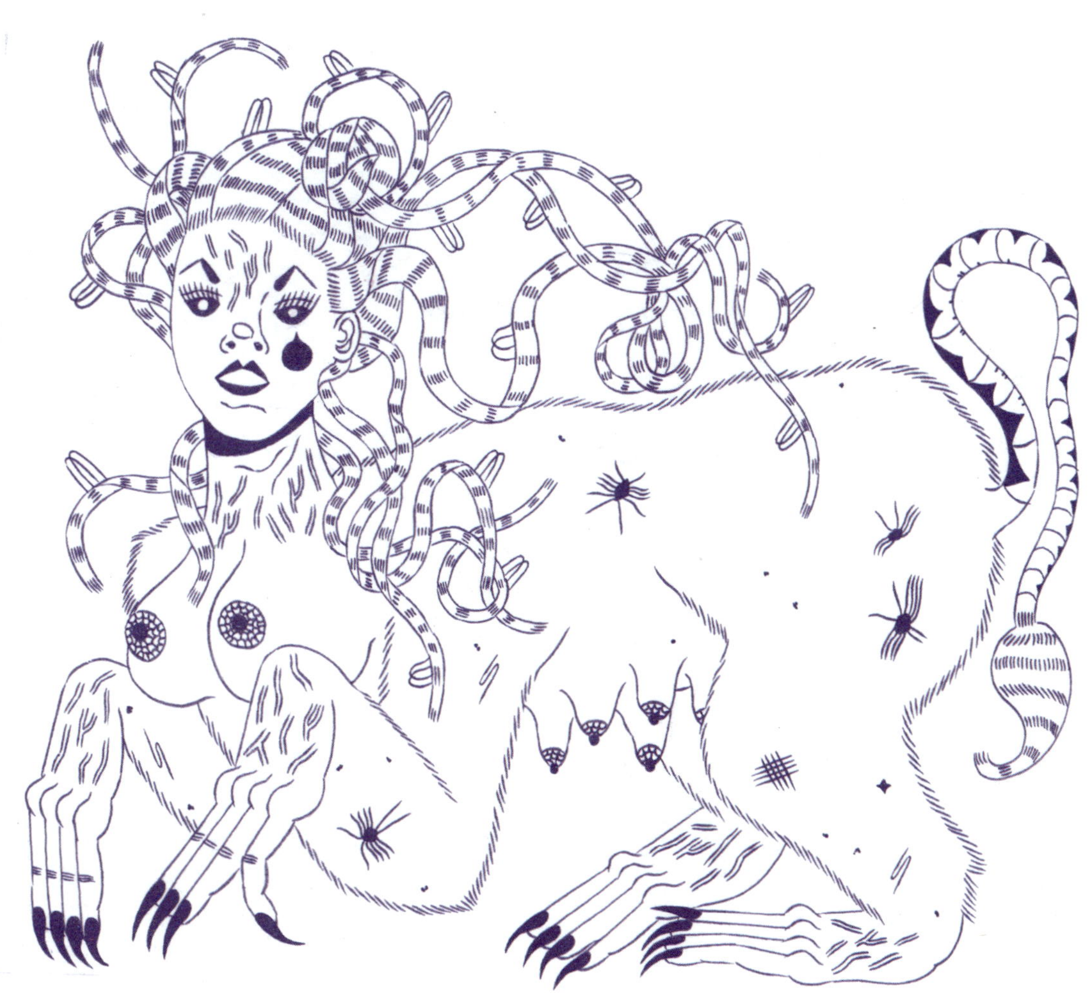

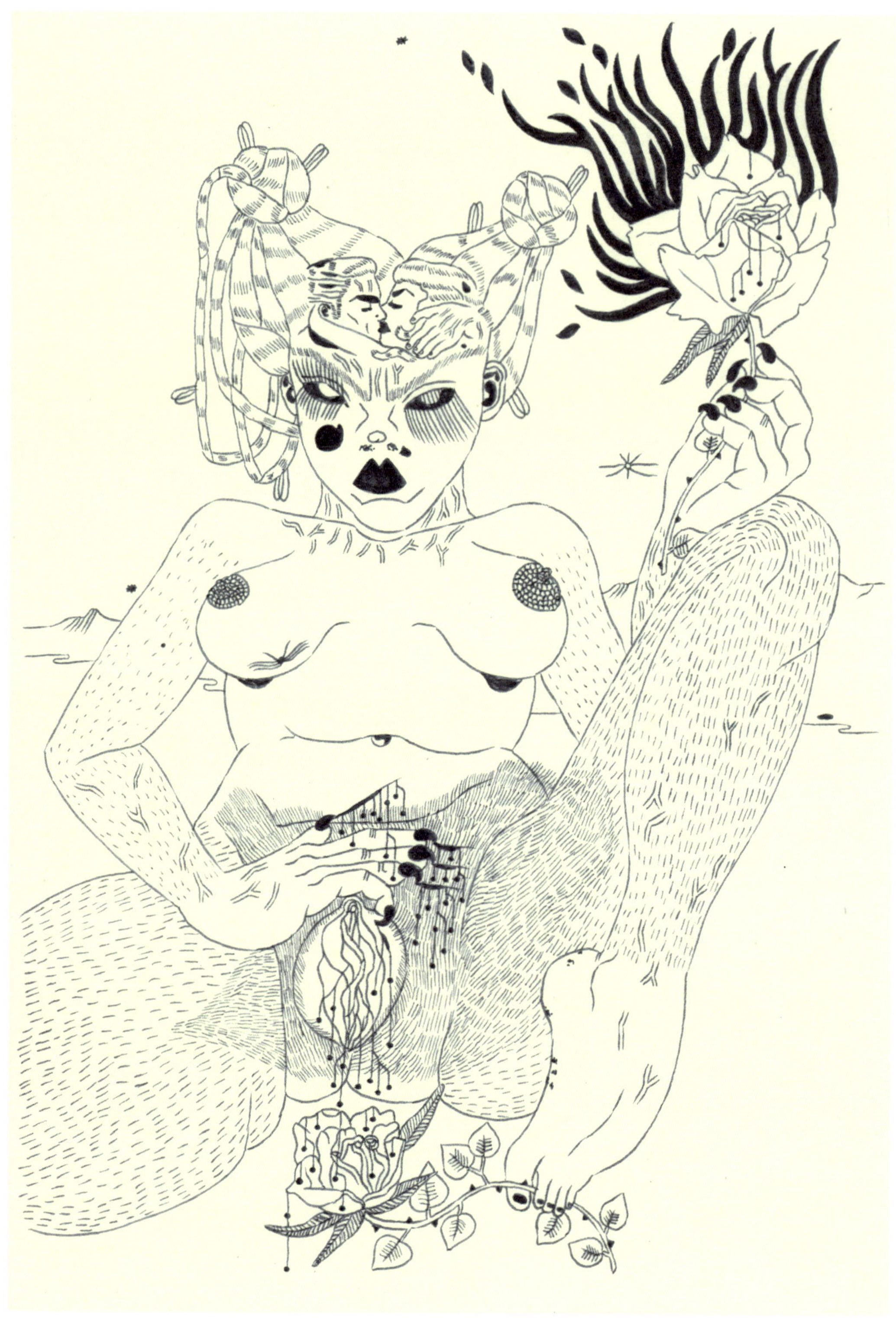

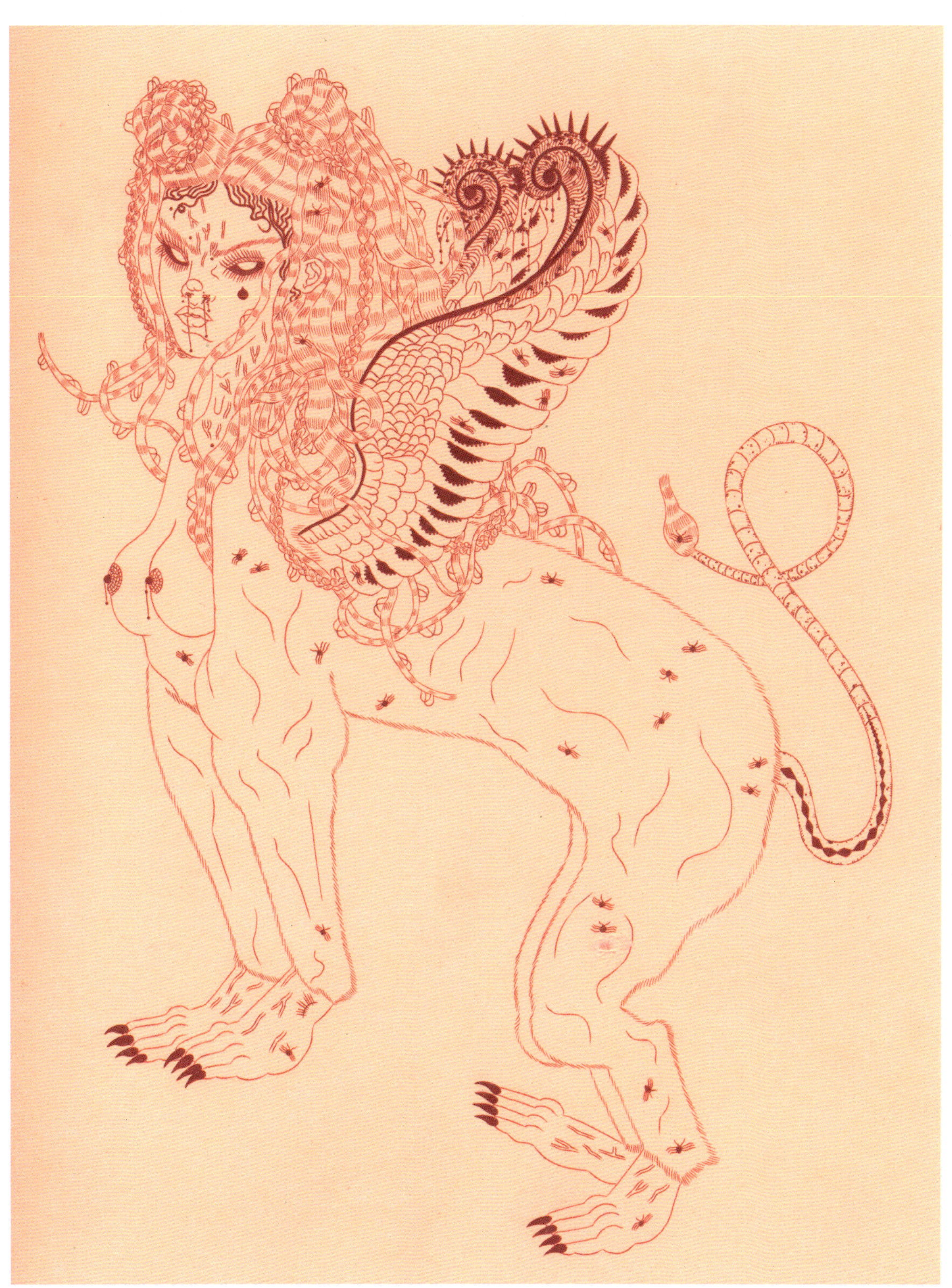

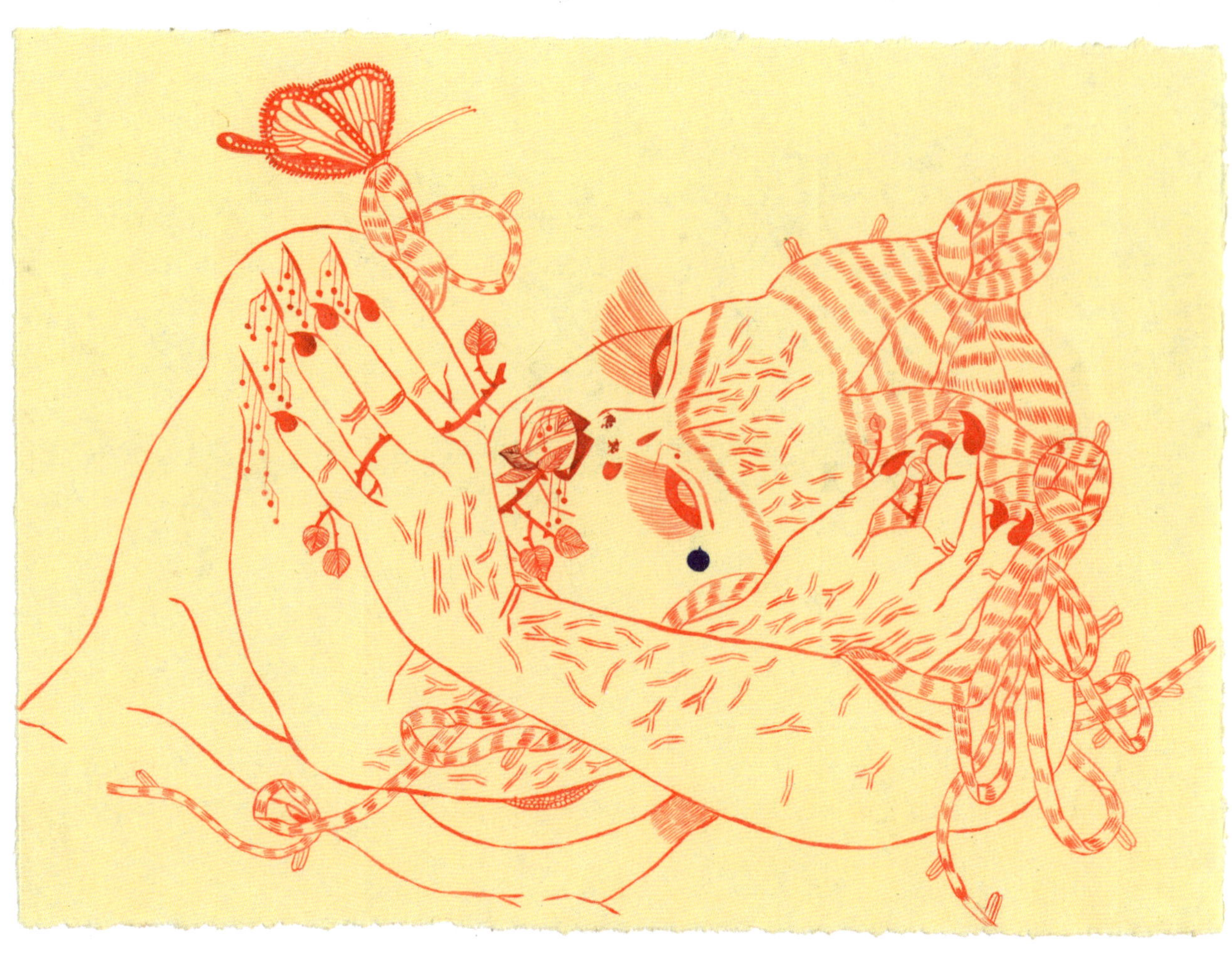

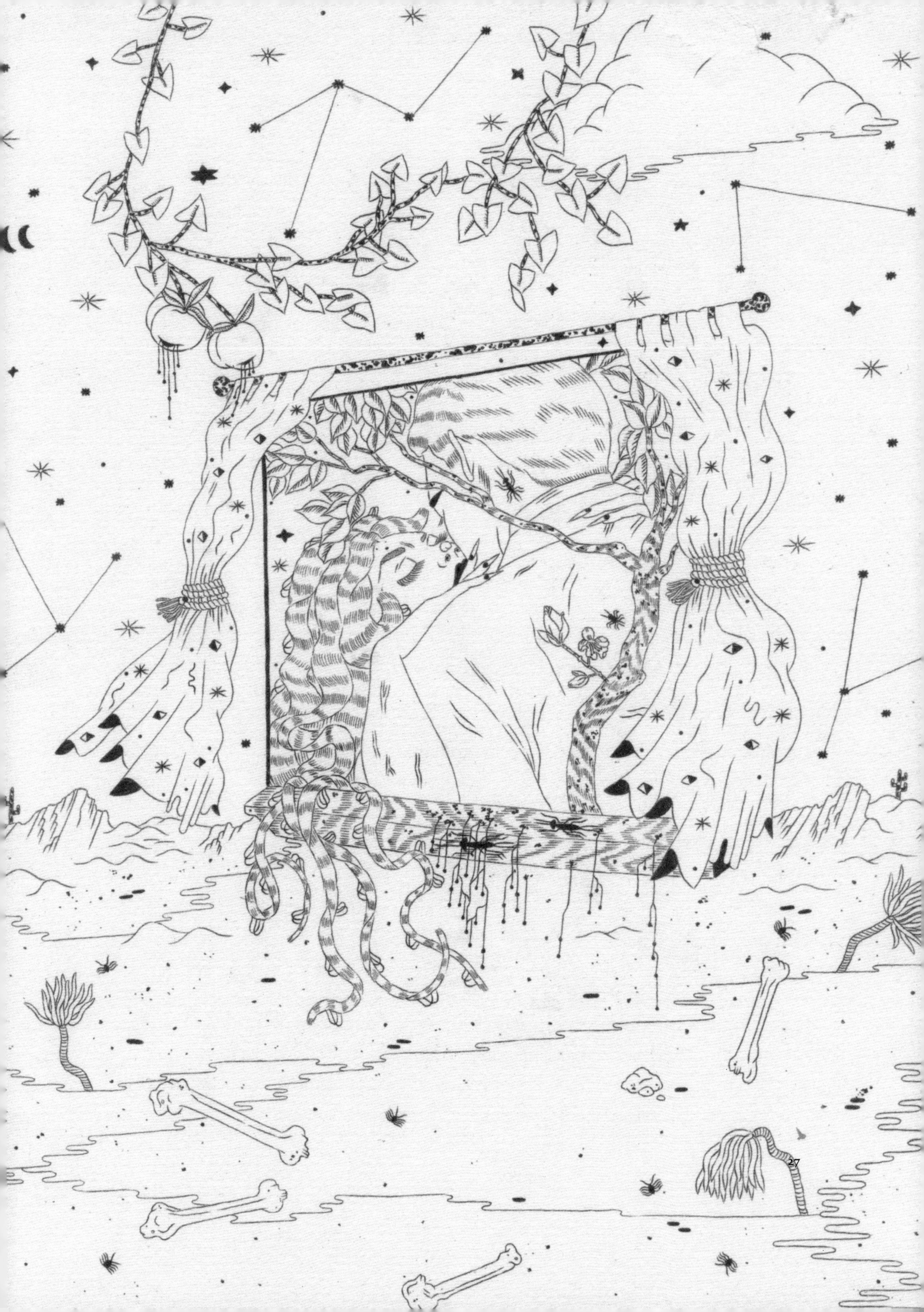

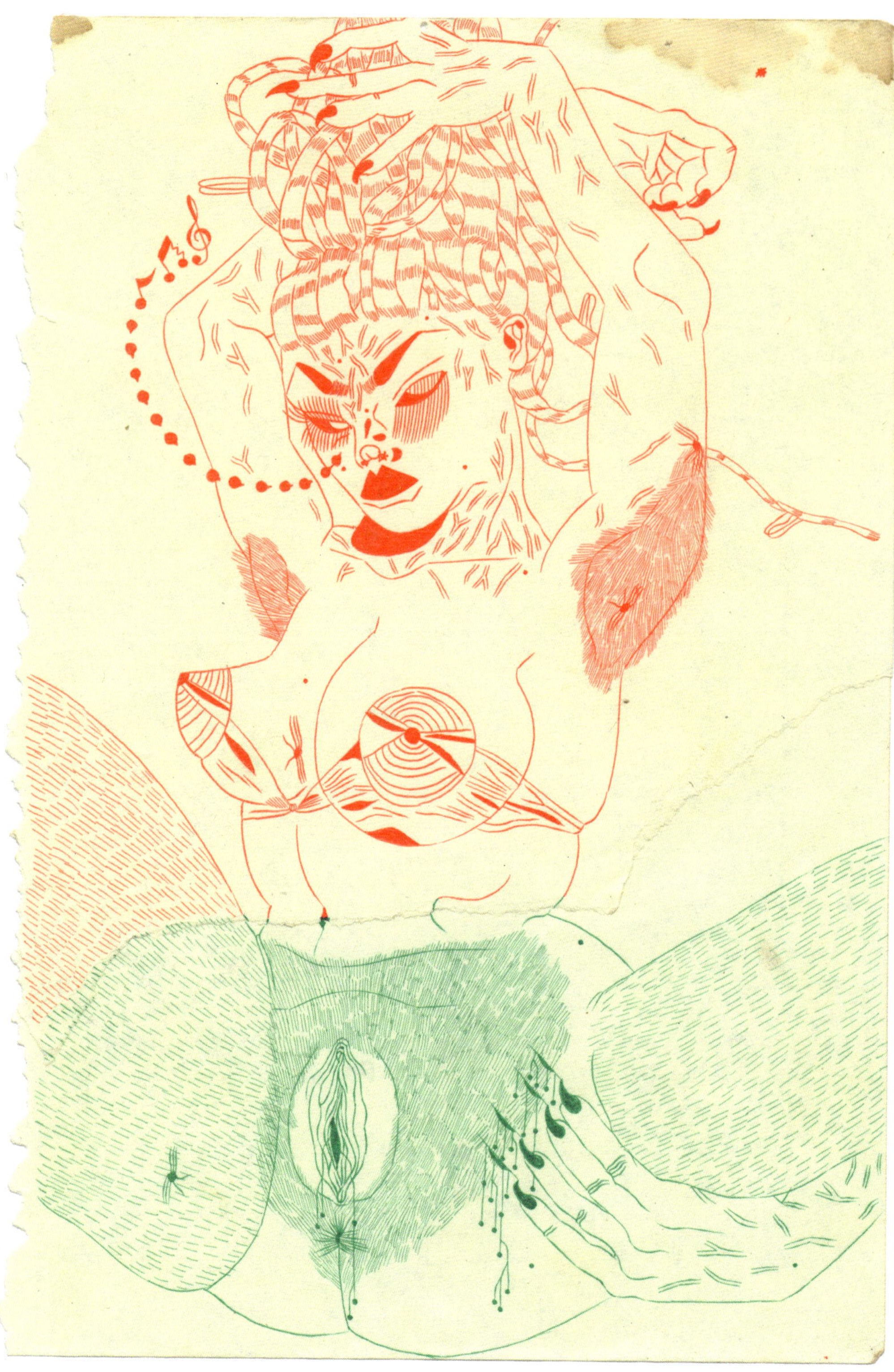

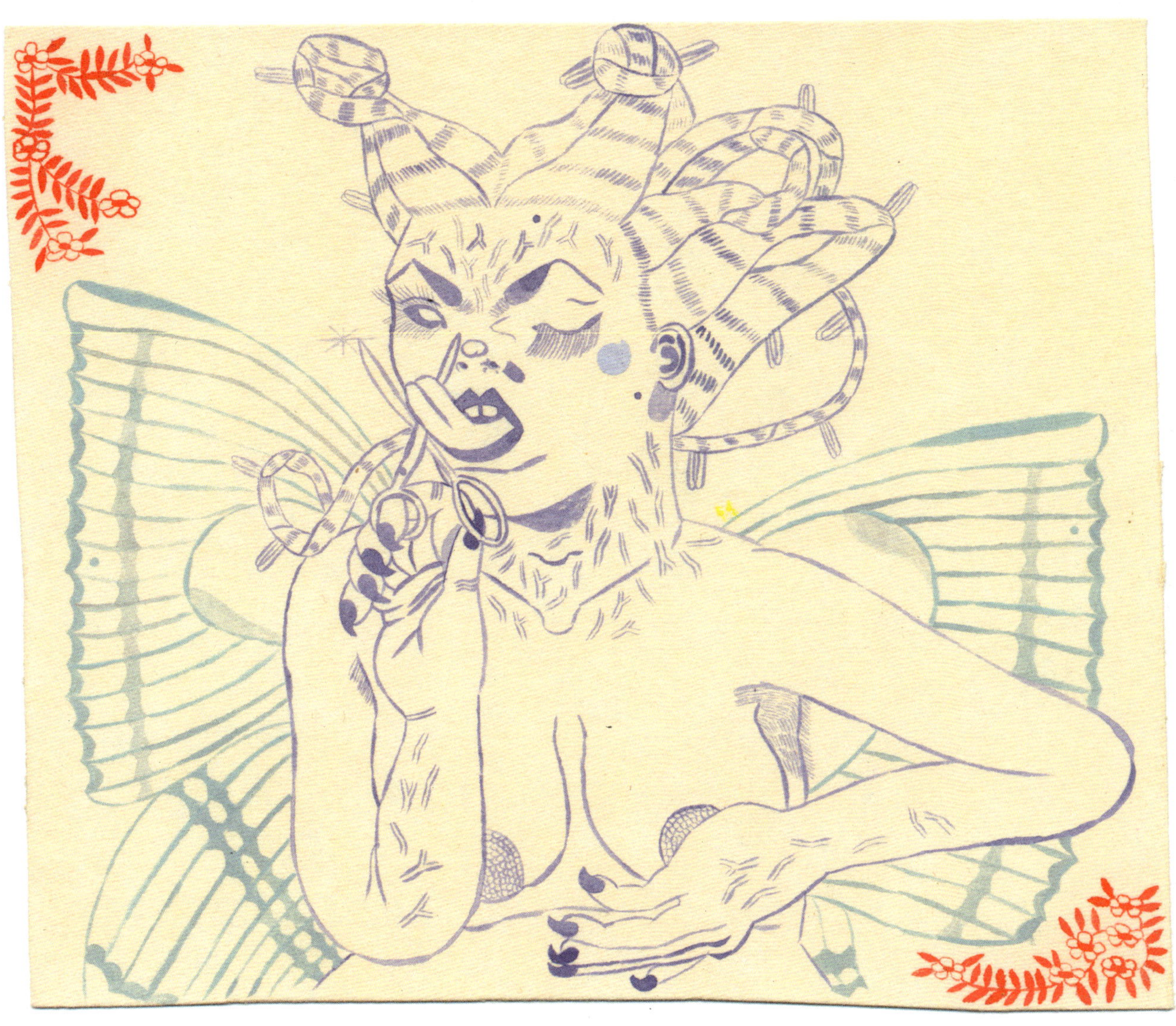

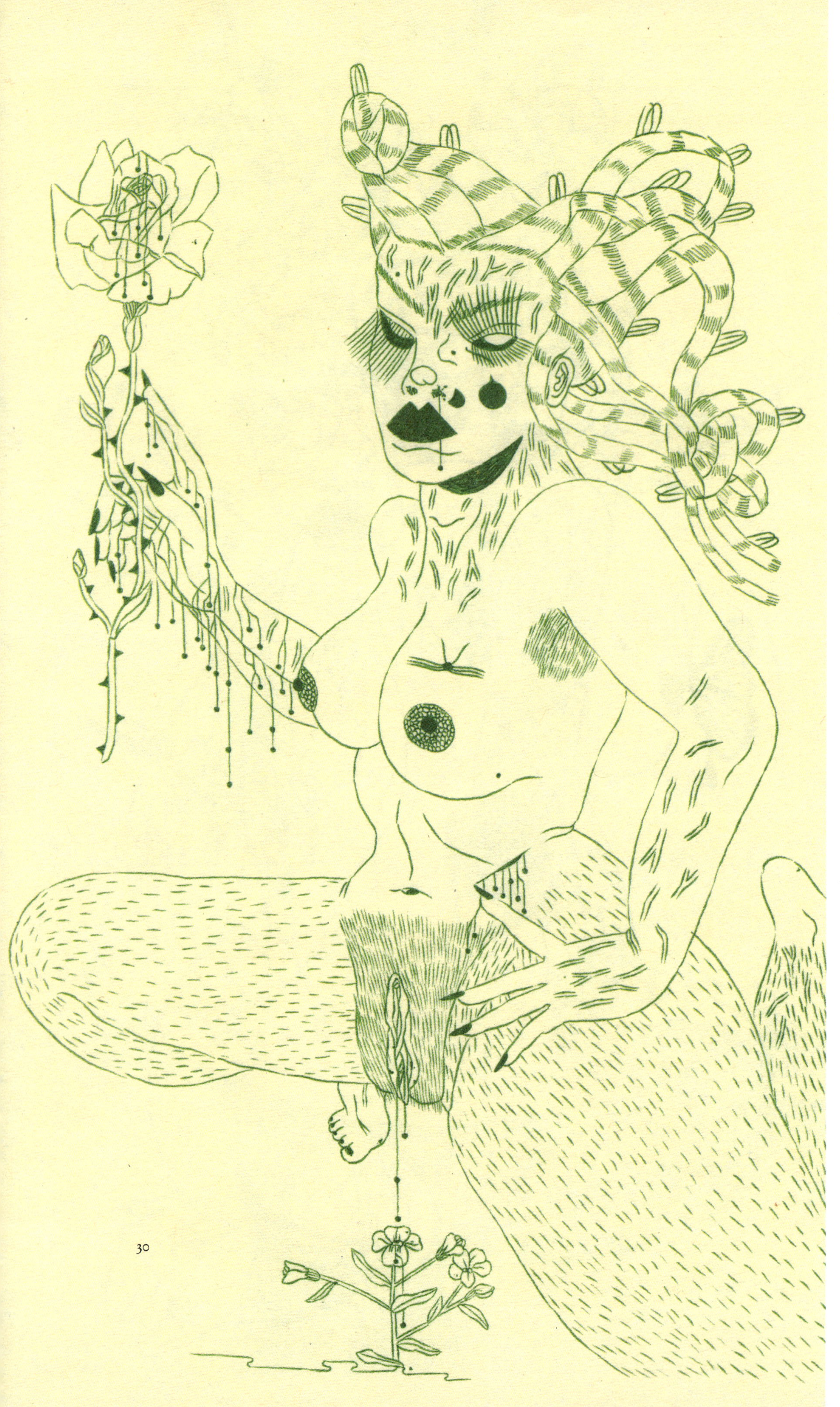

30

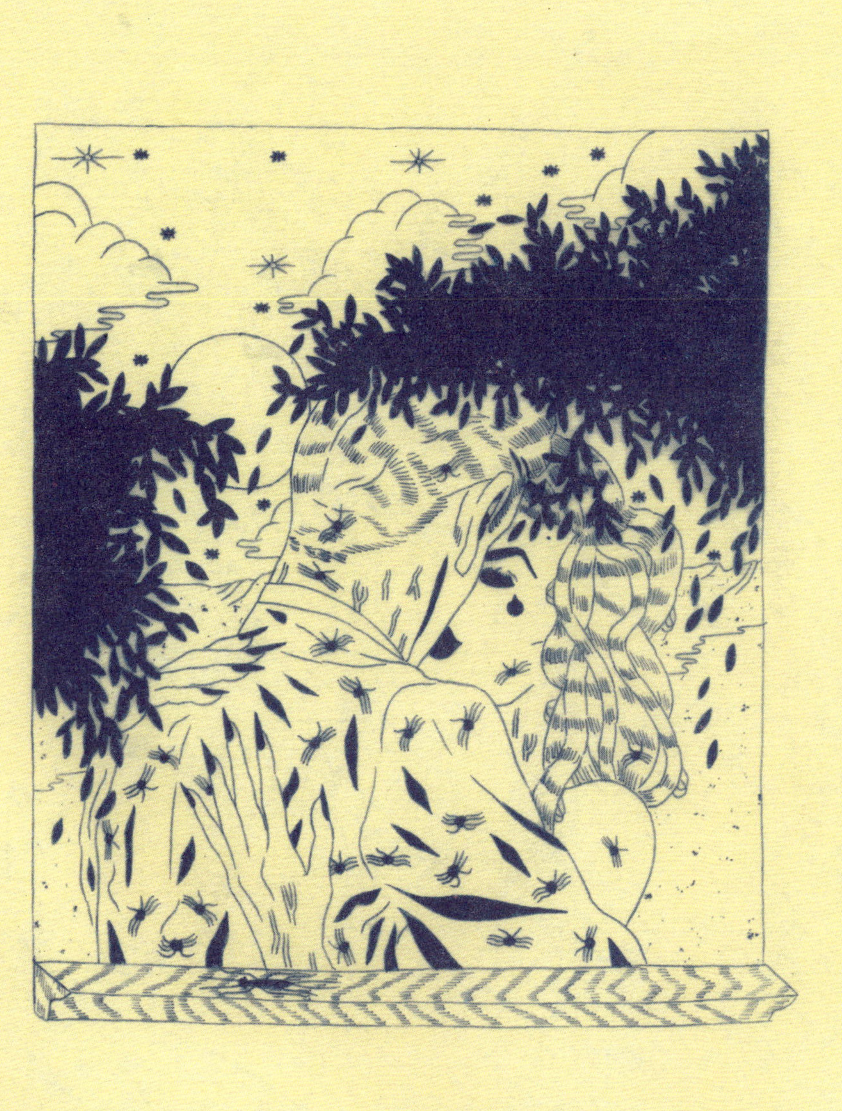

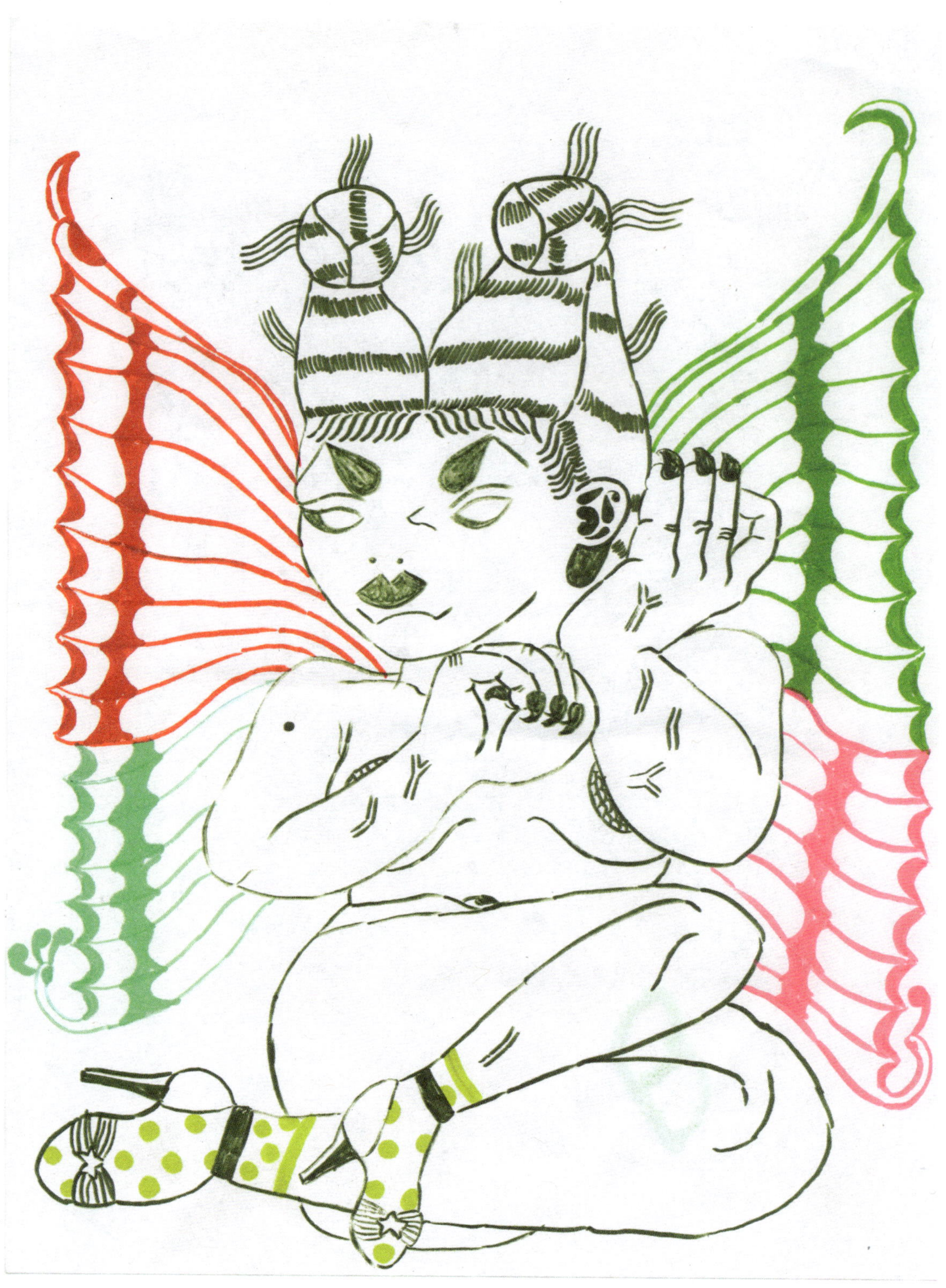

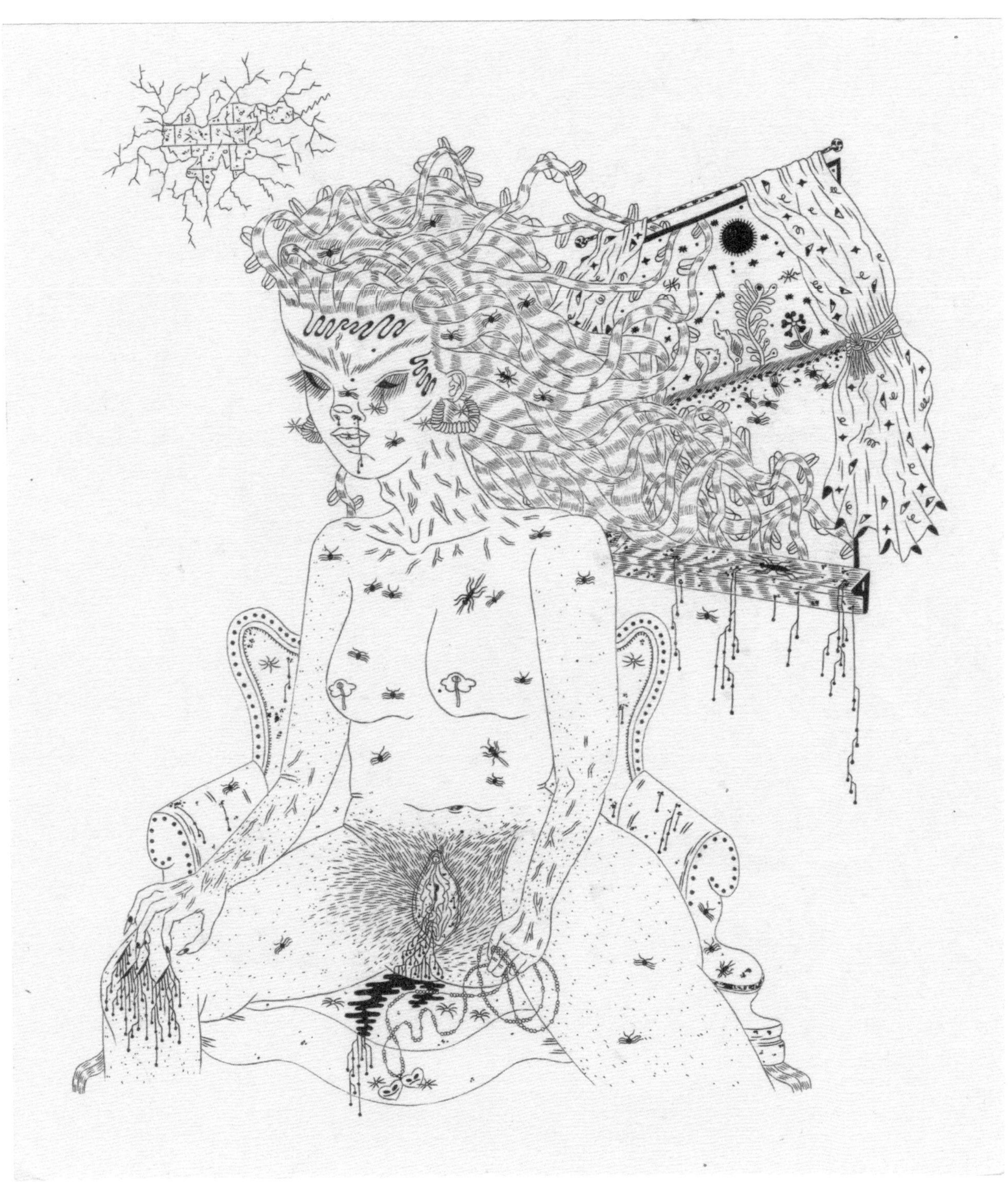

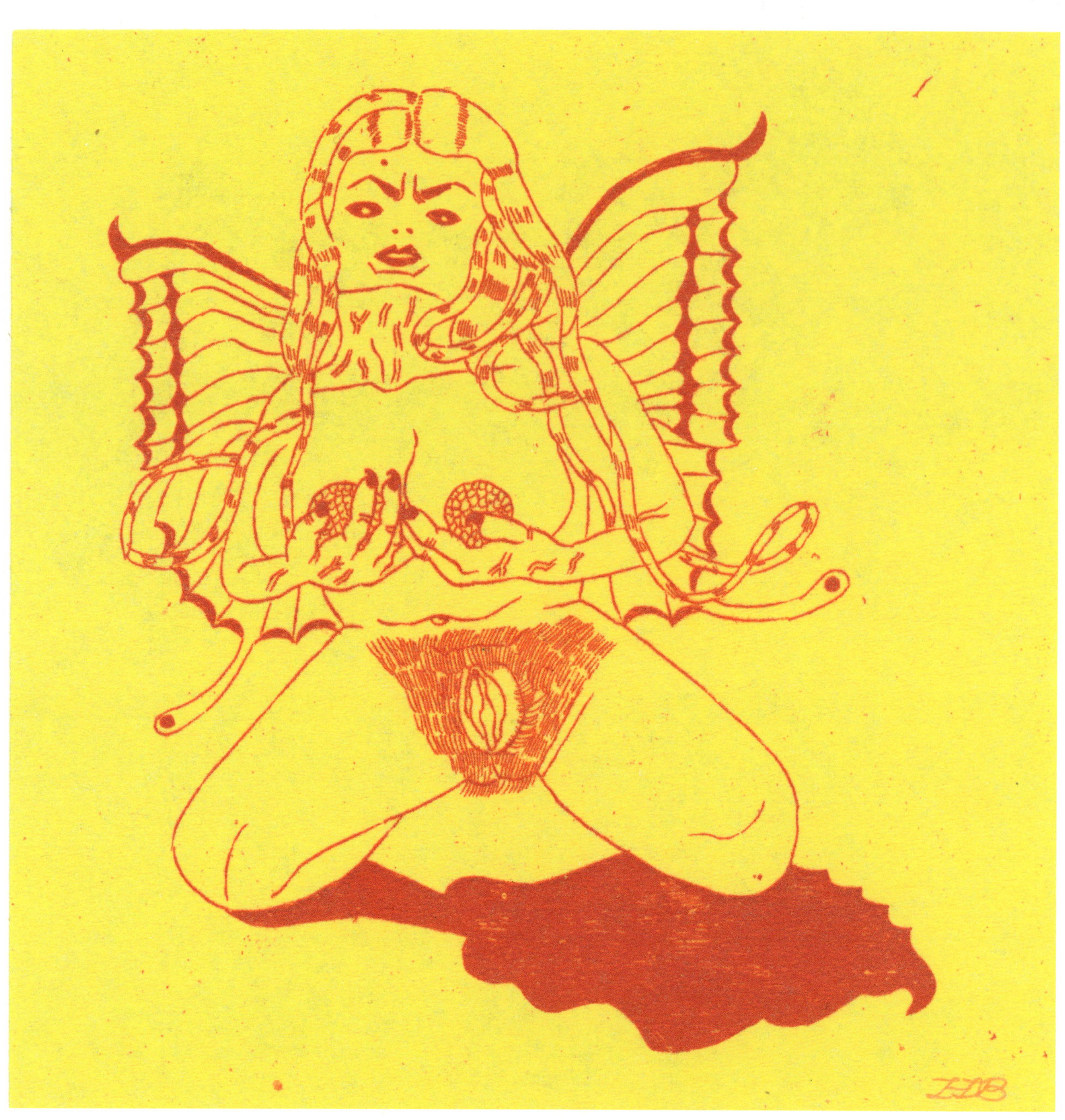

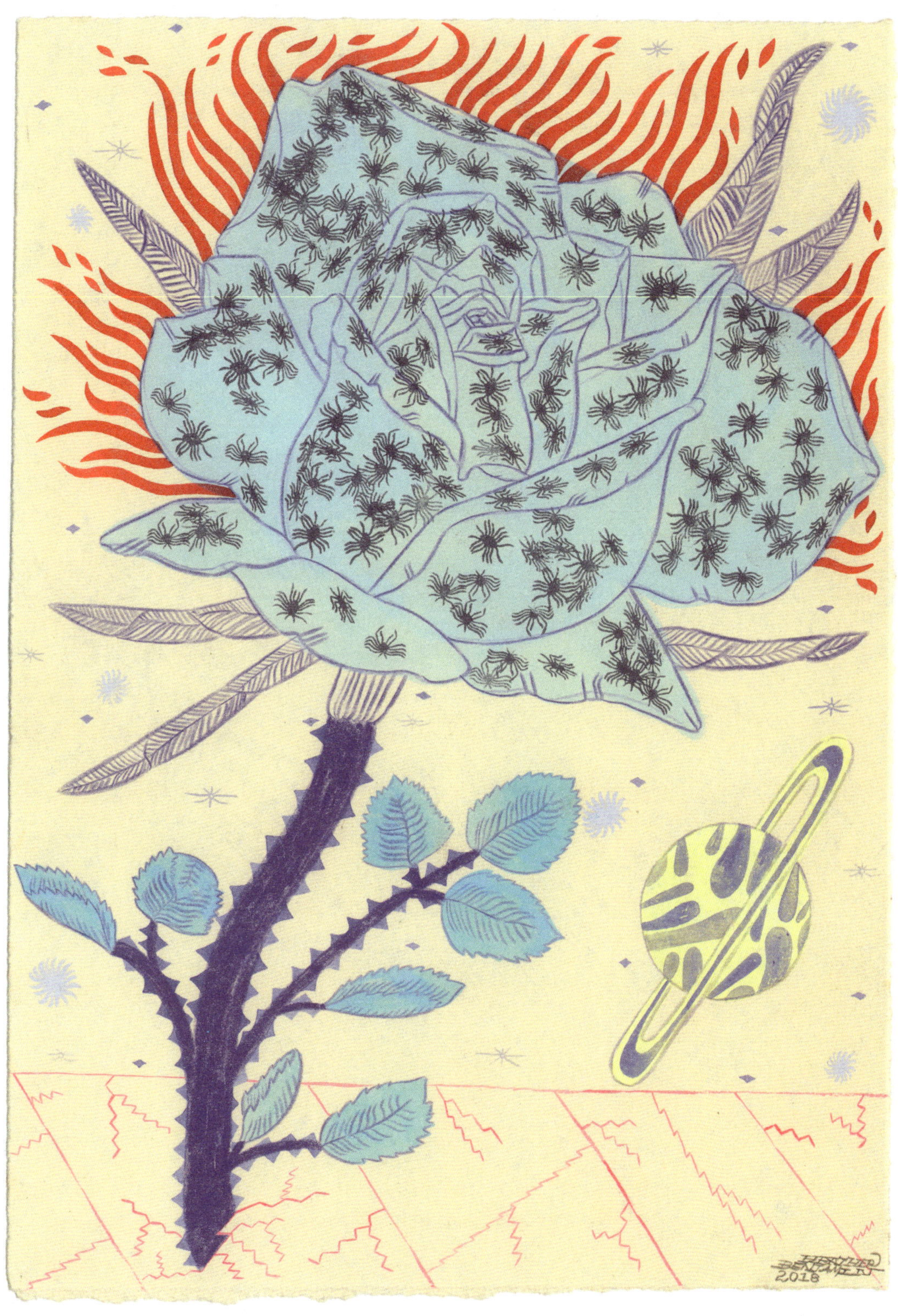

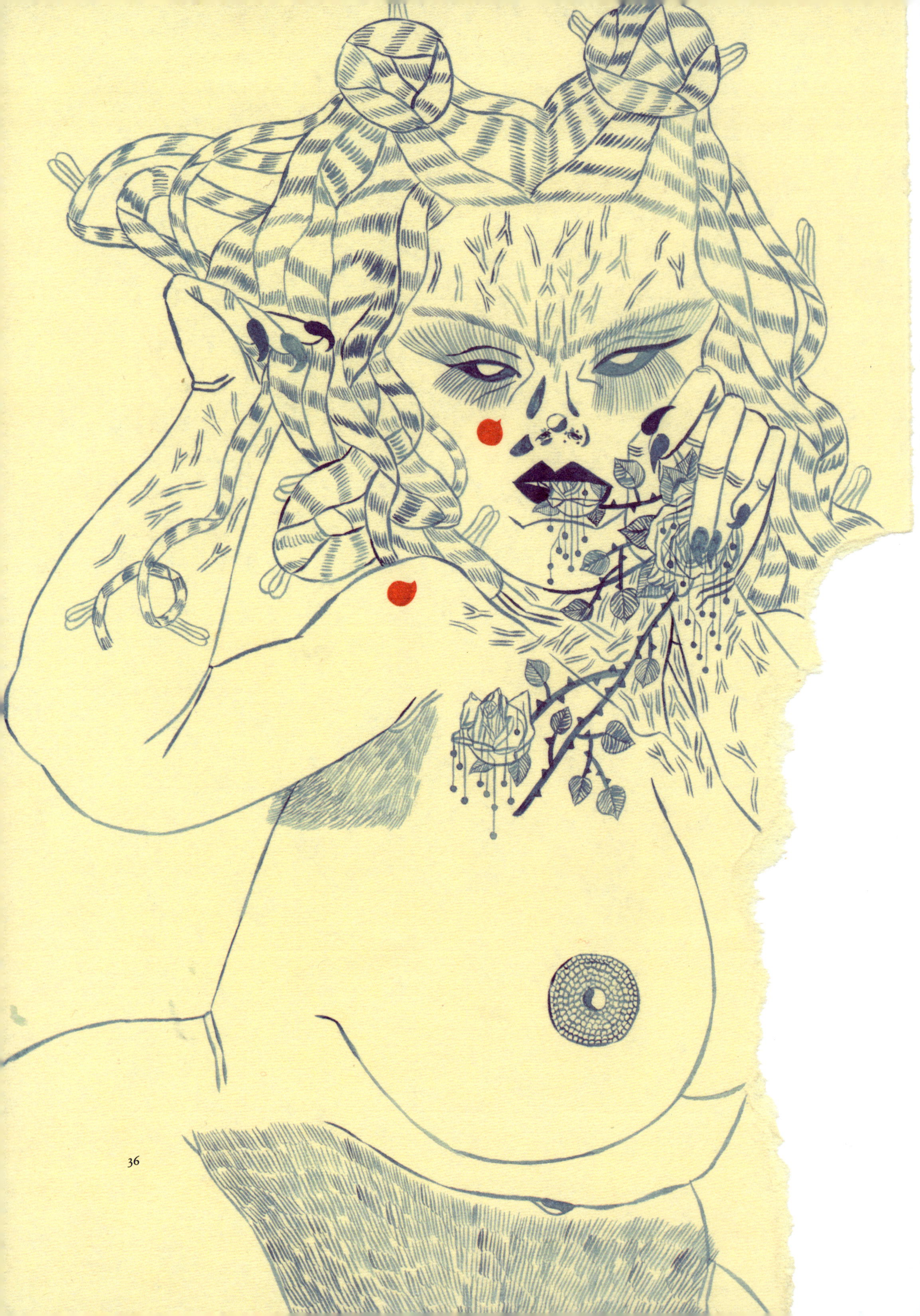

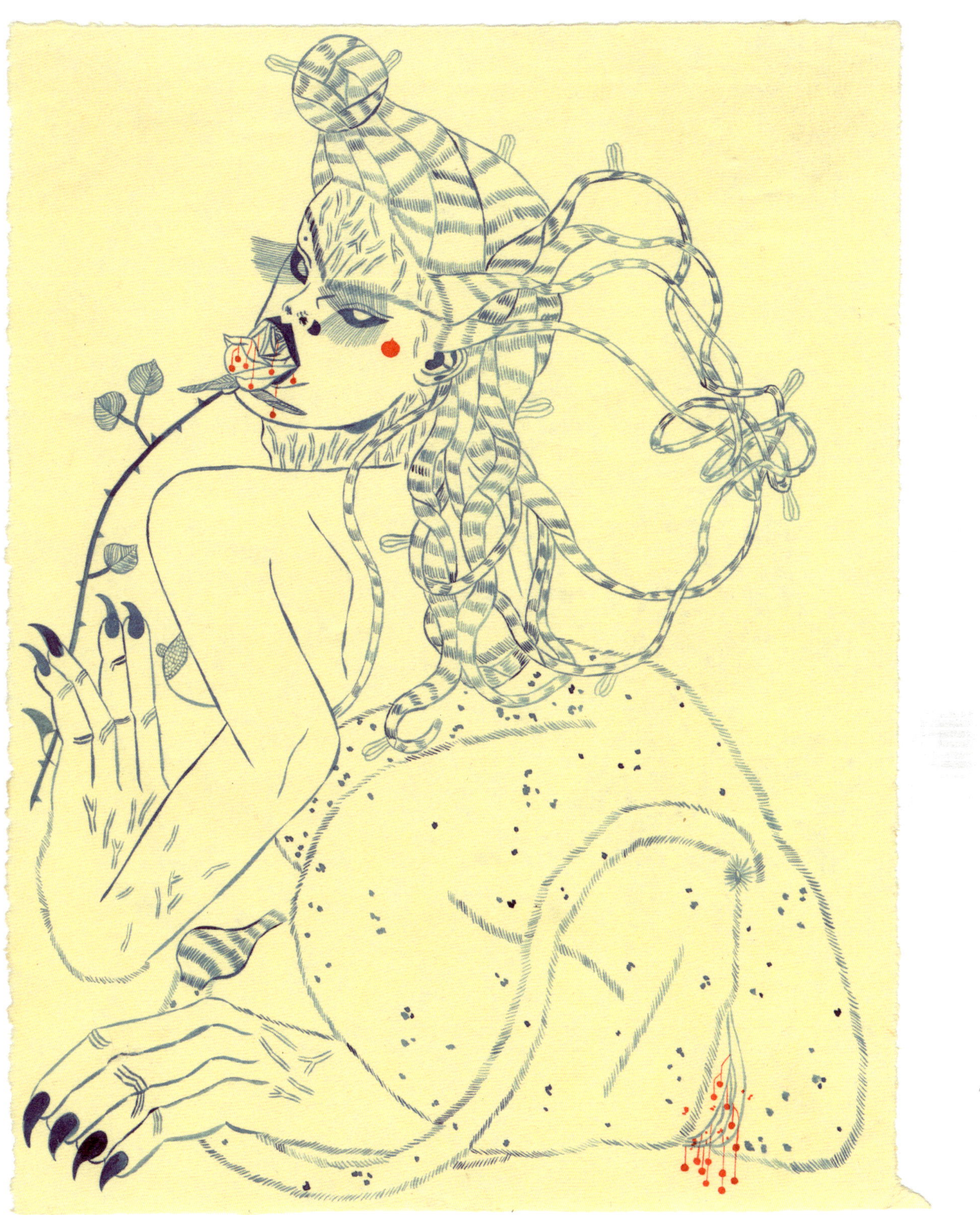

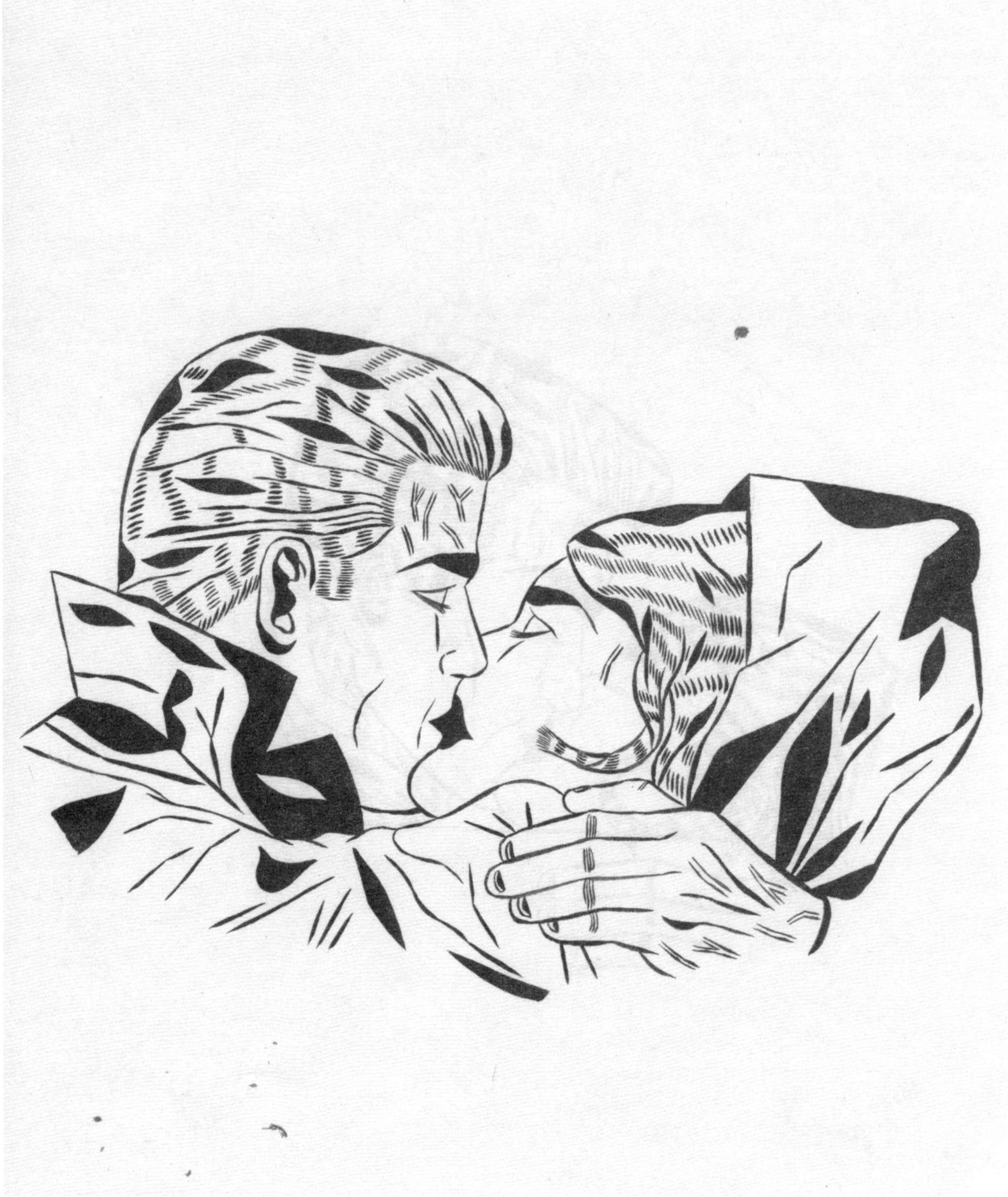

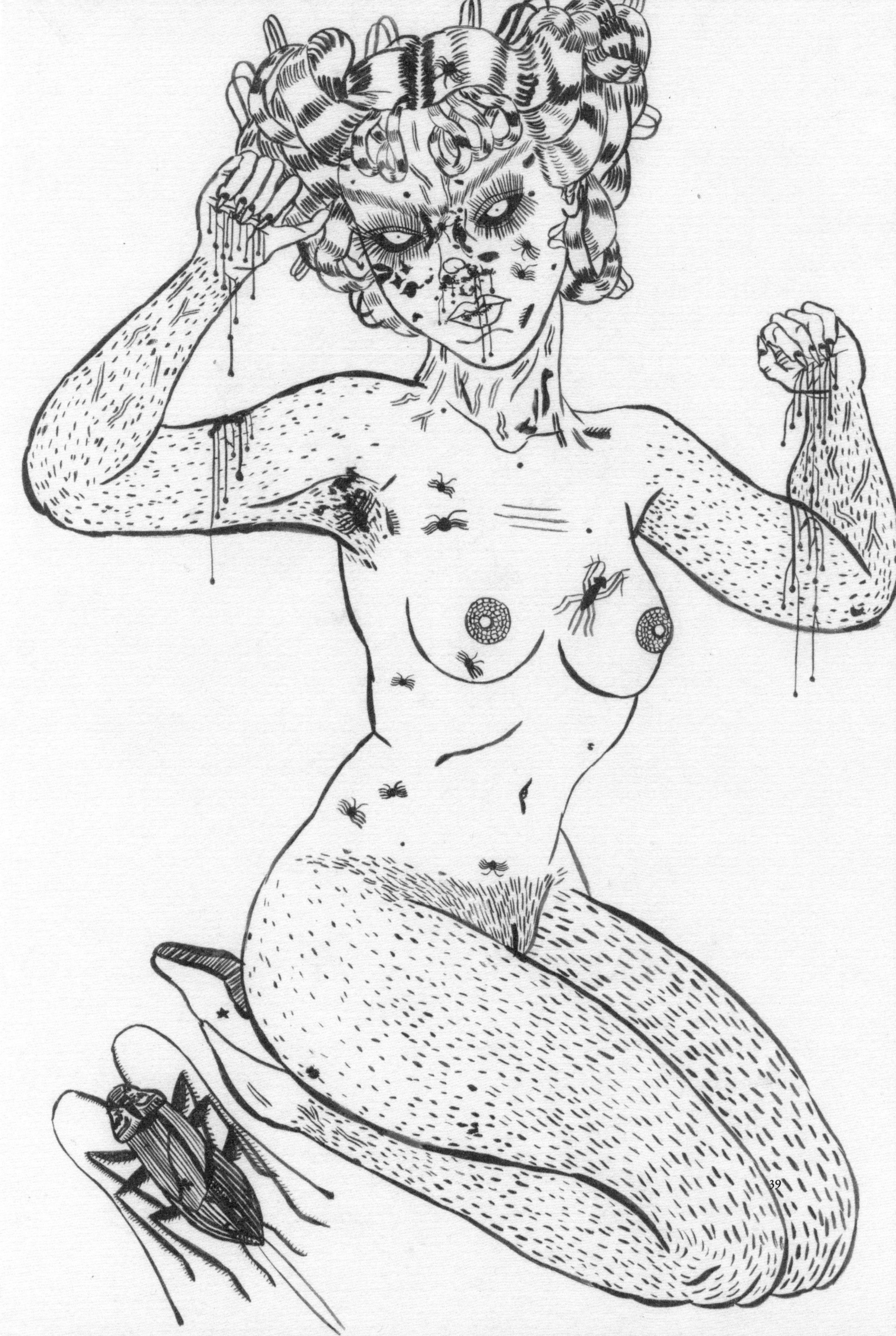

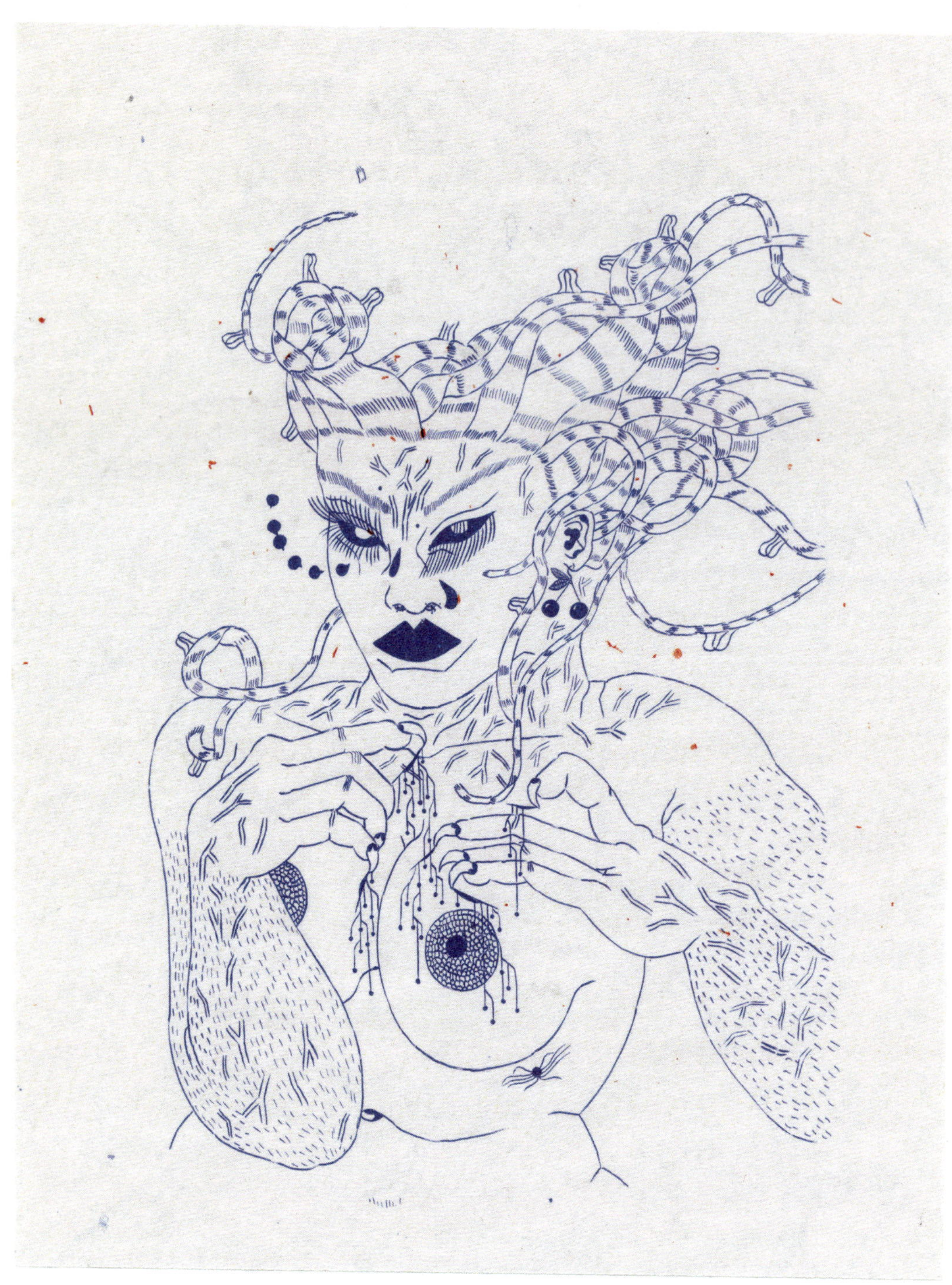

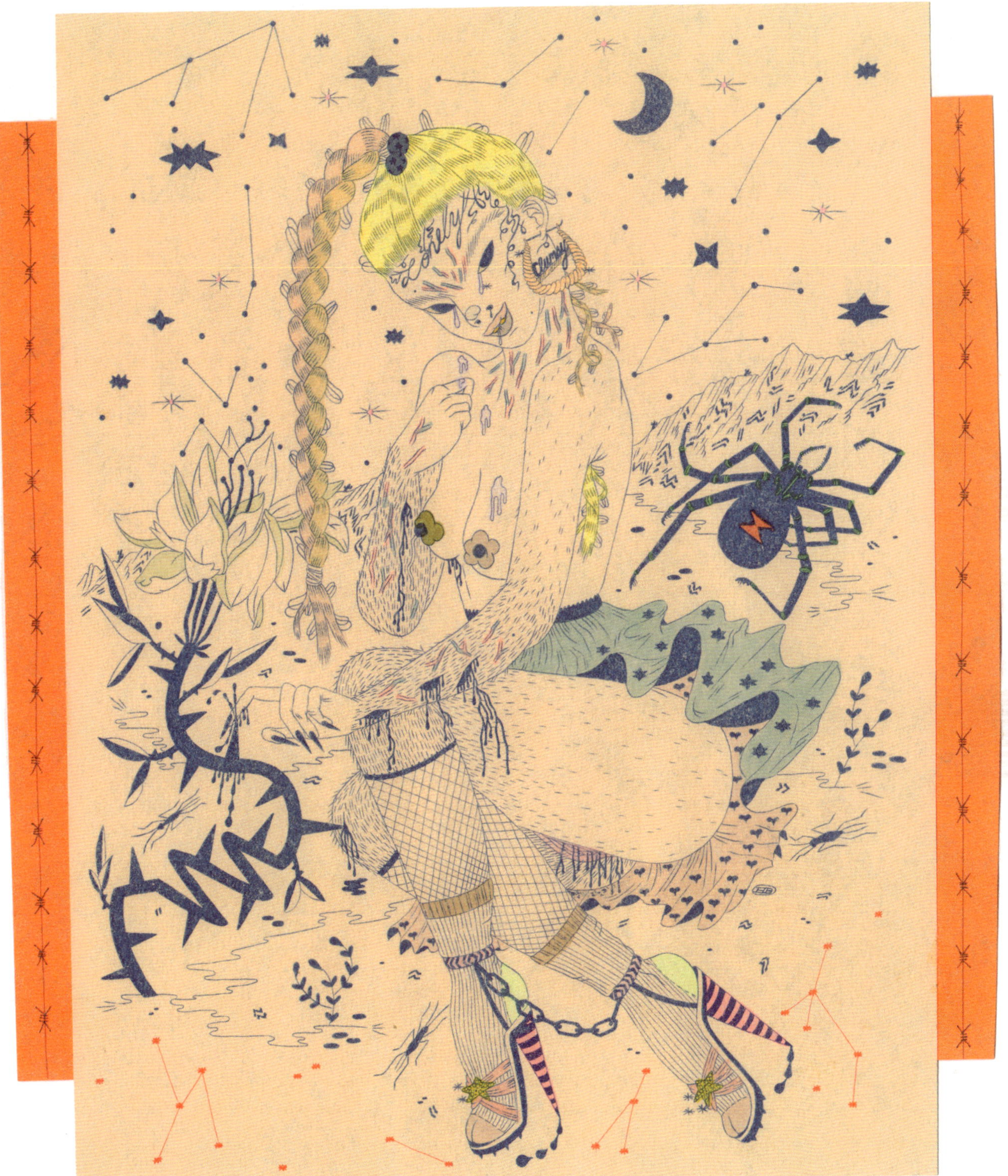

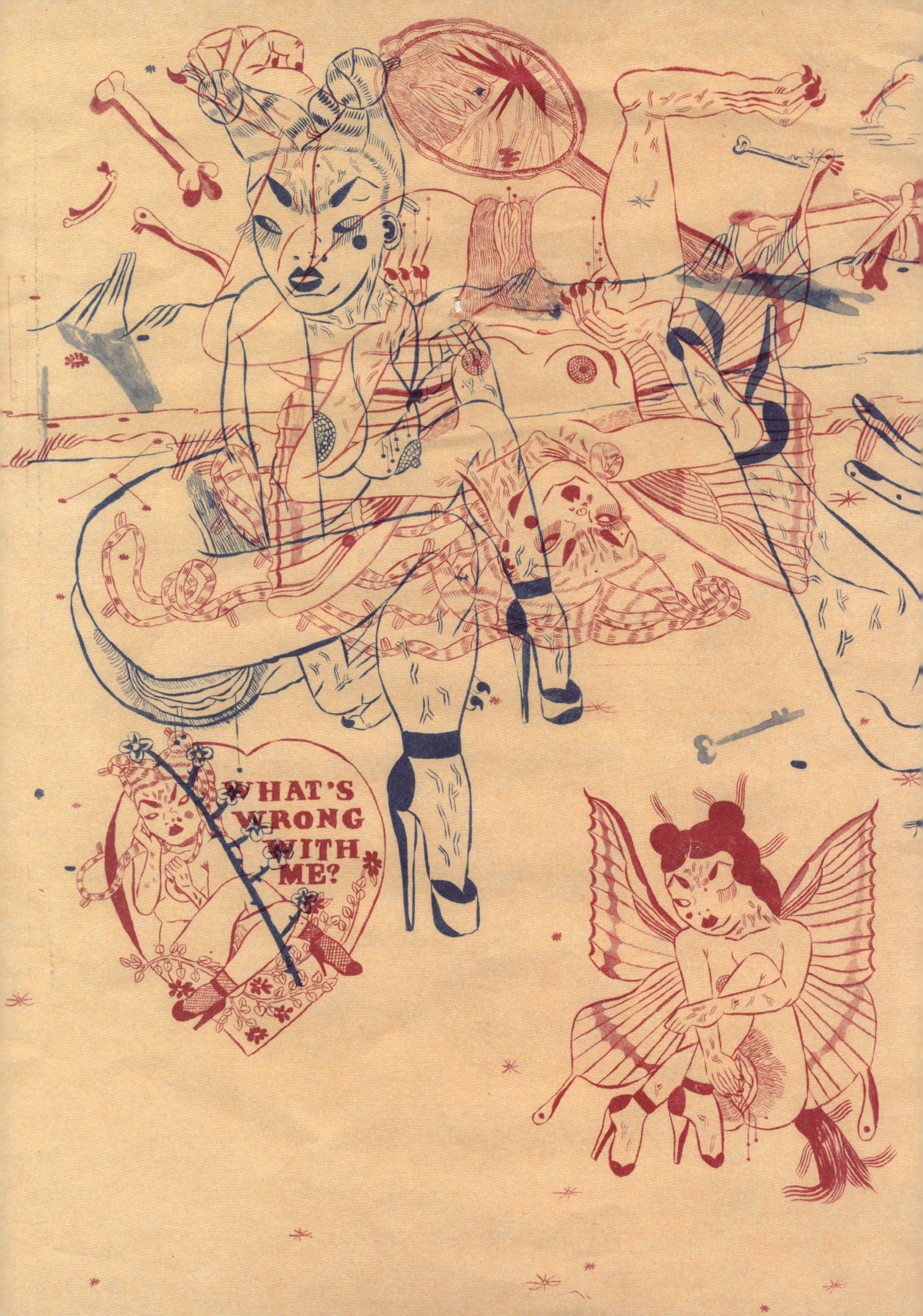

WHAT'S
WRONG
WITH
ME?

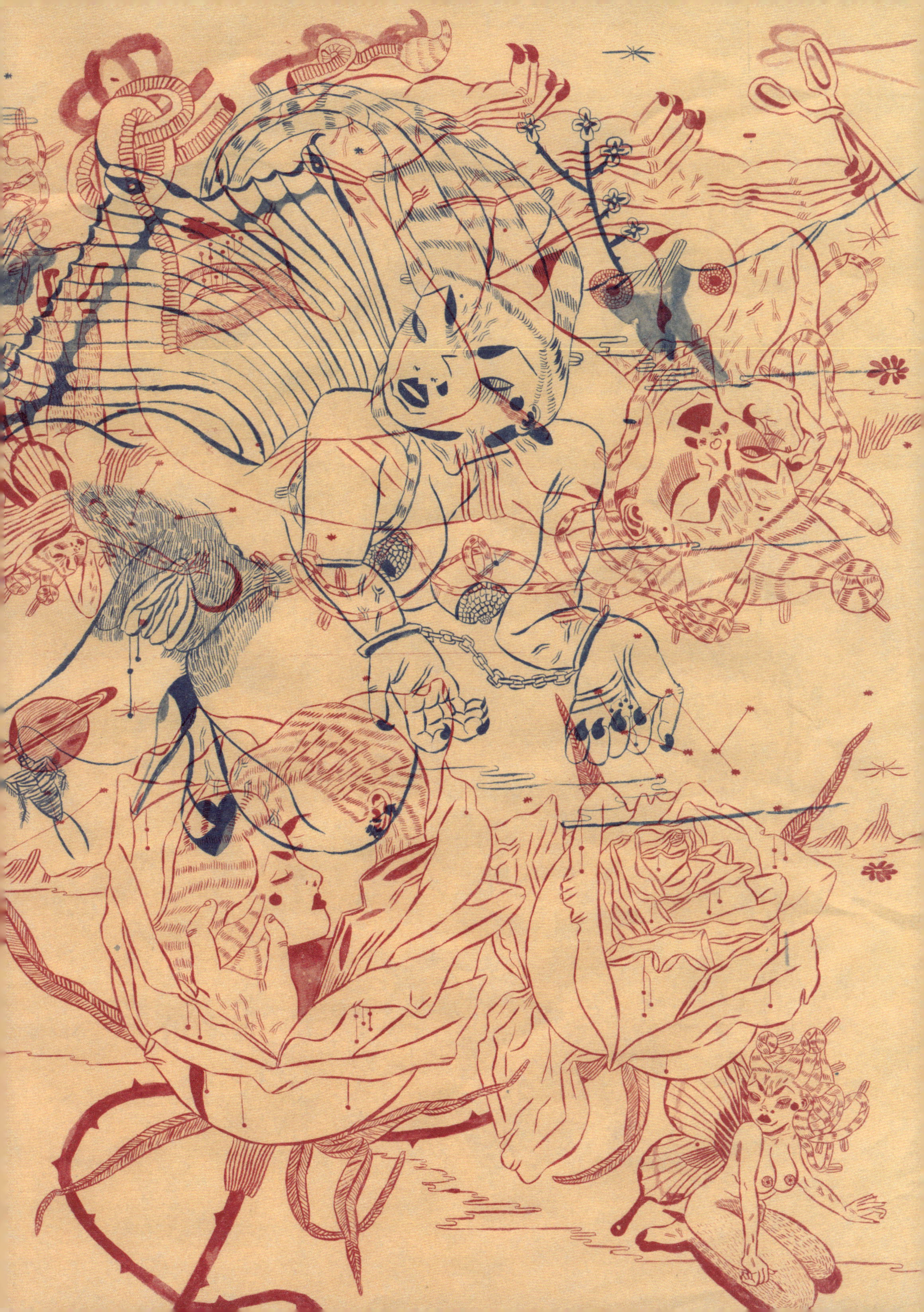

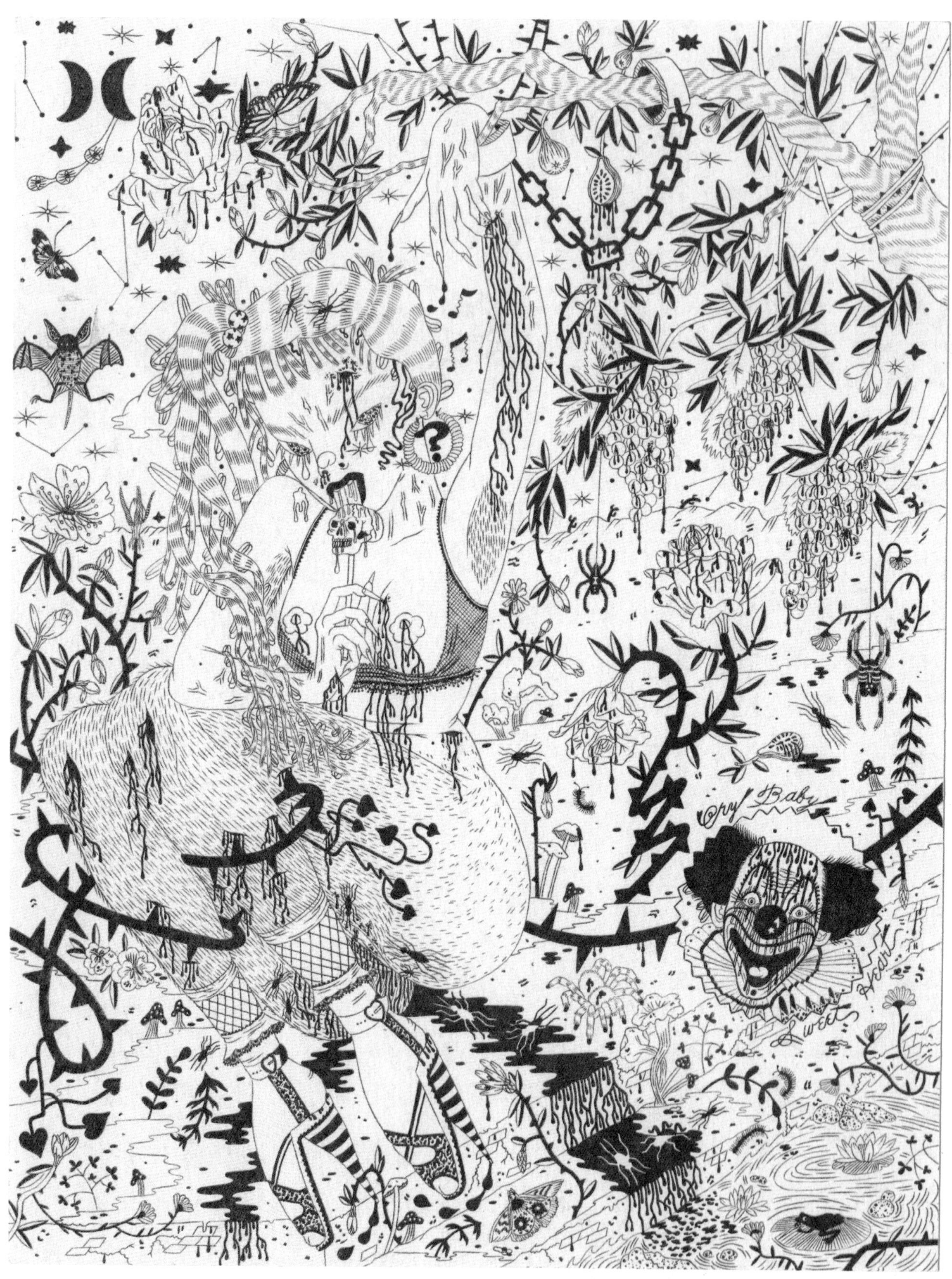

Cry Baby
Sweet Heart

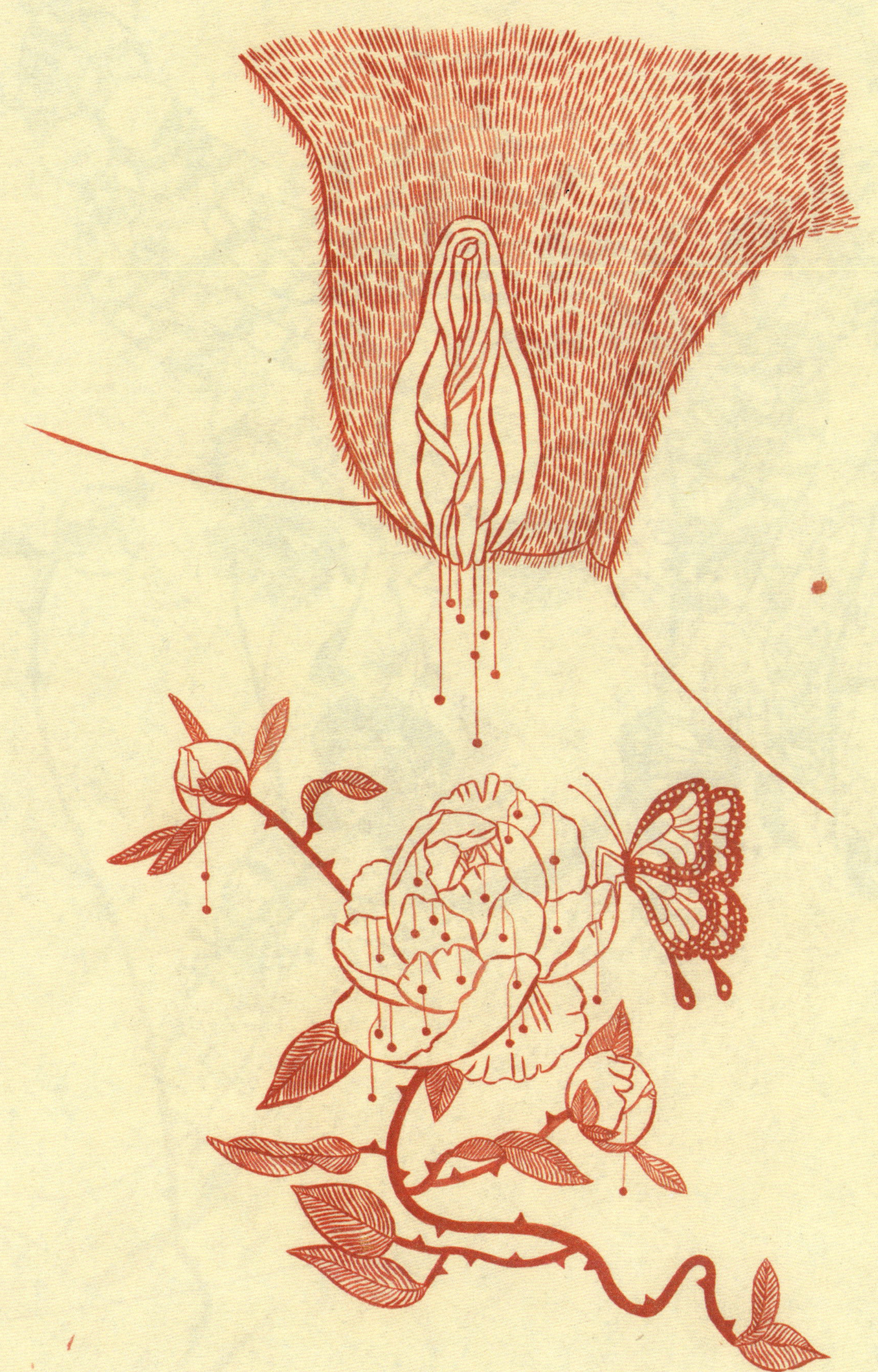

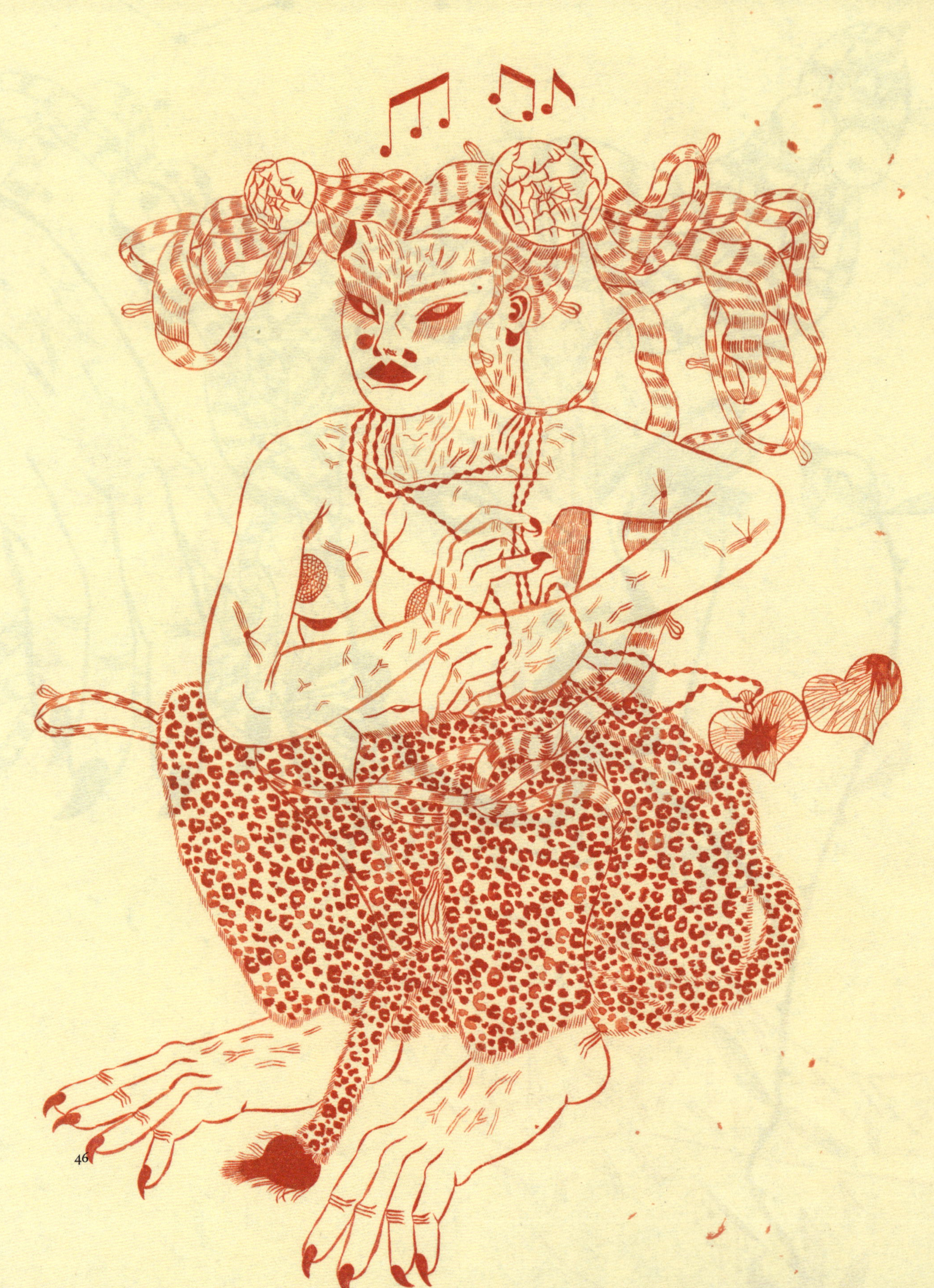

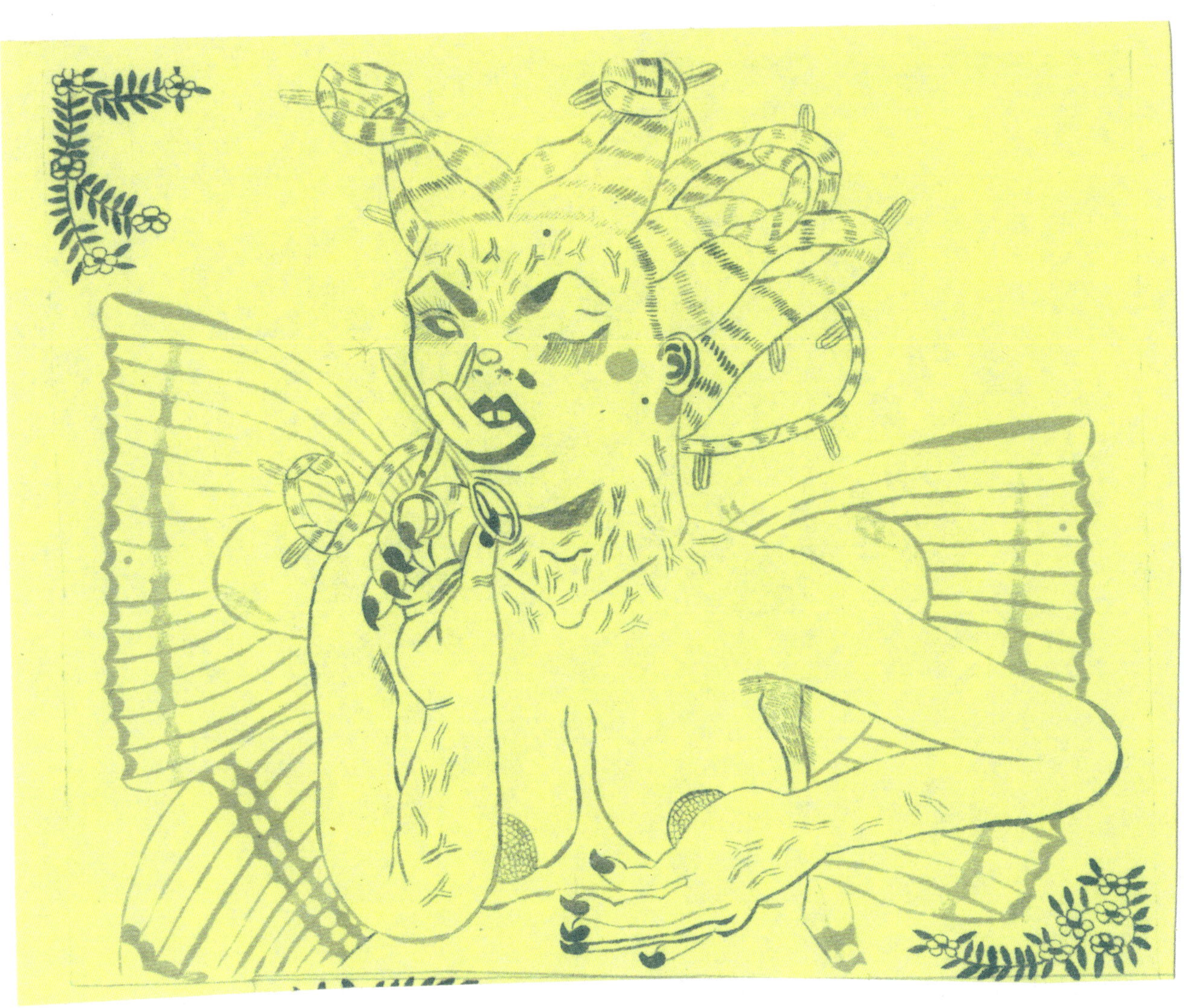

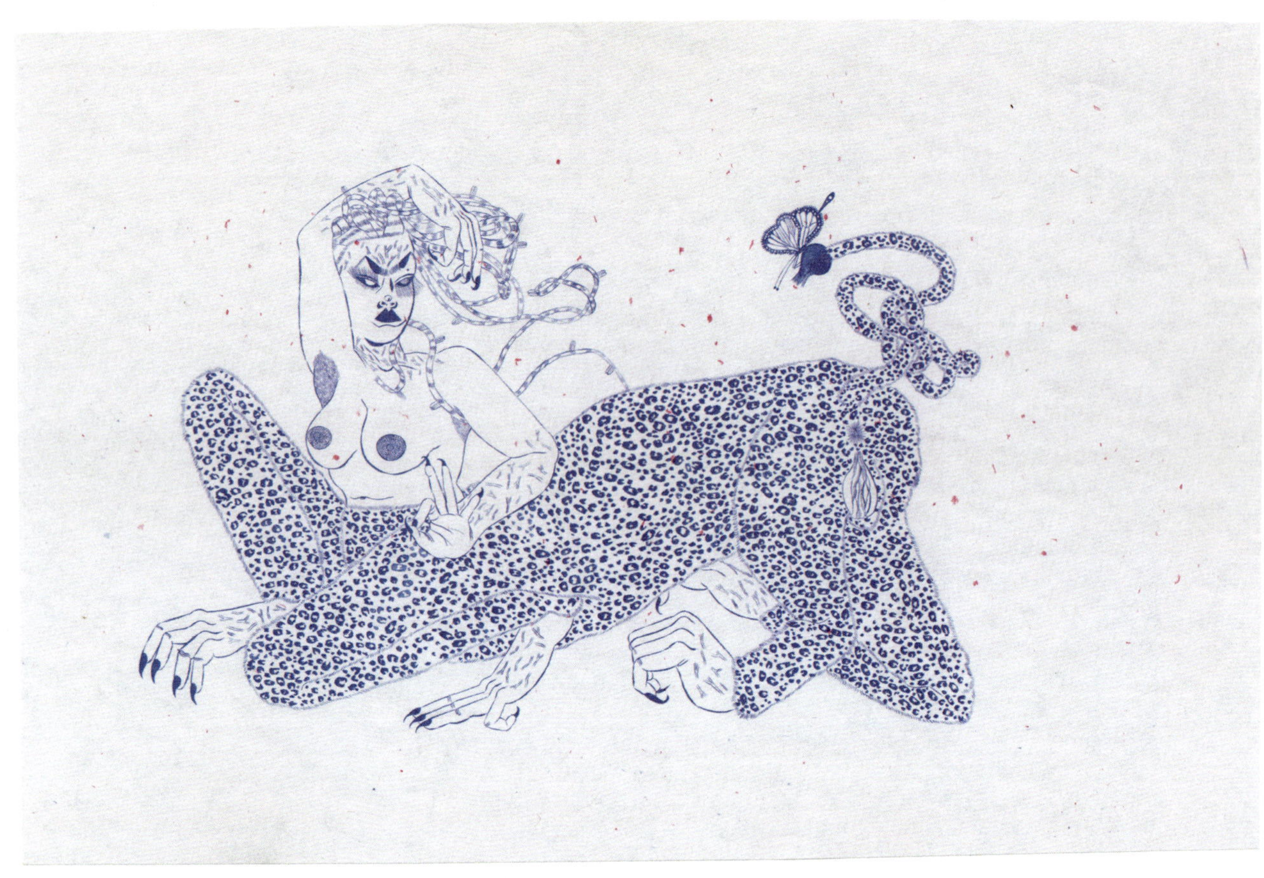

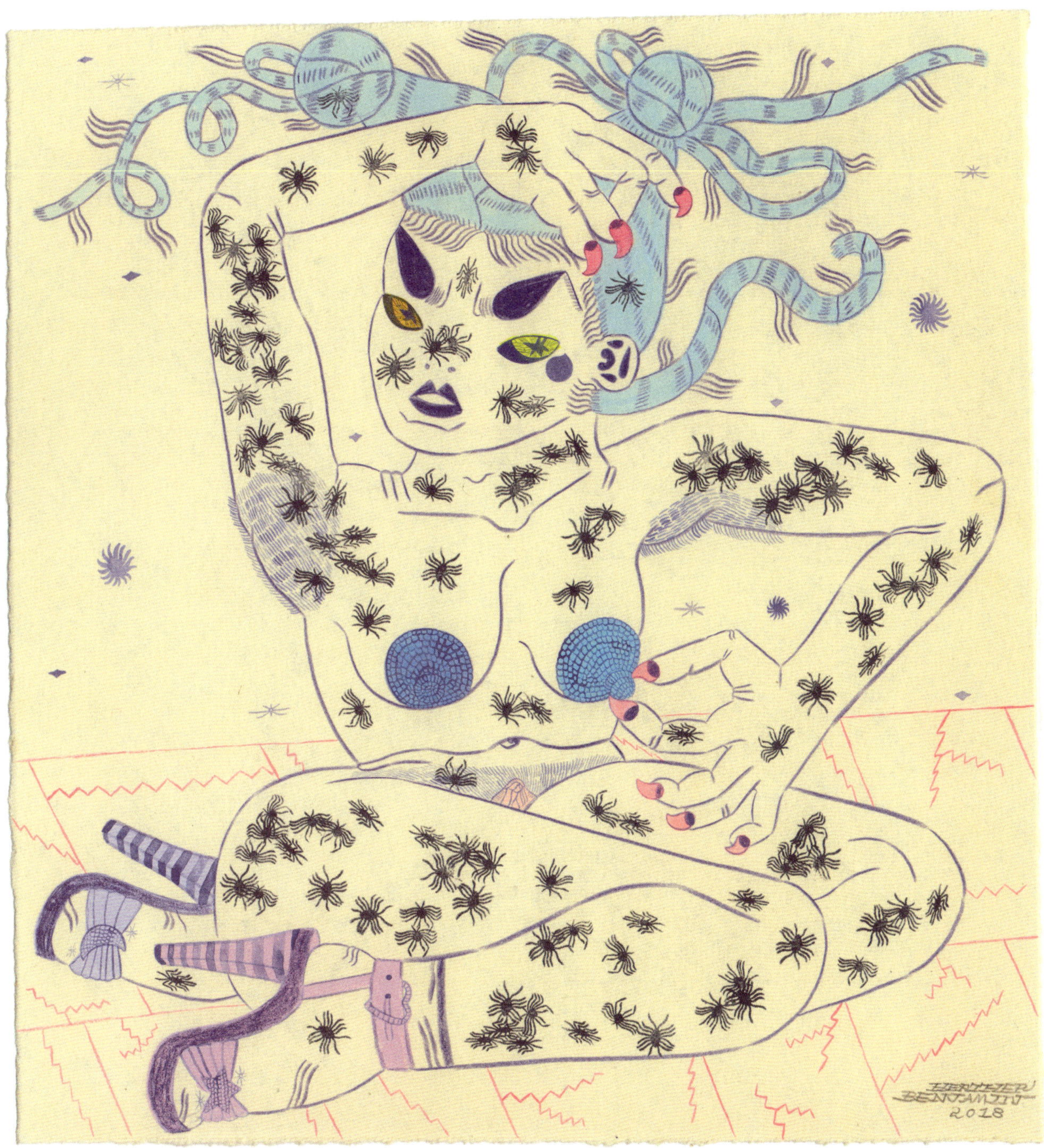

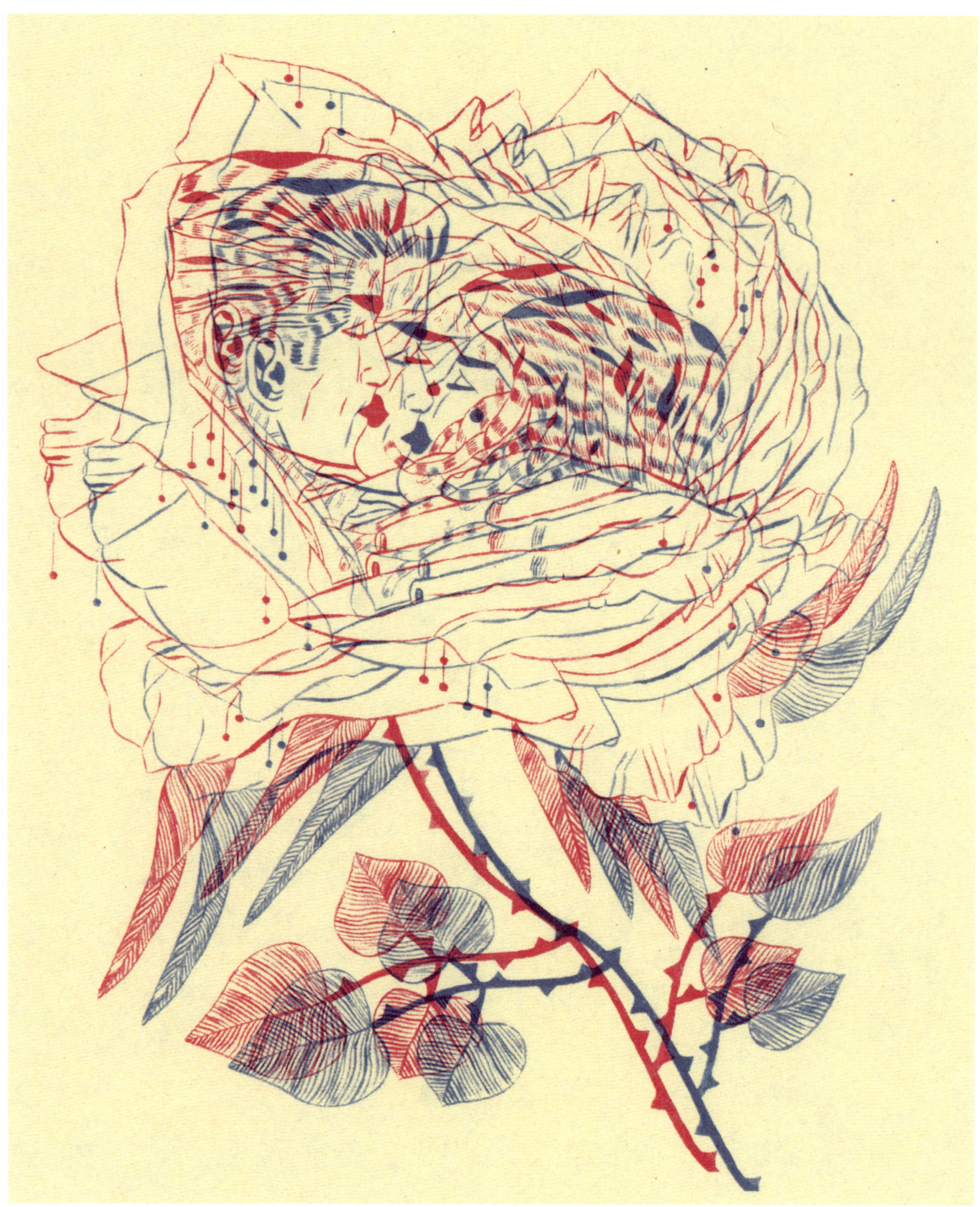

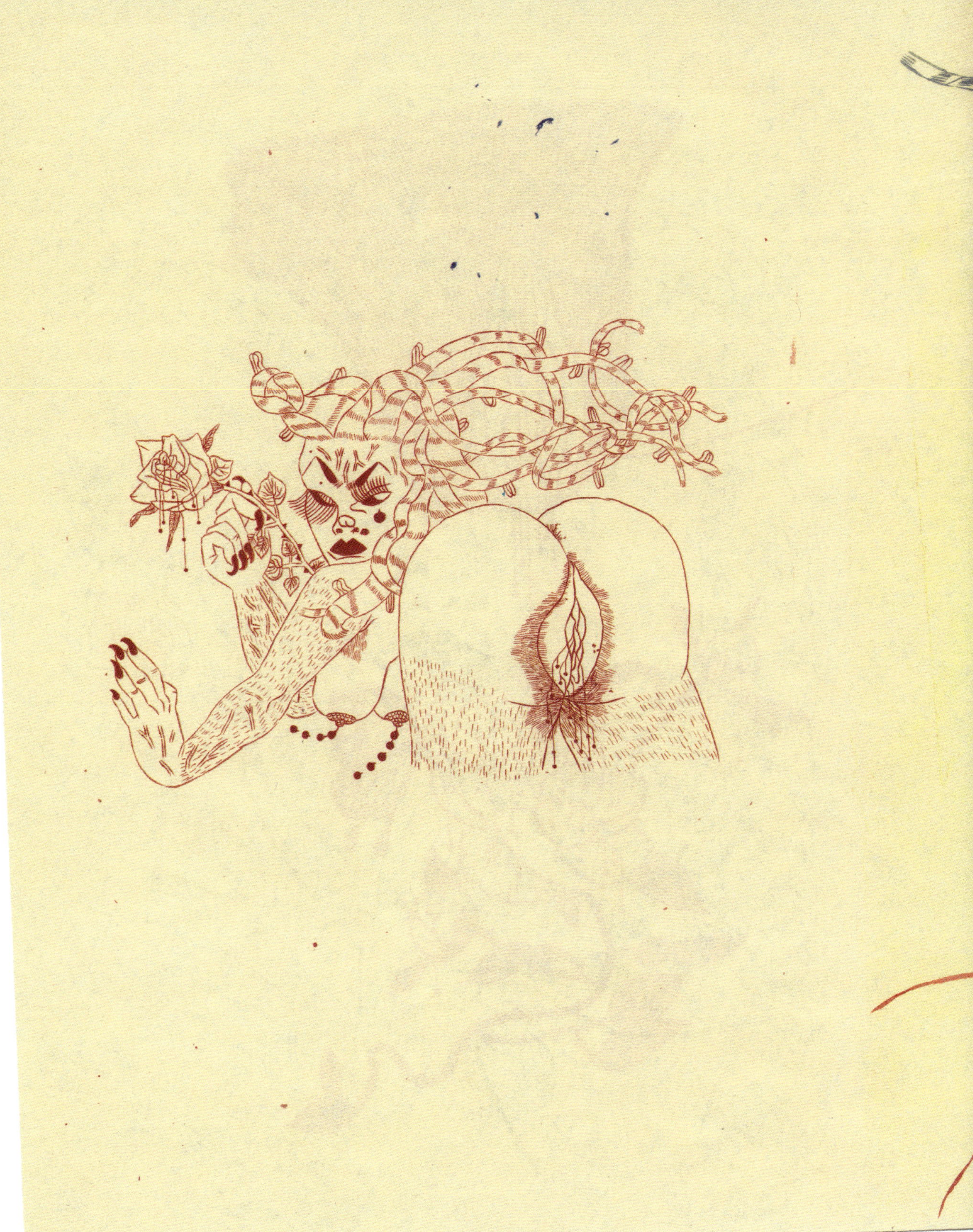

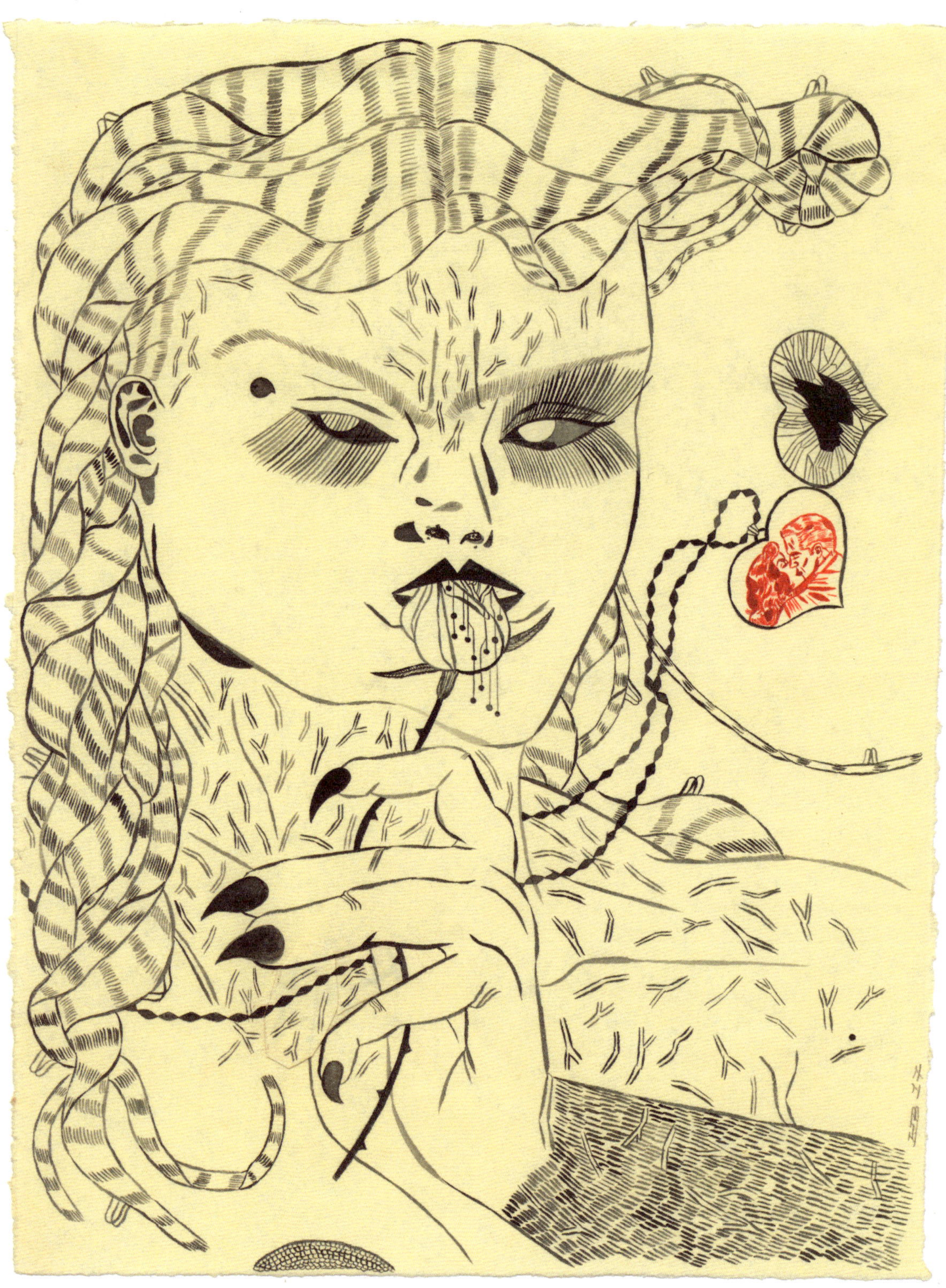

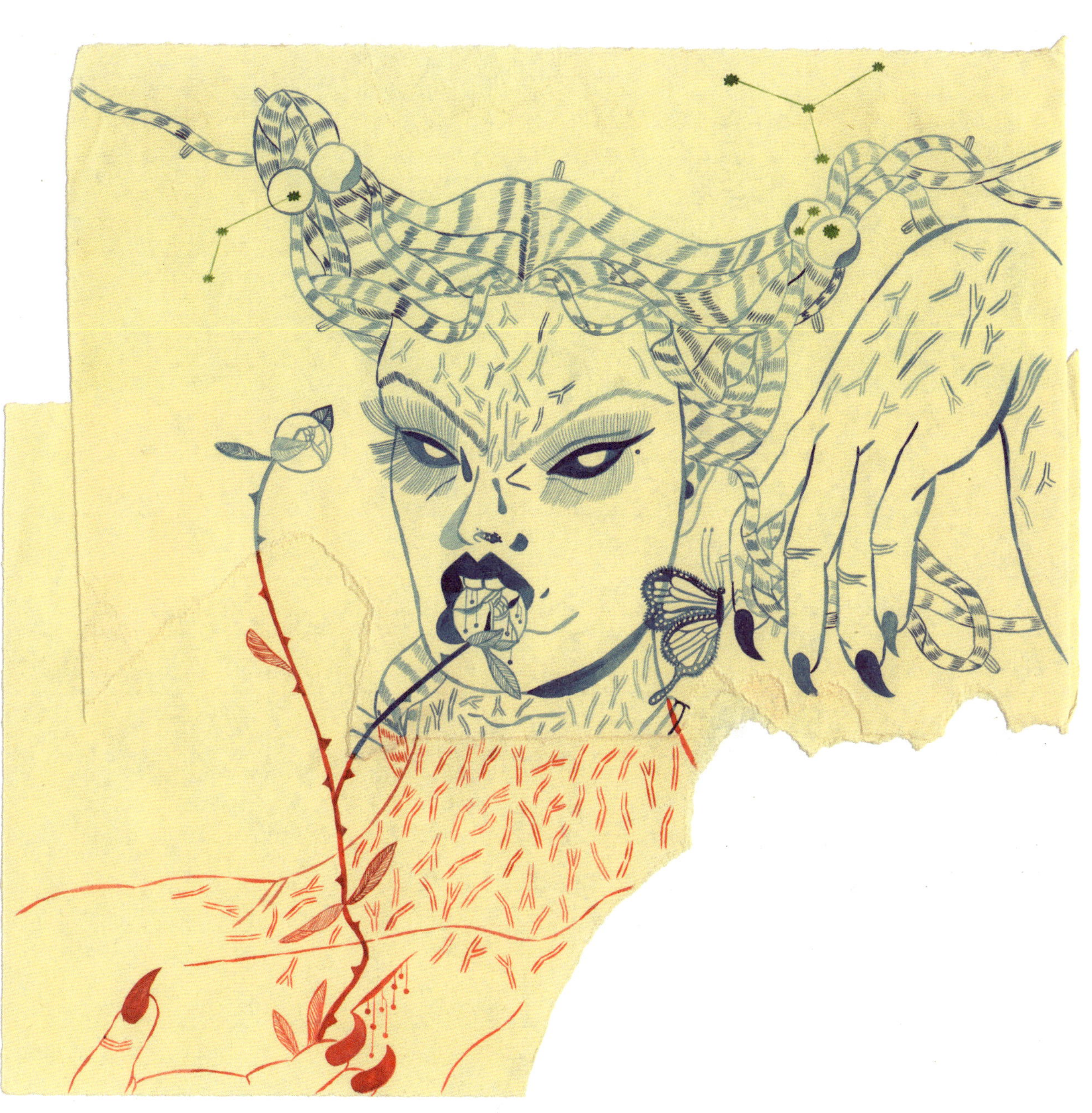

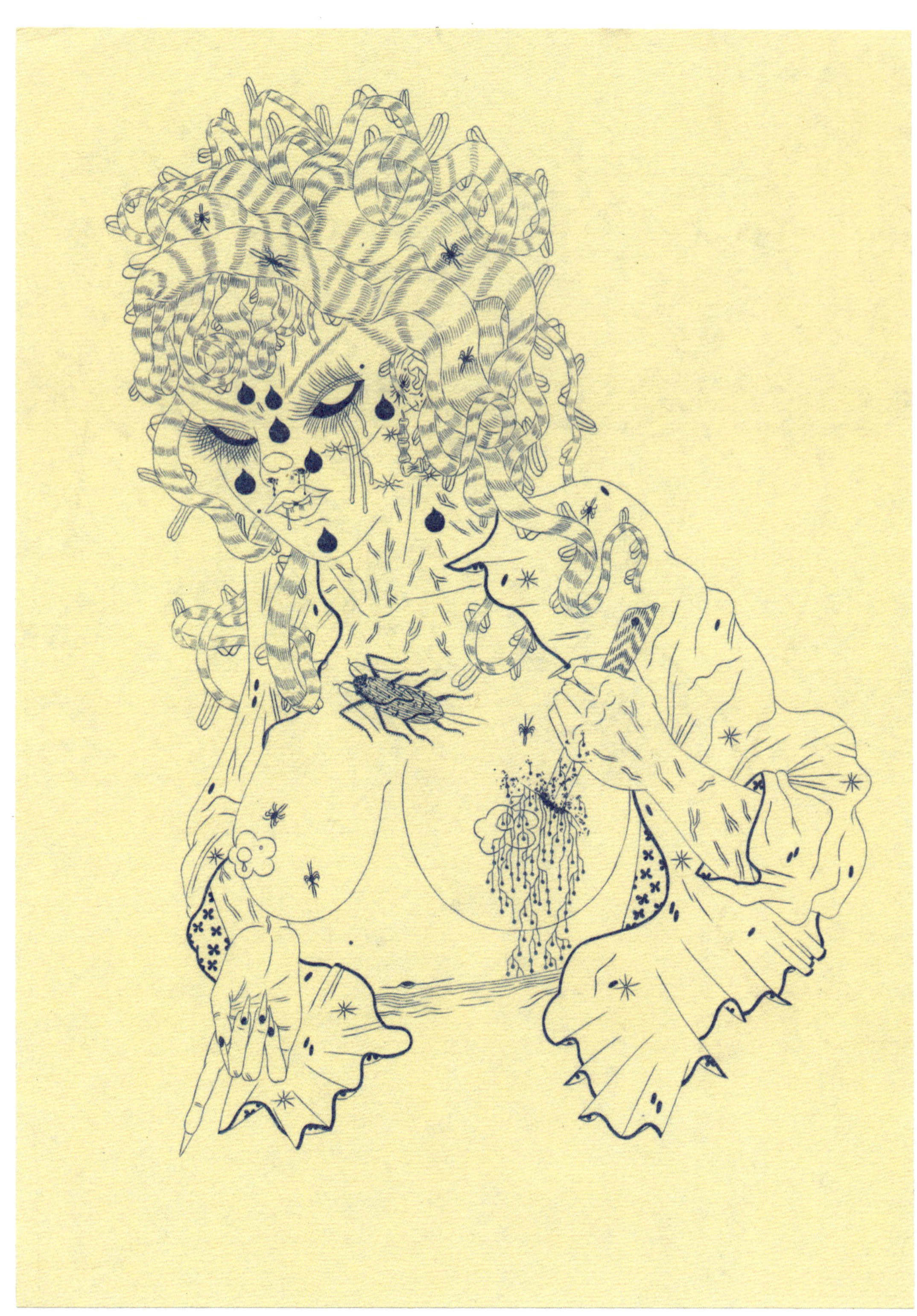

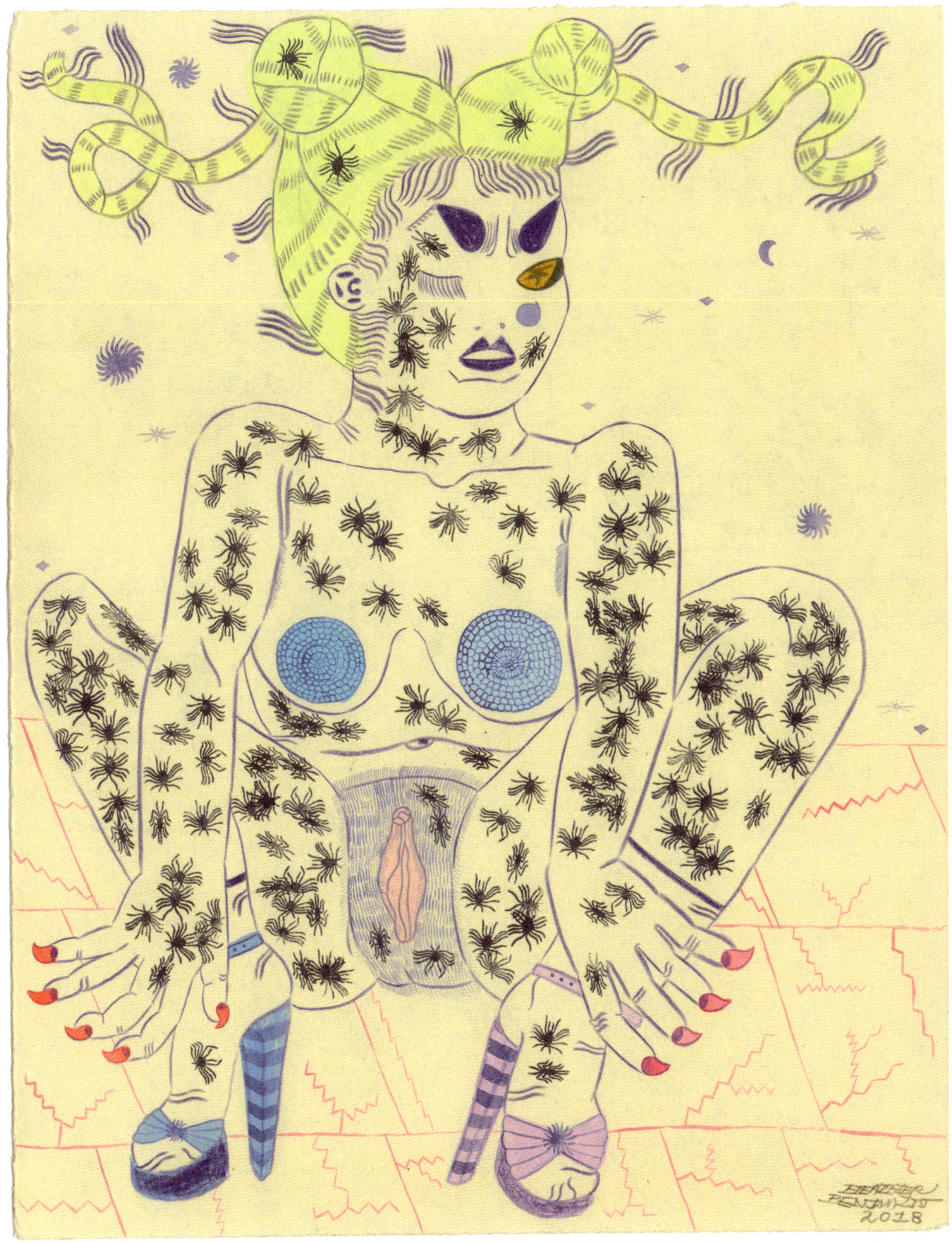

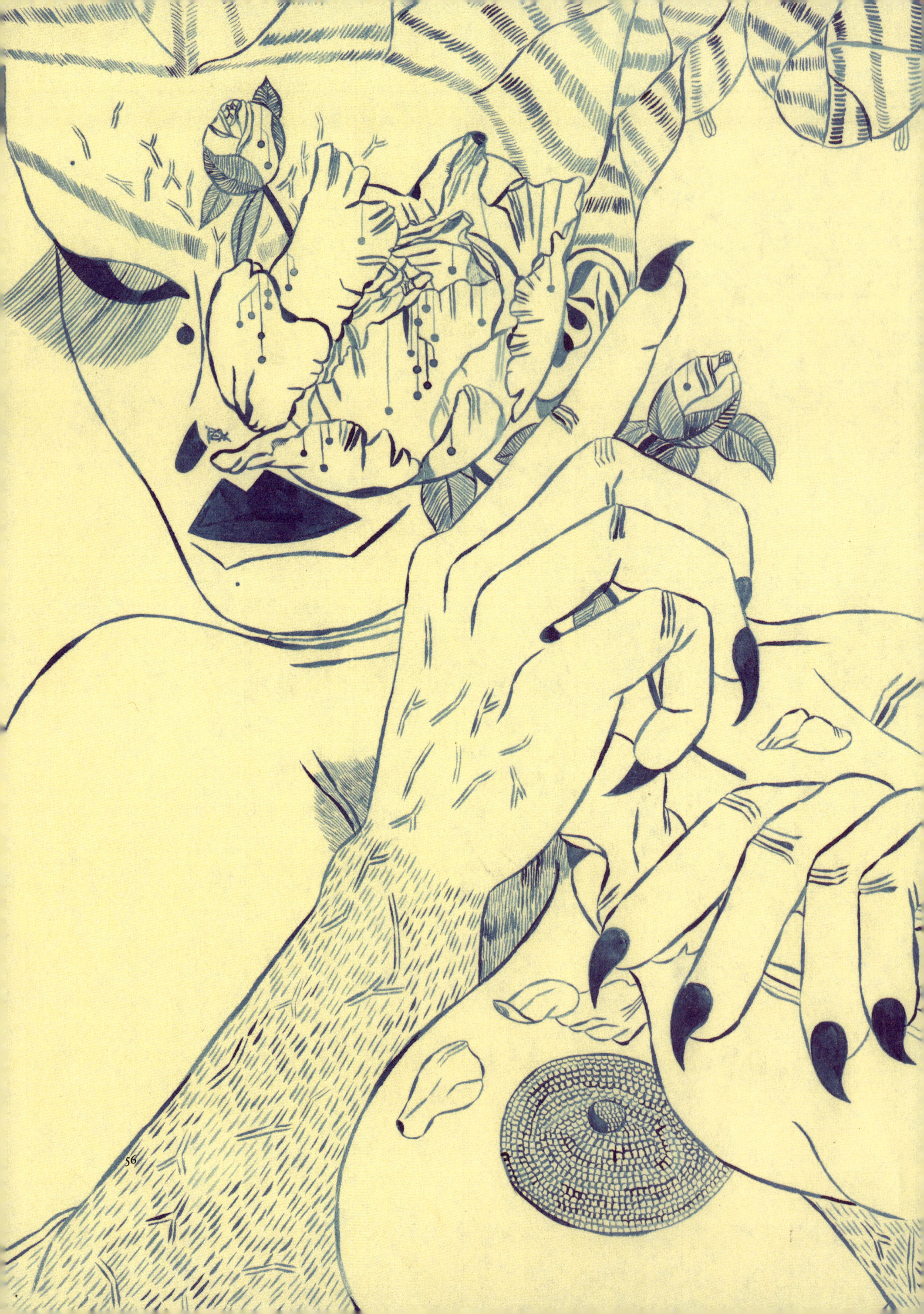

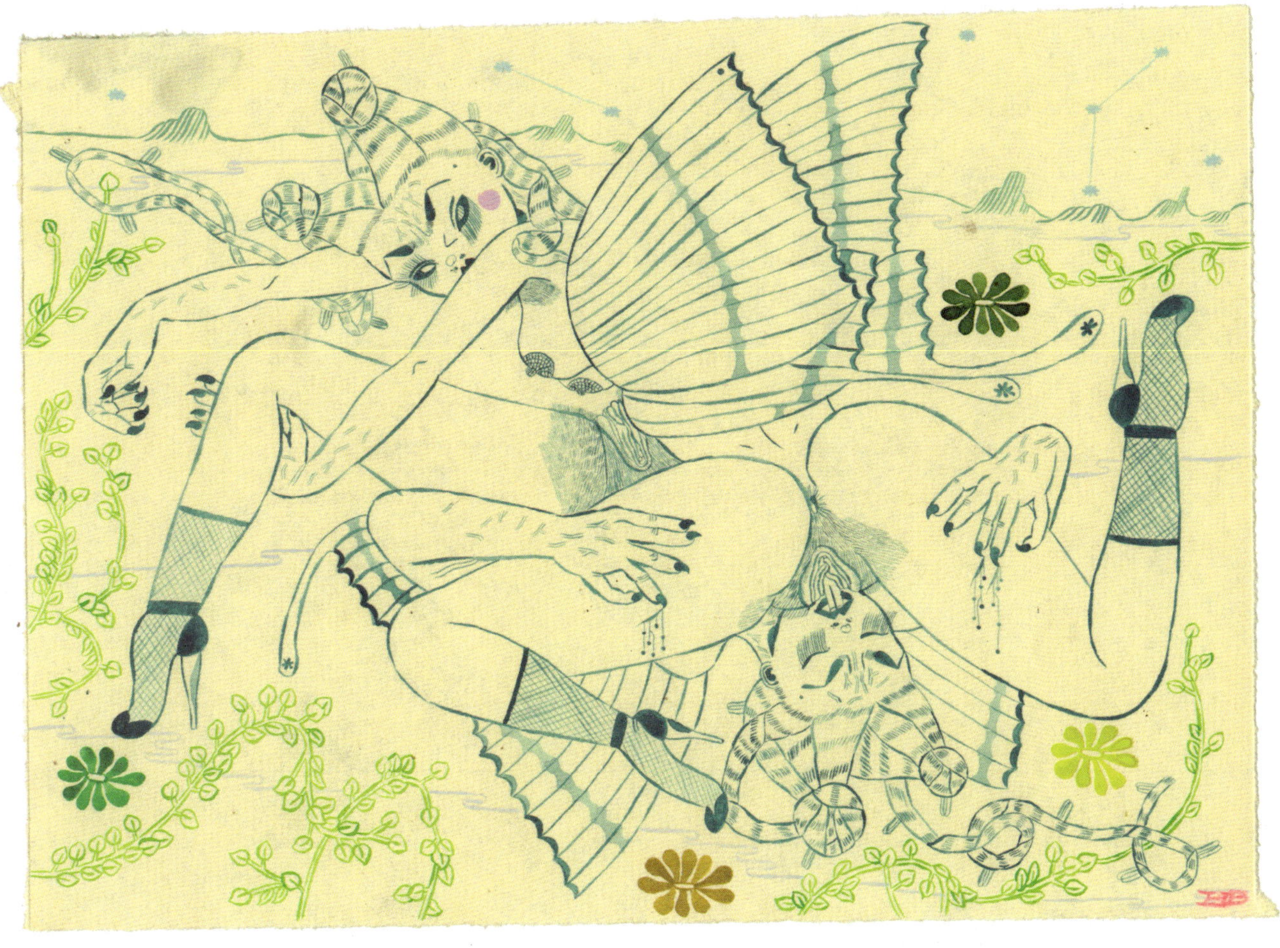

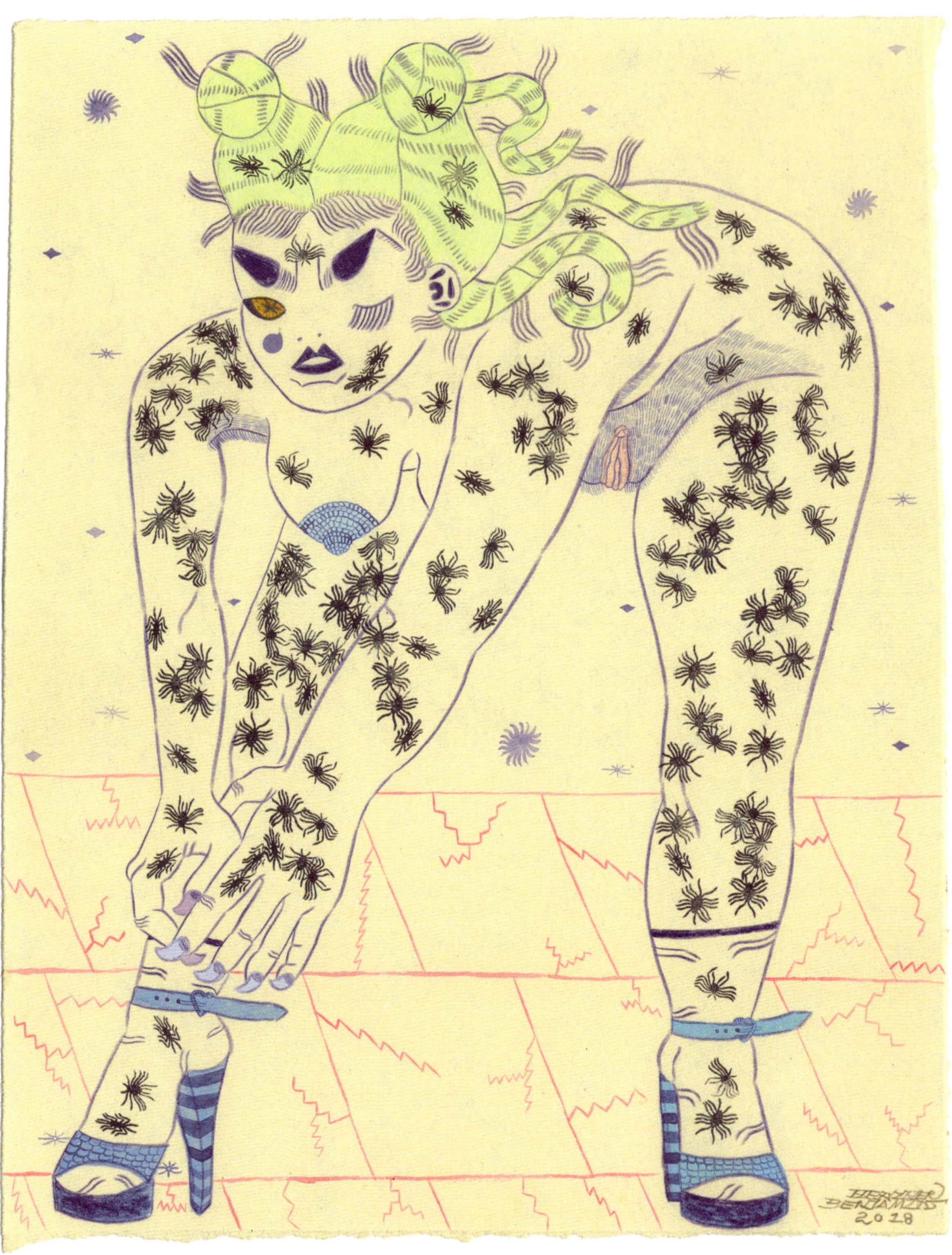

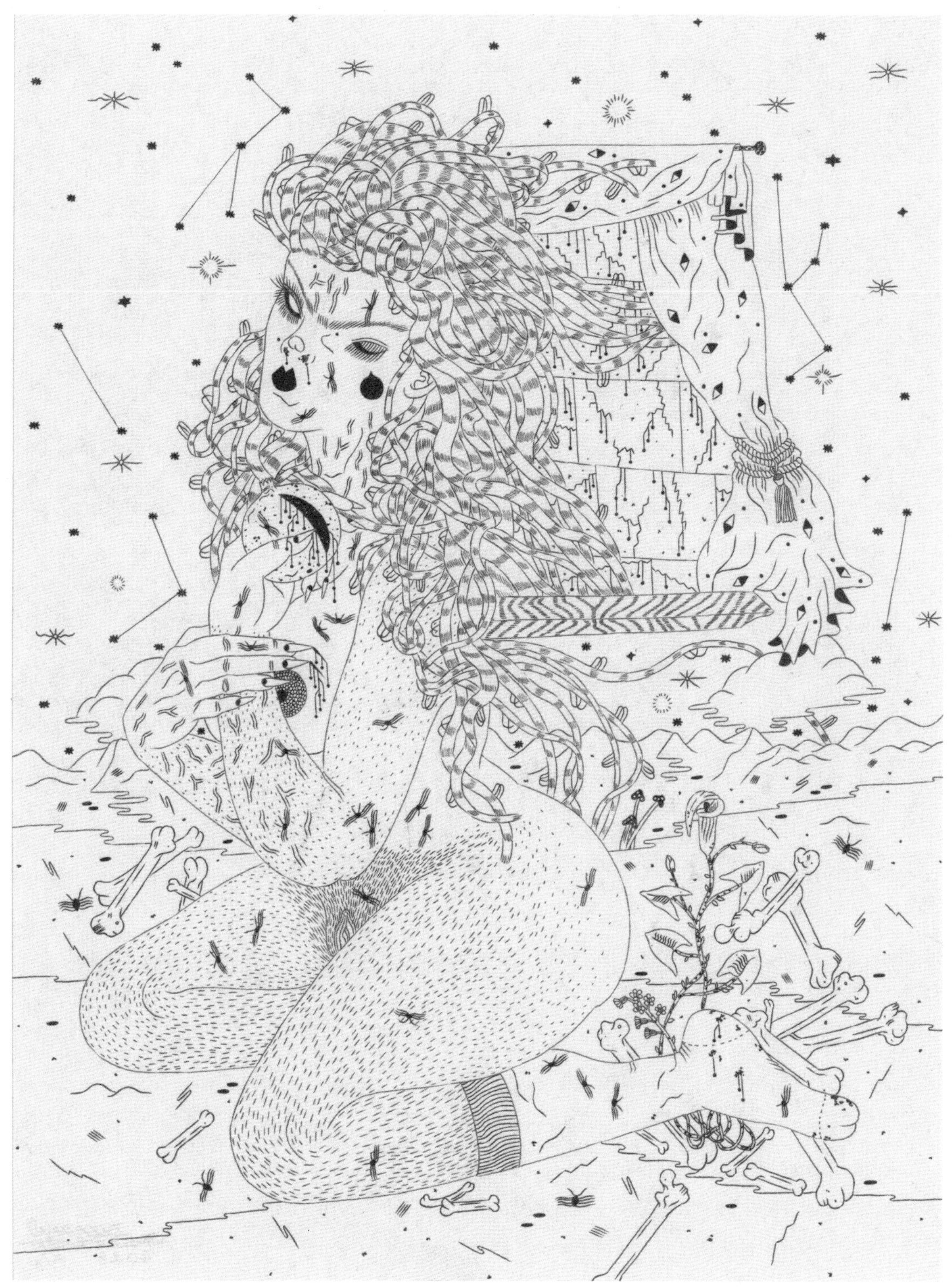

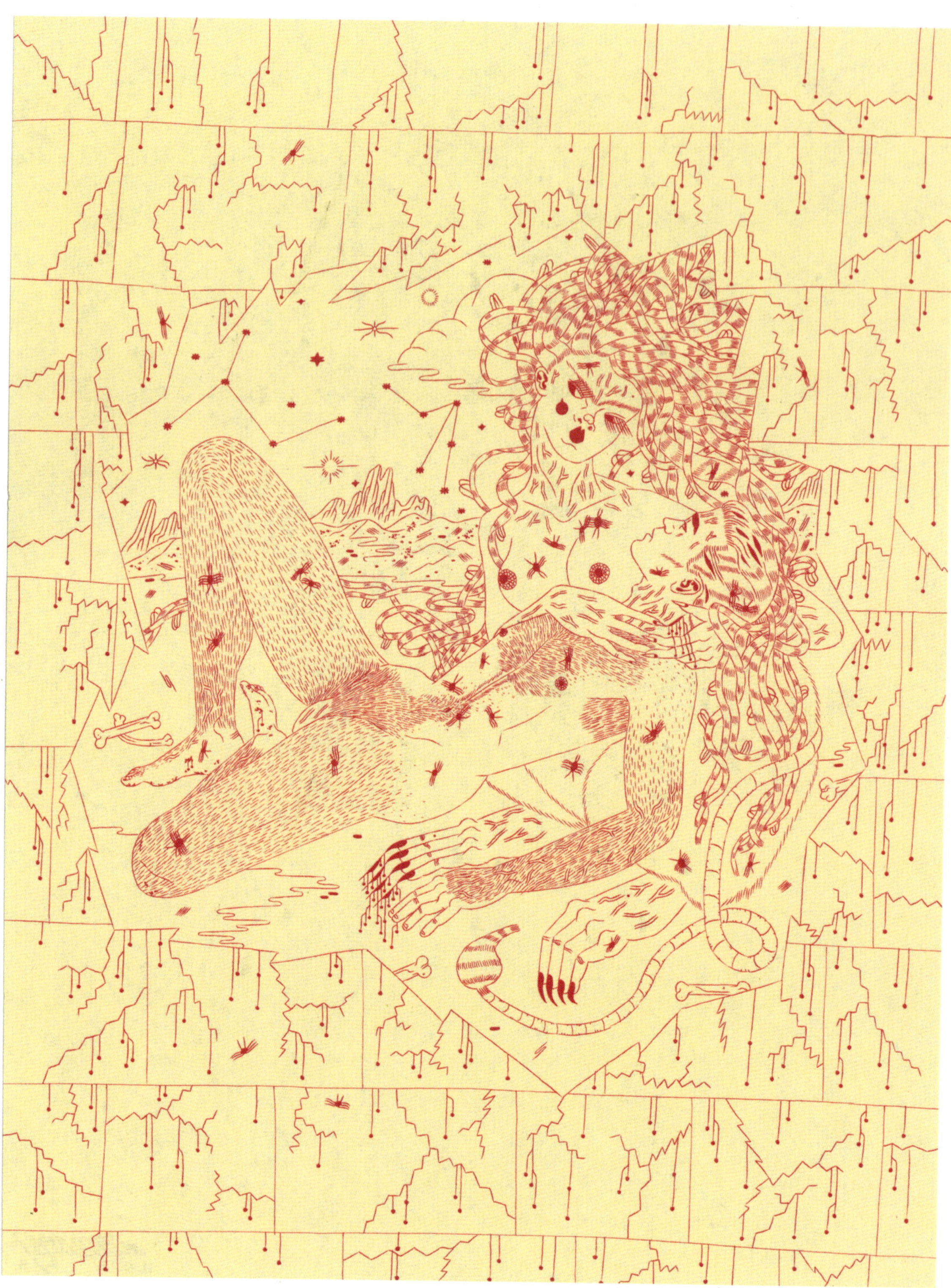

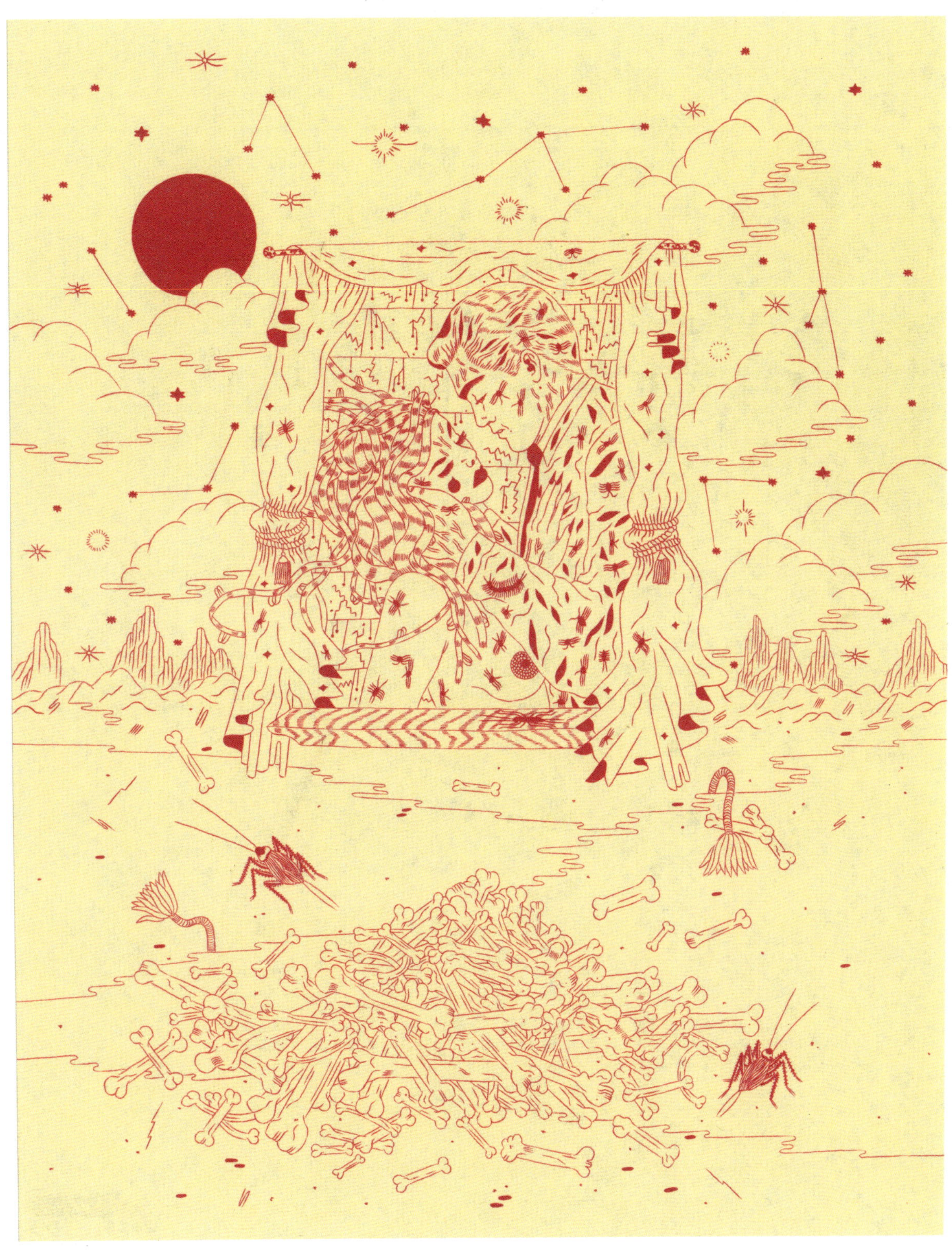

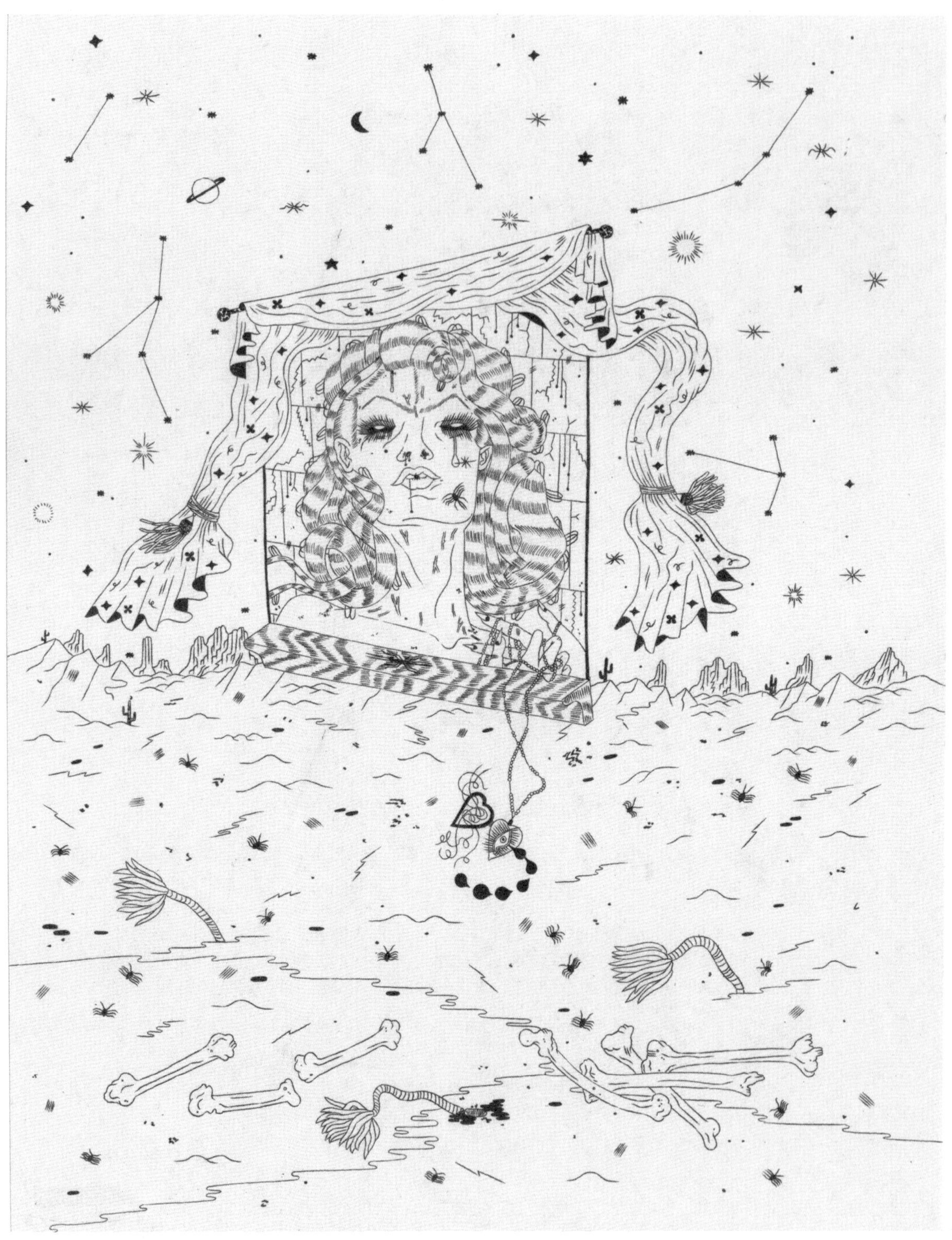

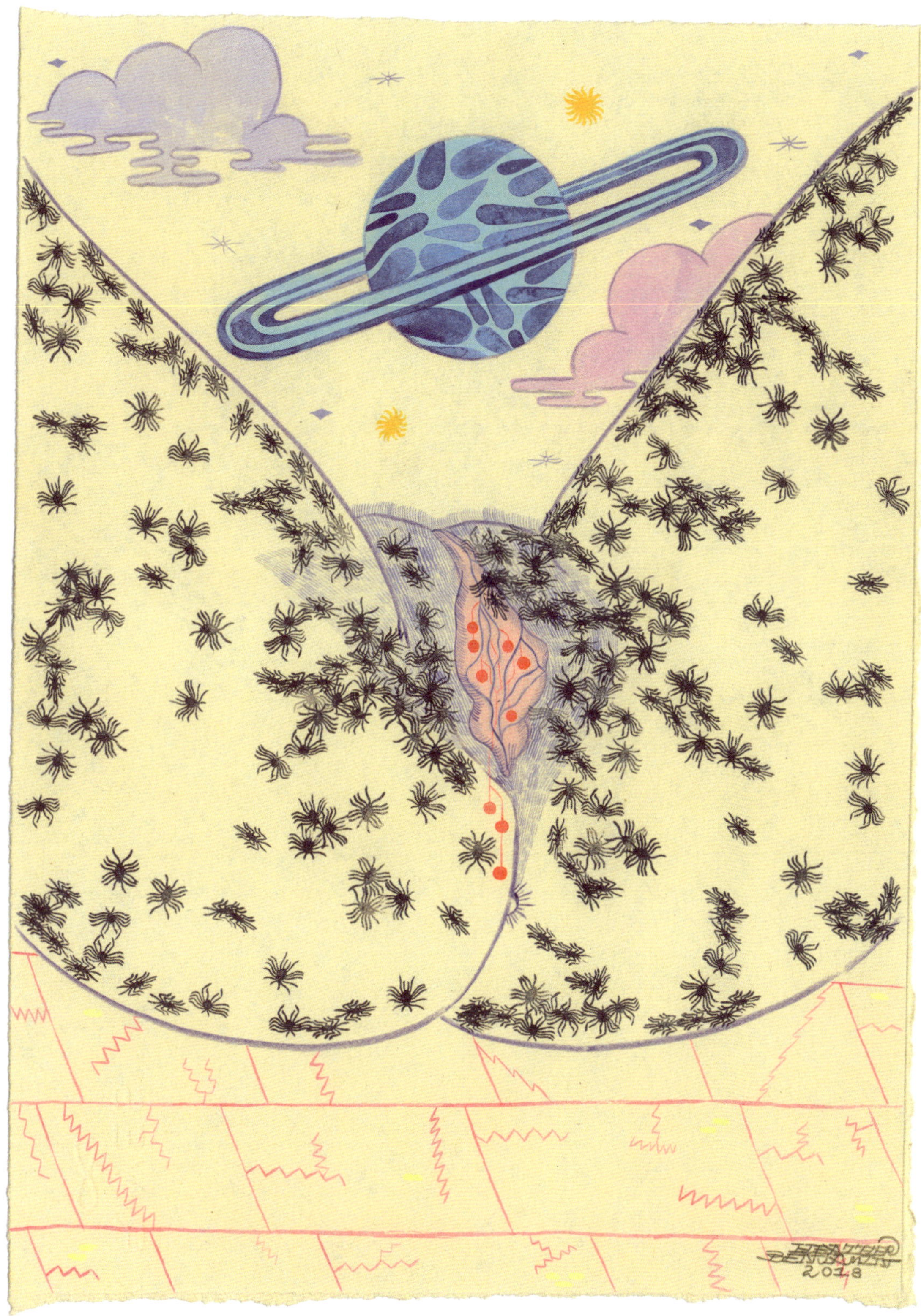

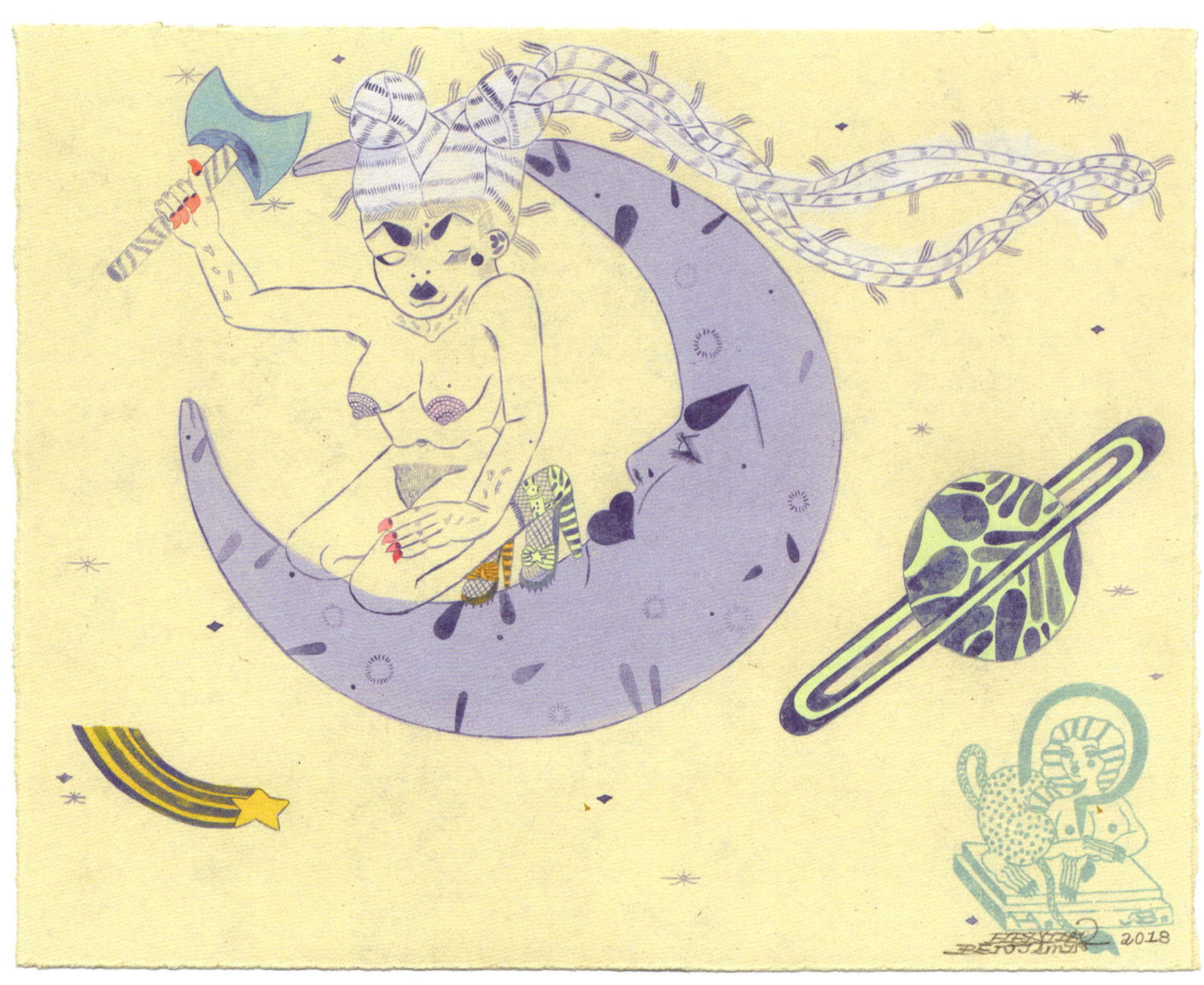

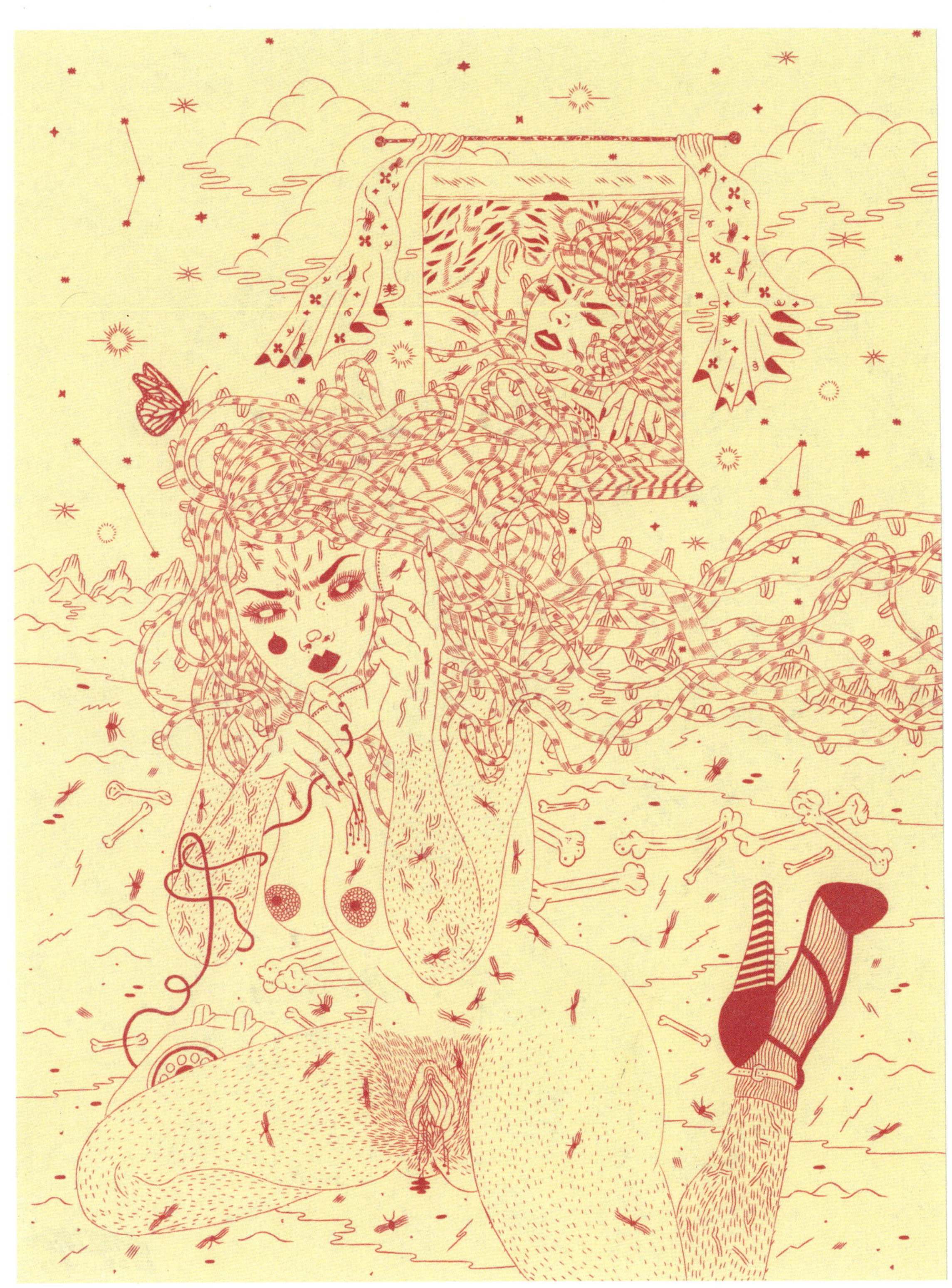

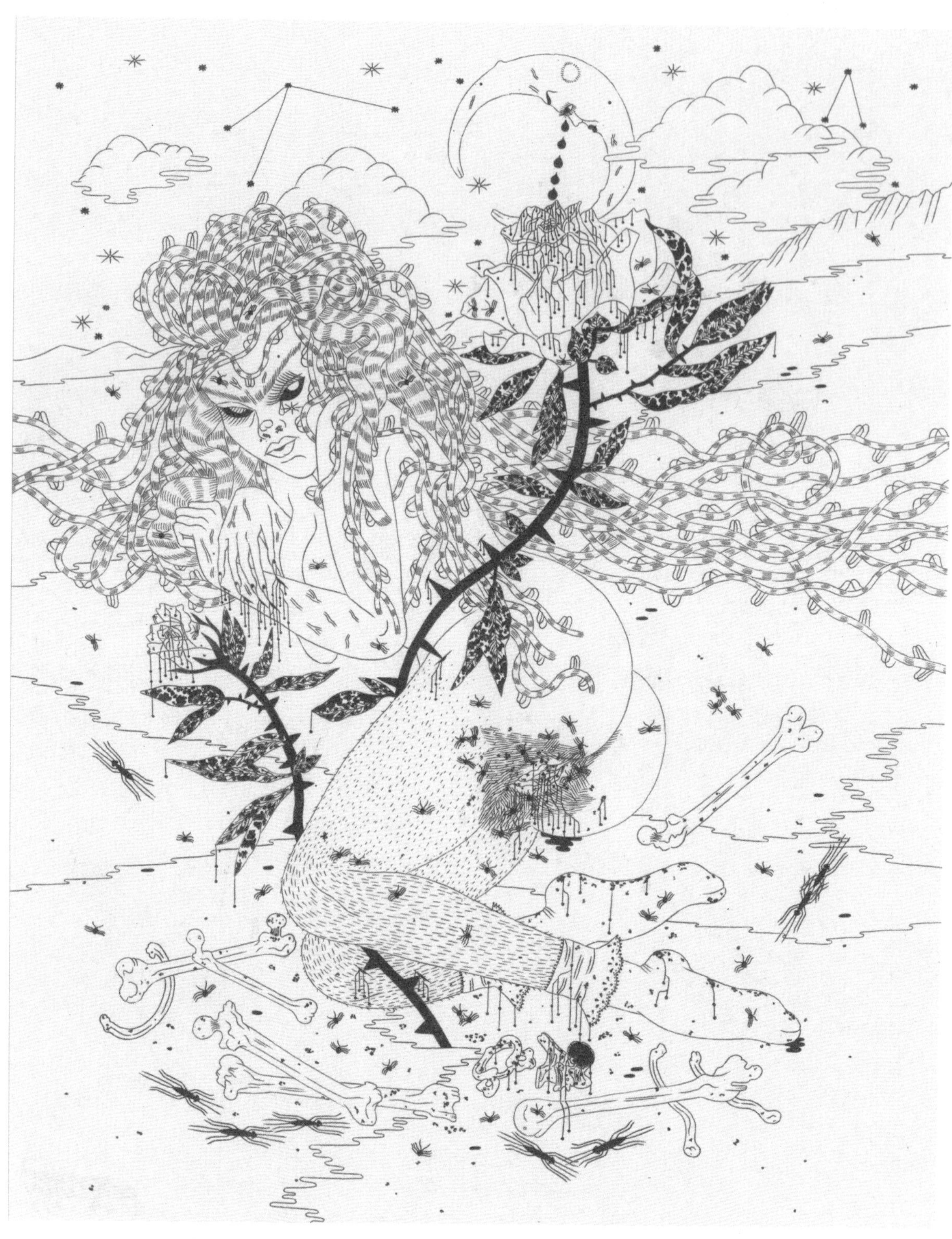

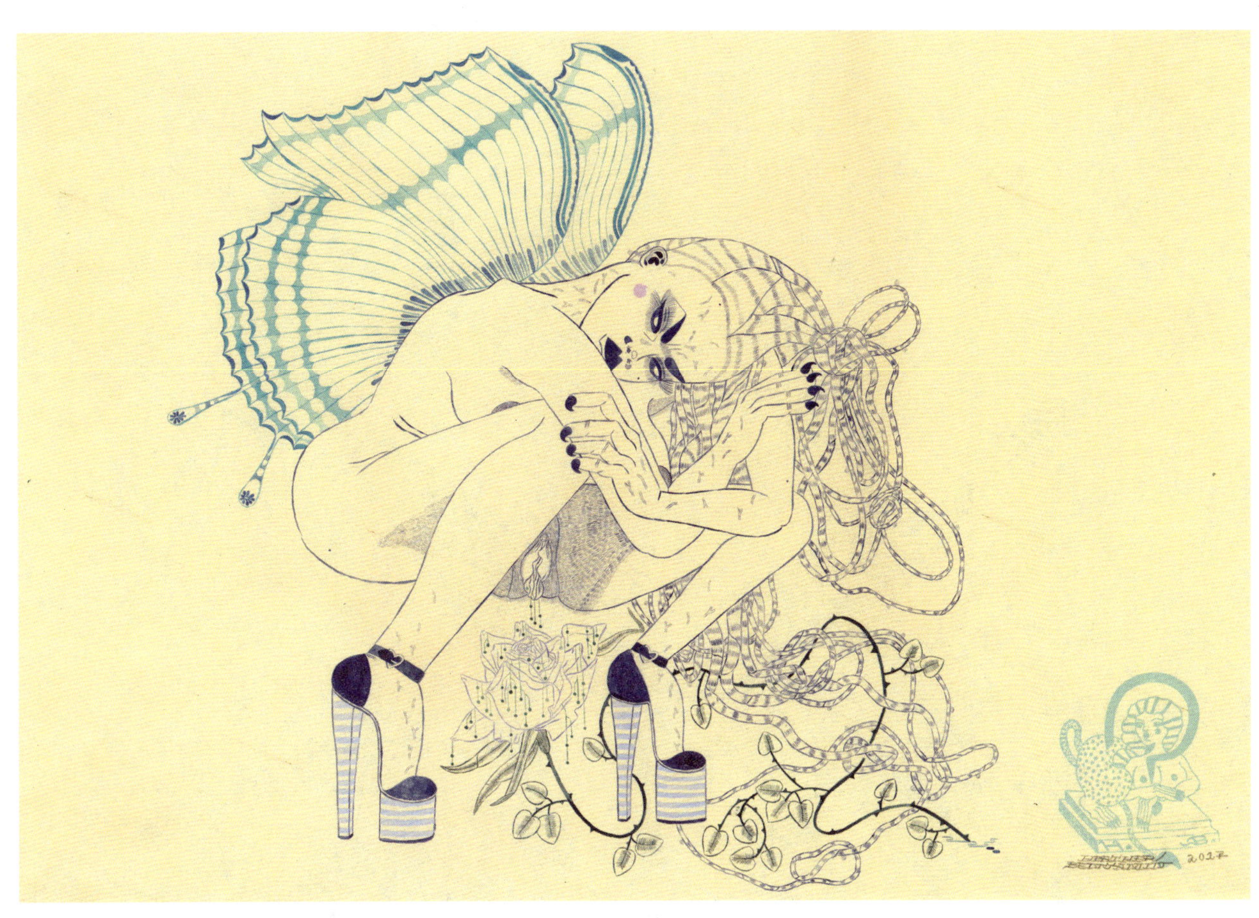

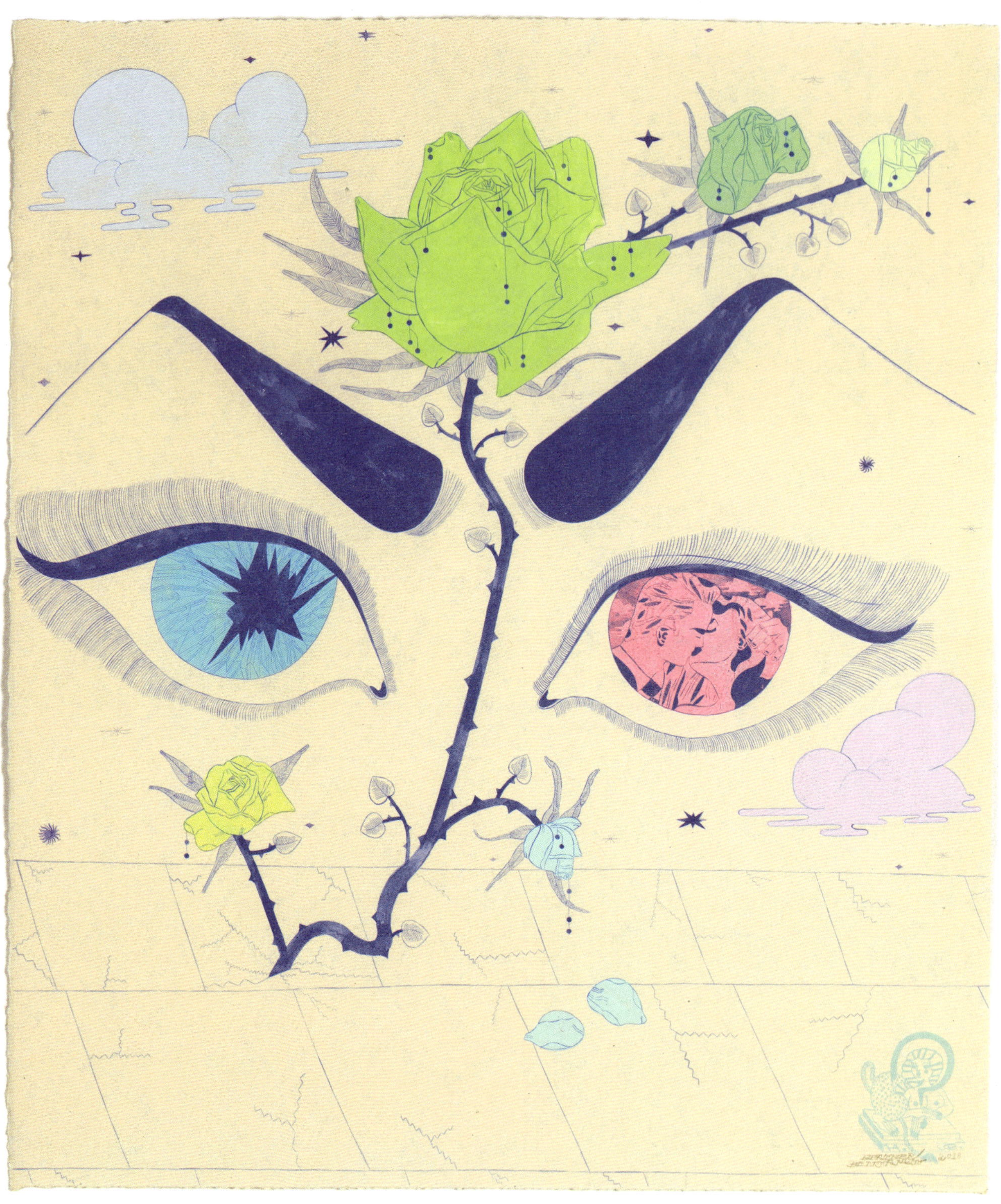

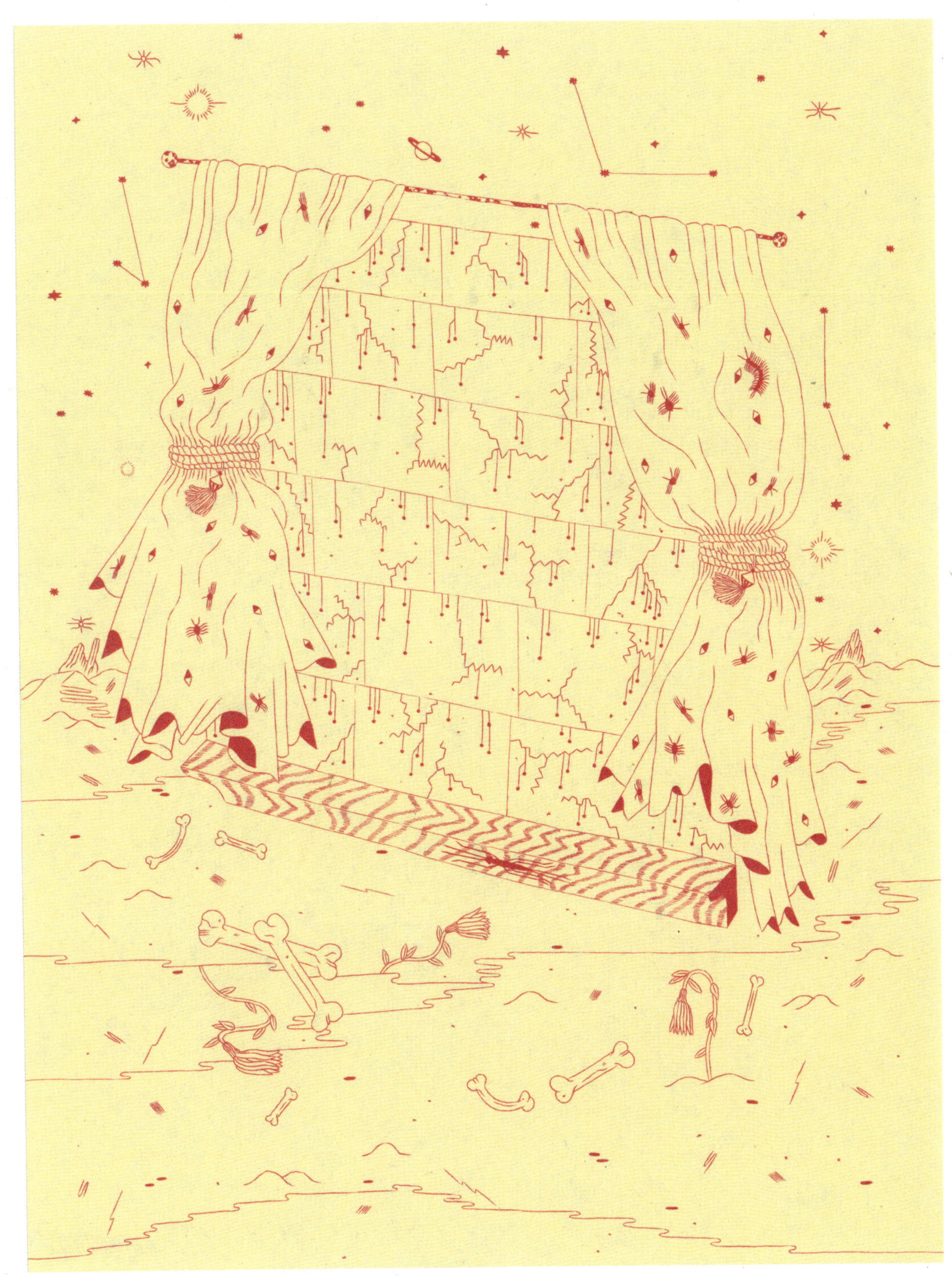

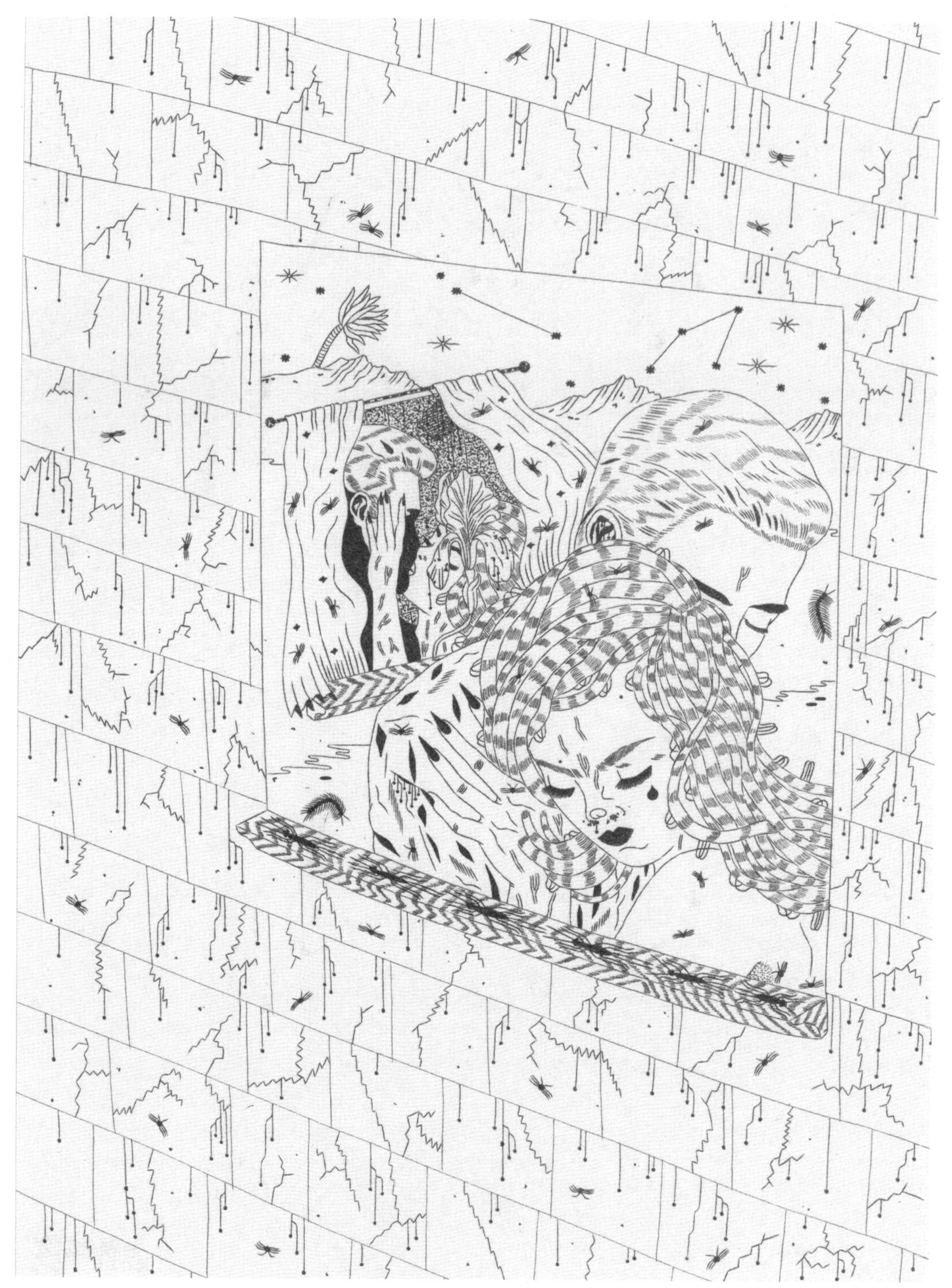

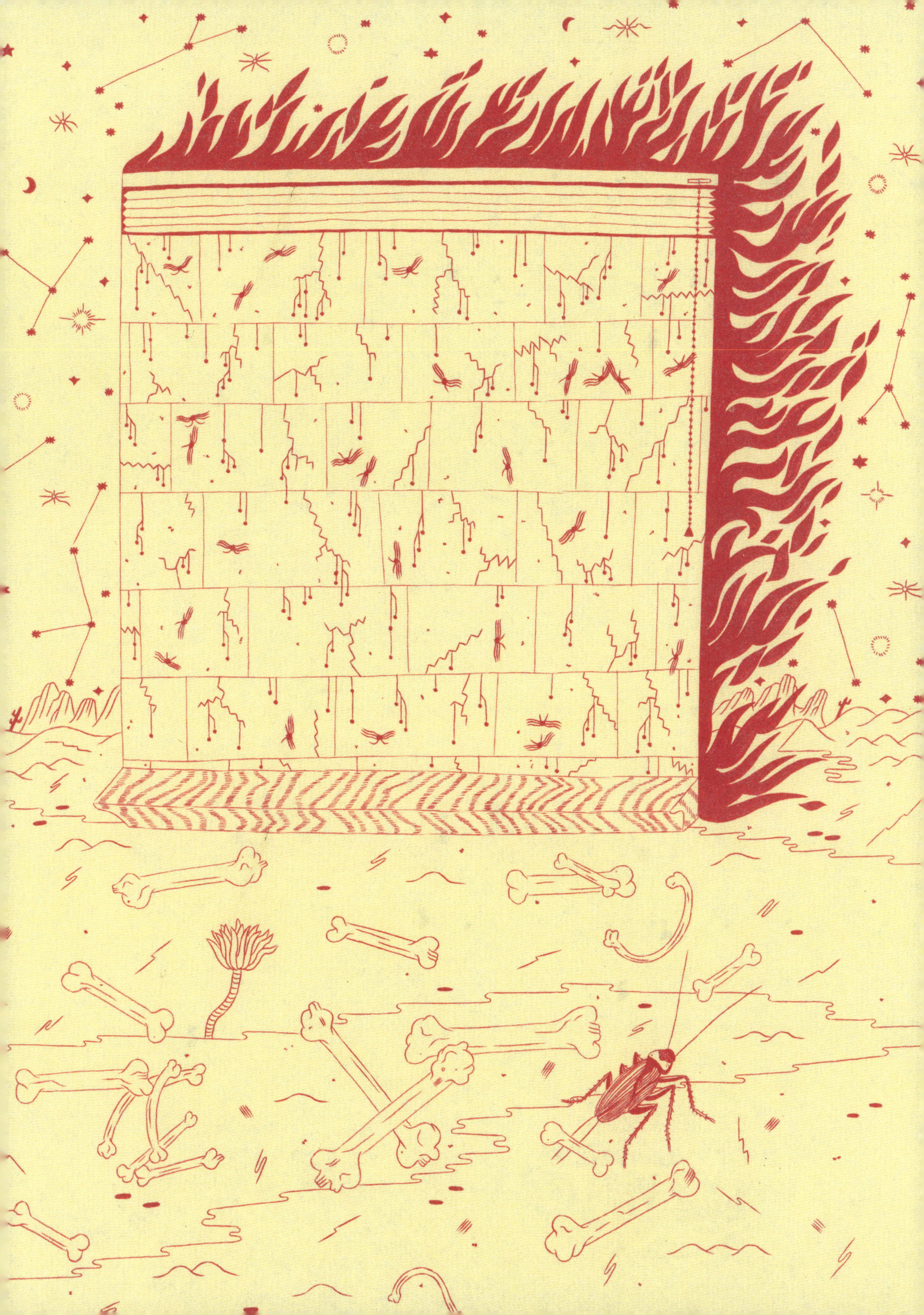

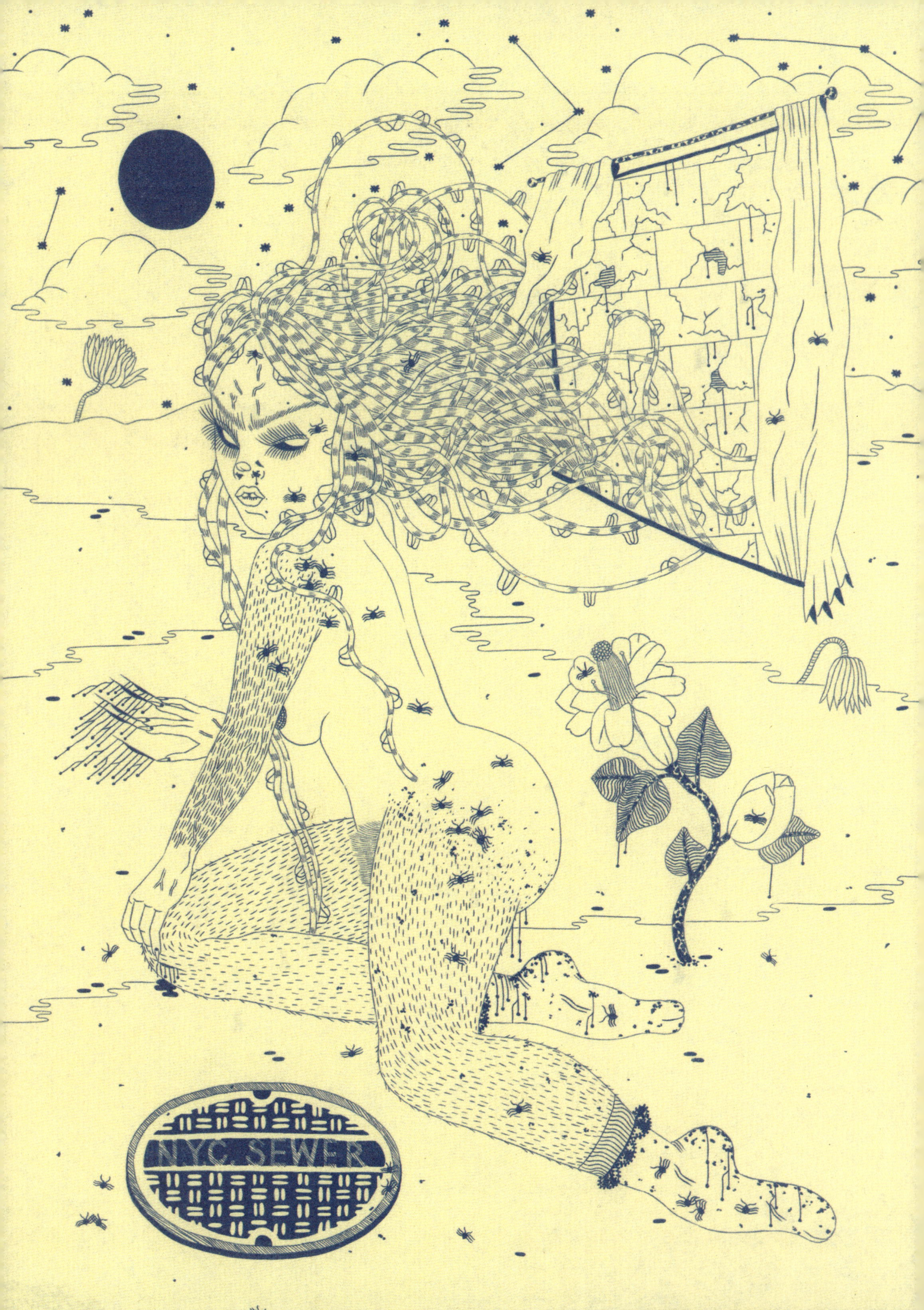

NYC SEWER

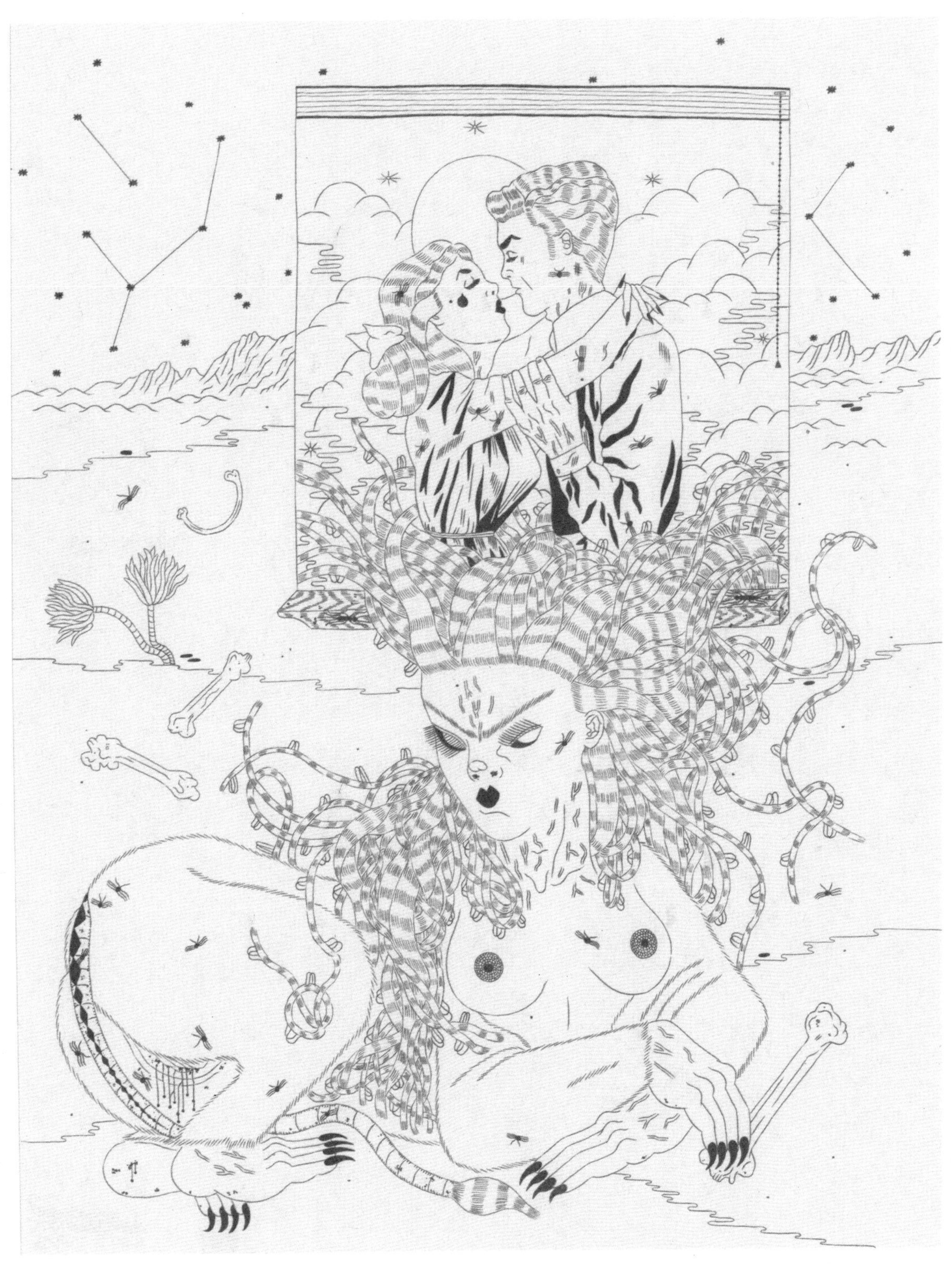

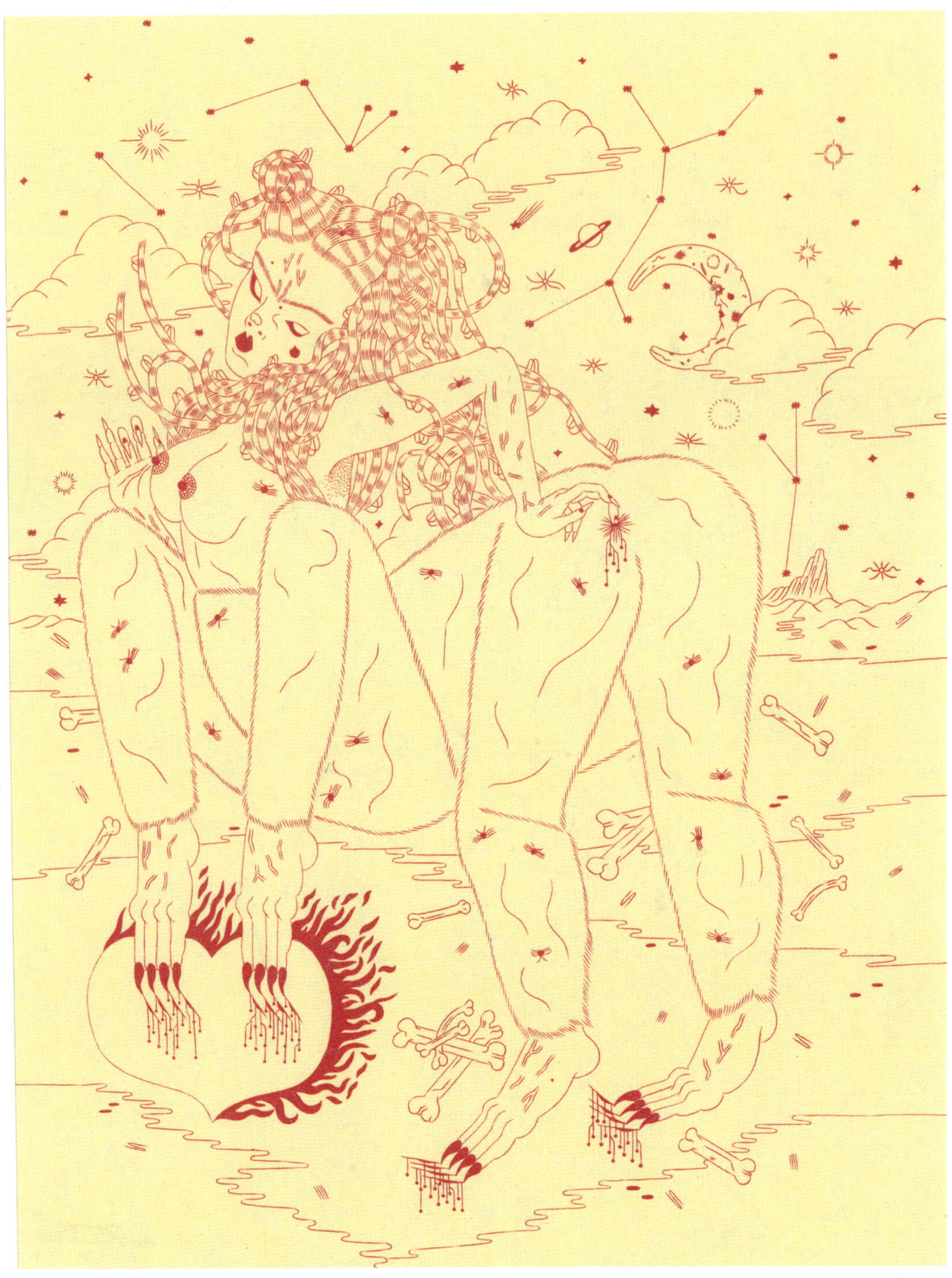

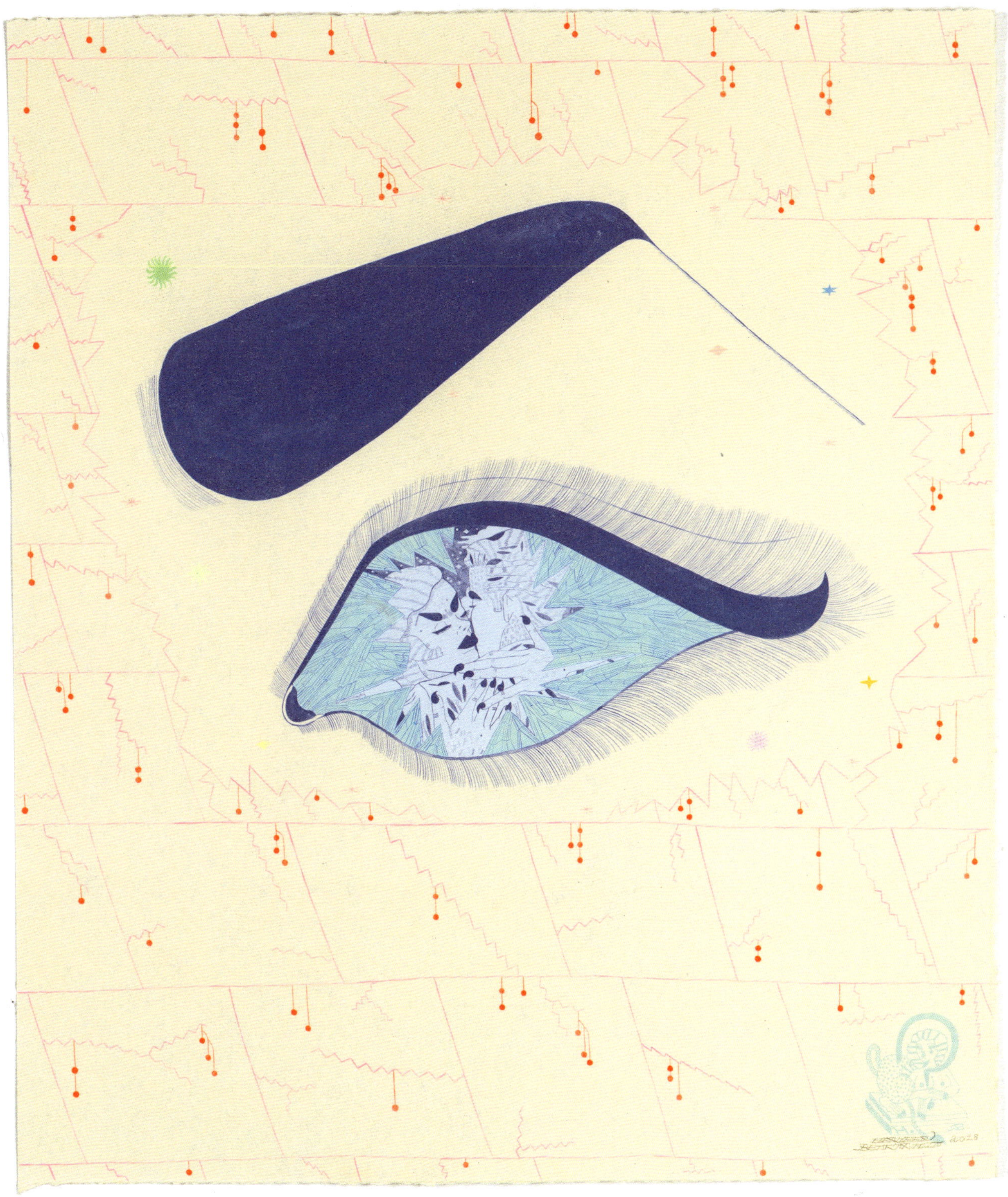

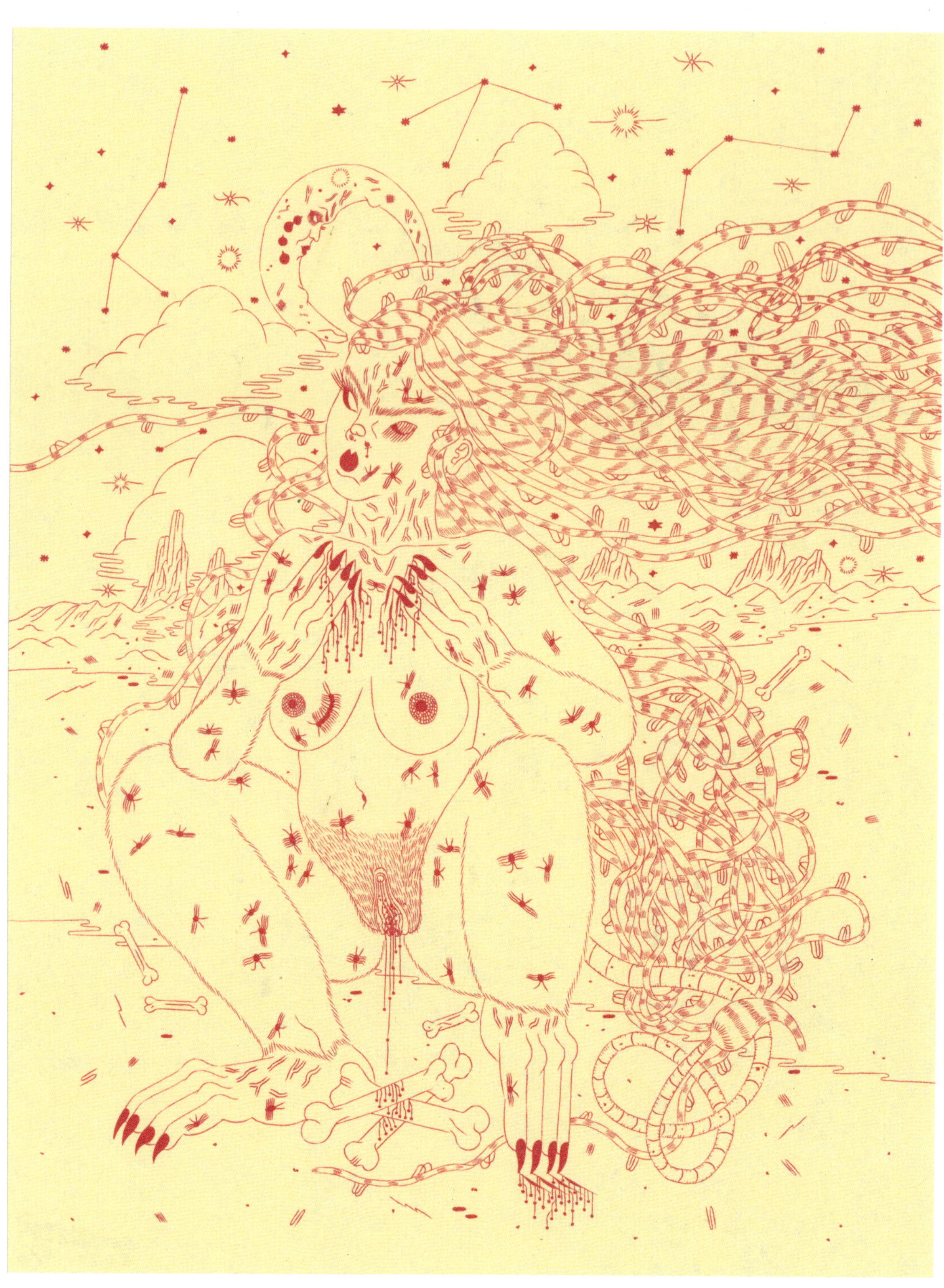

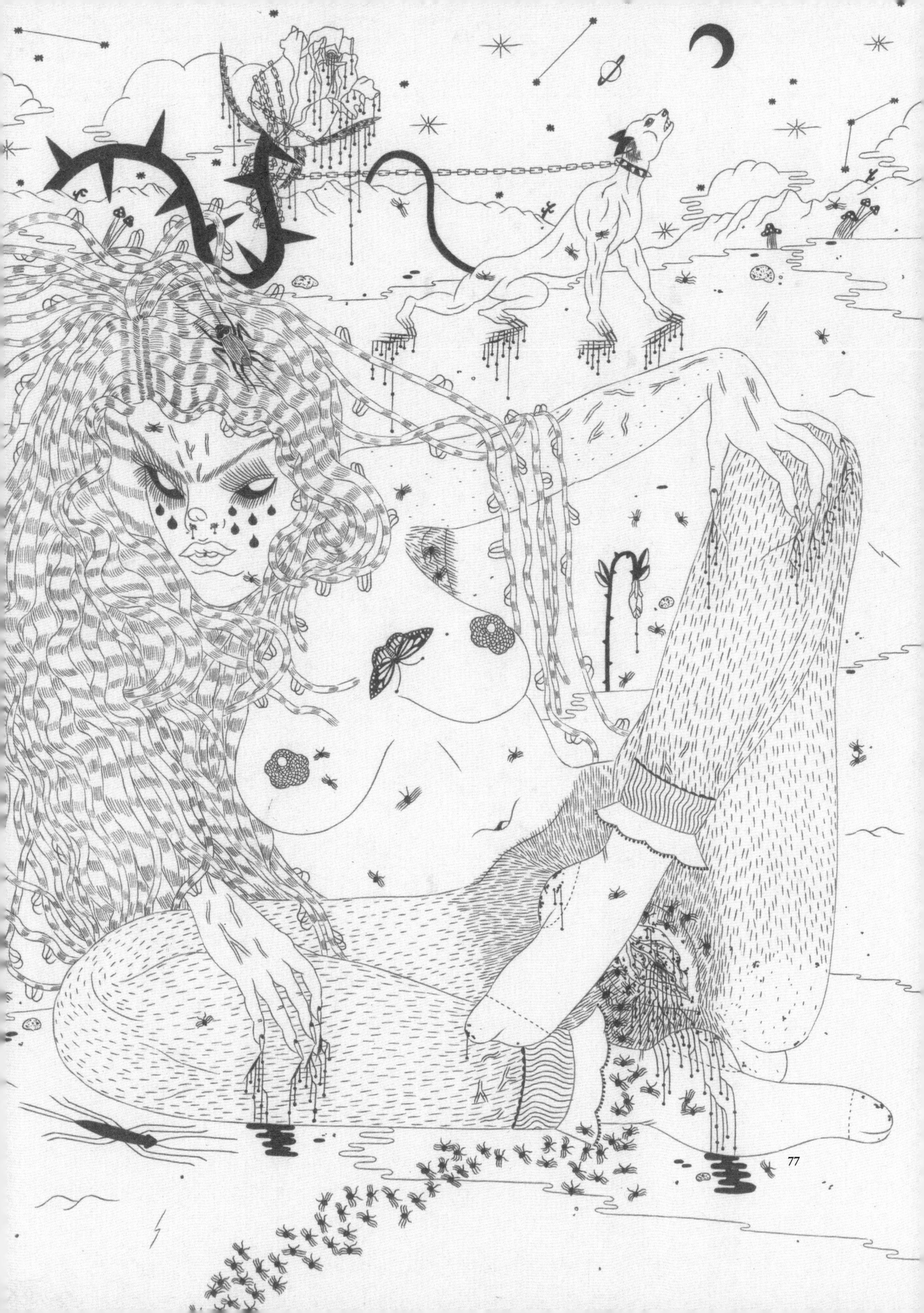

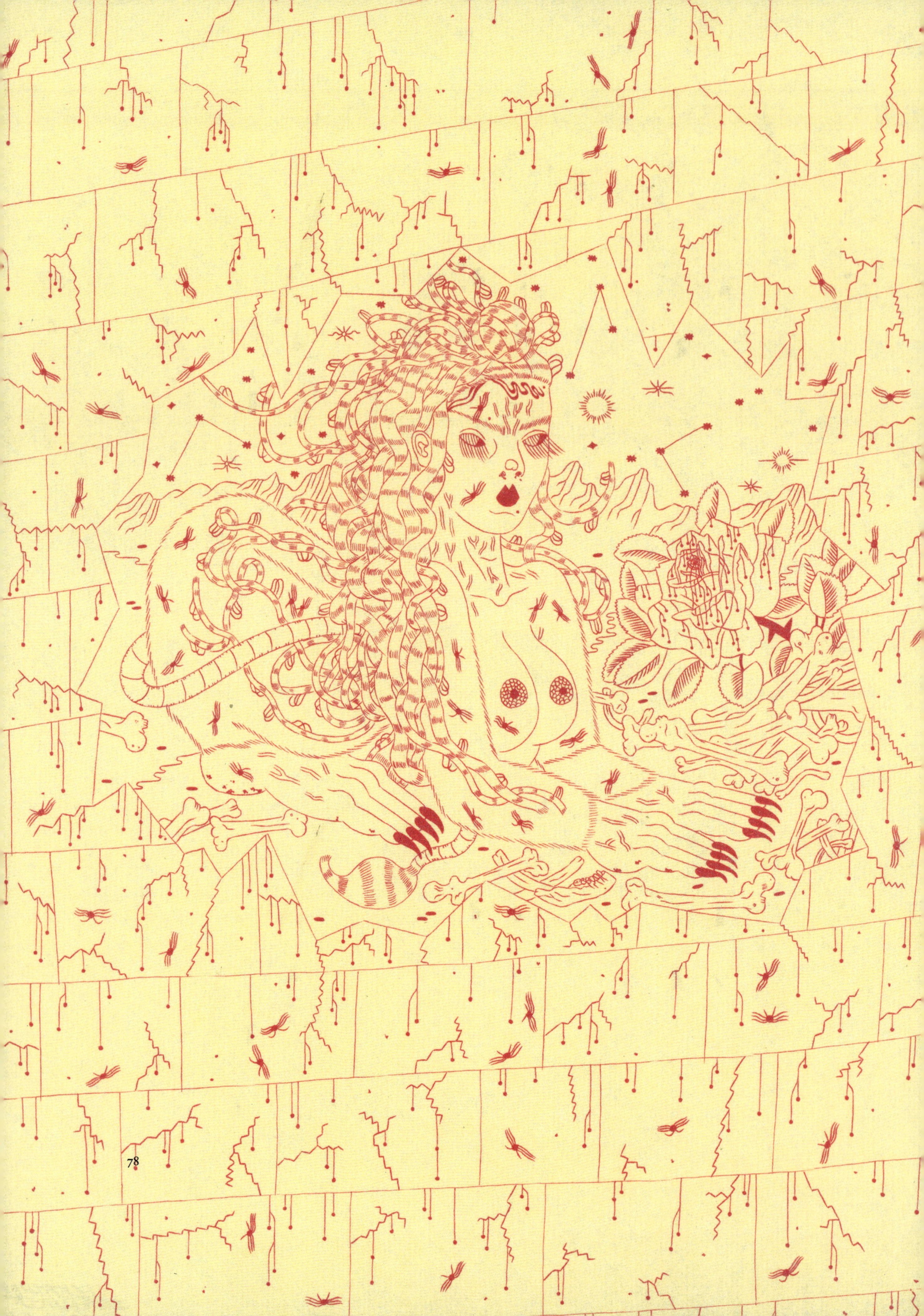

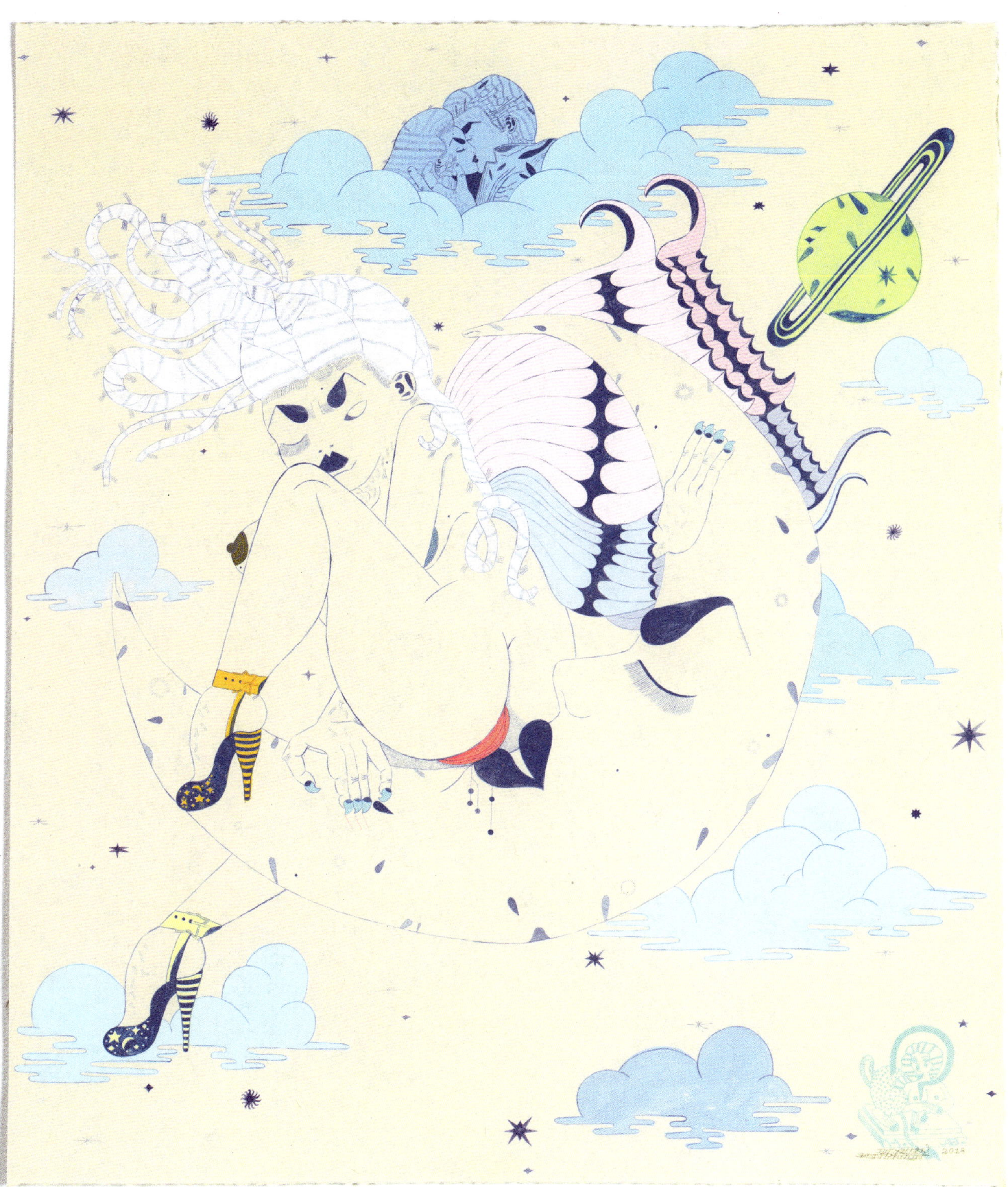

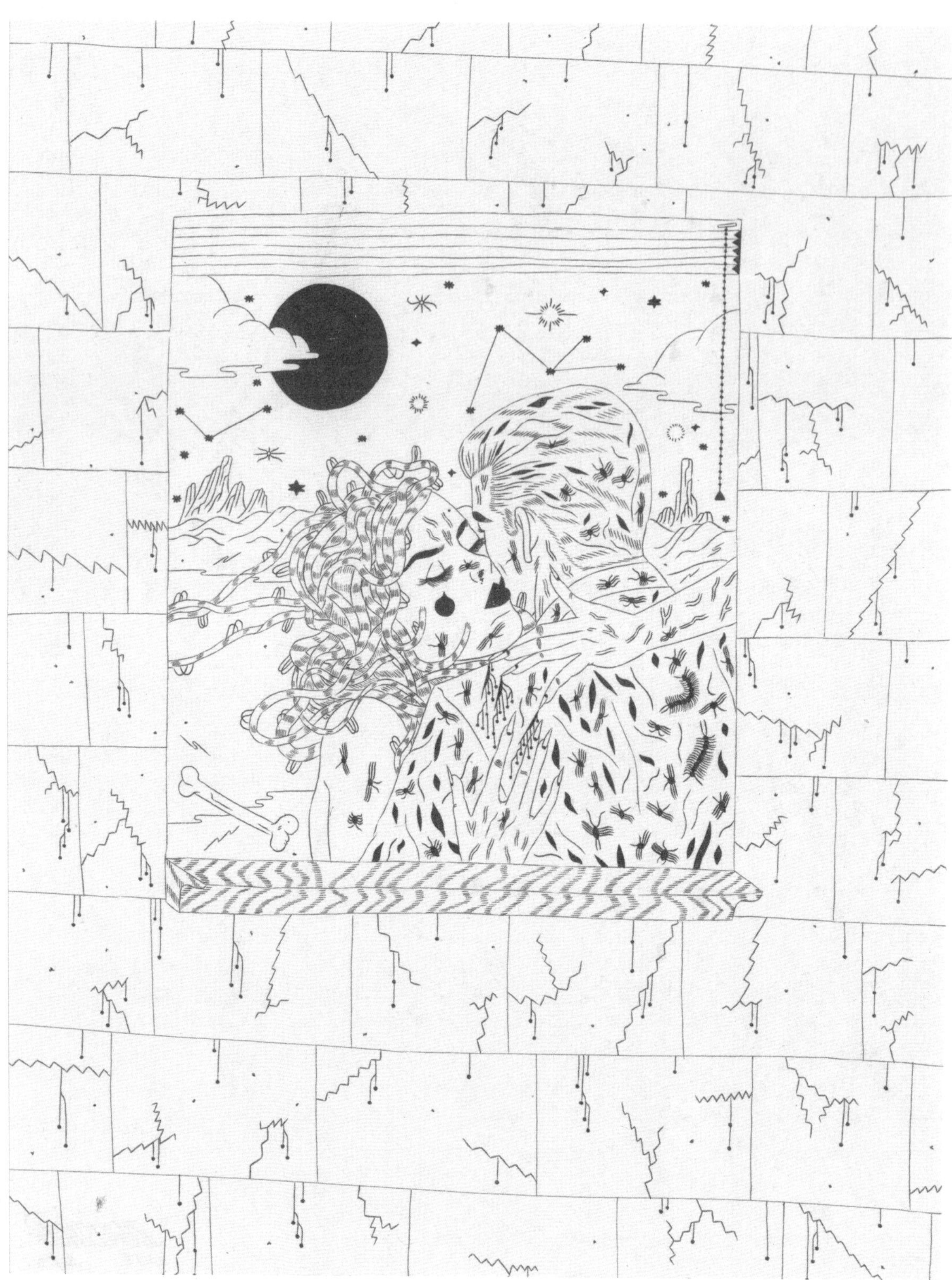

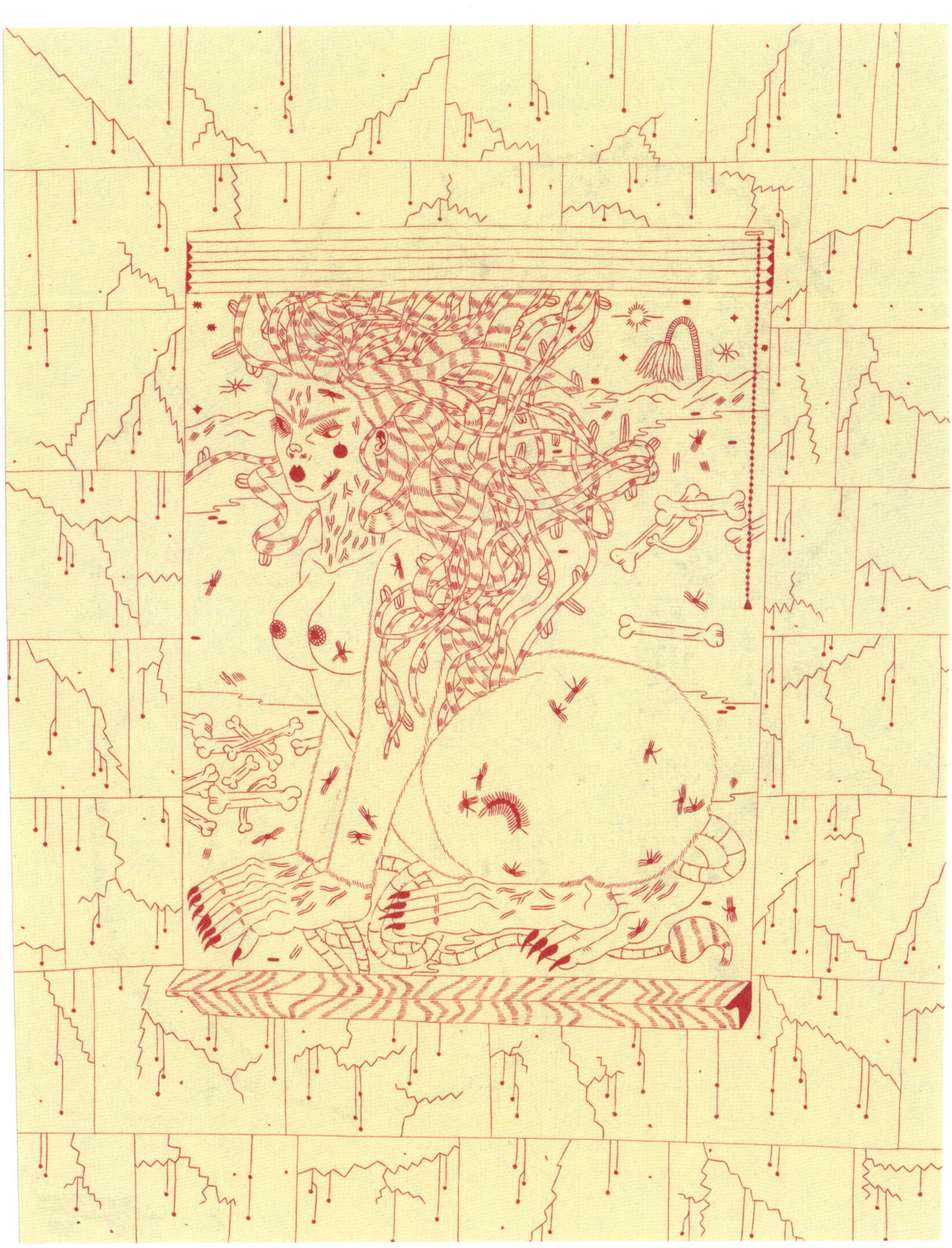

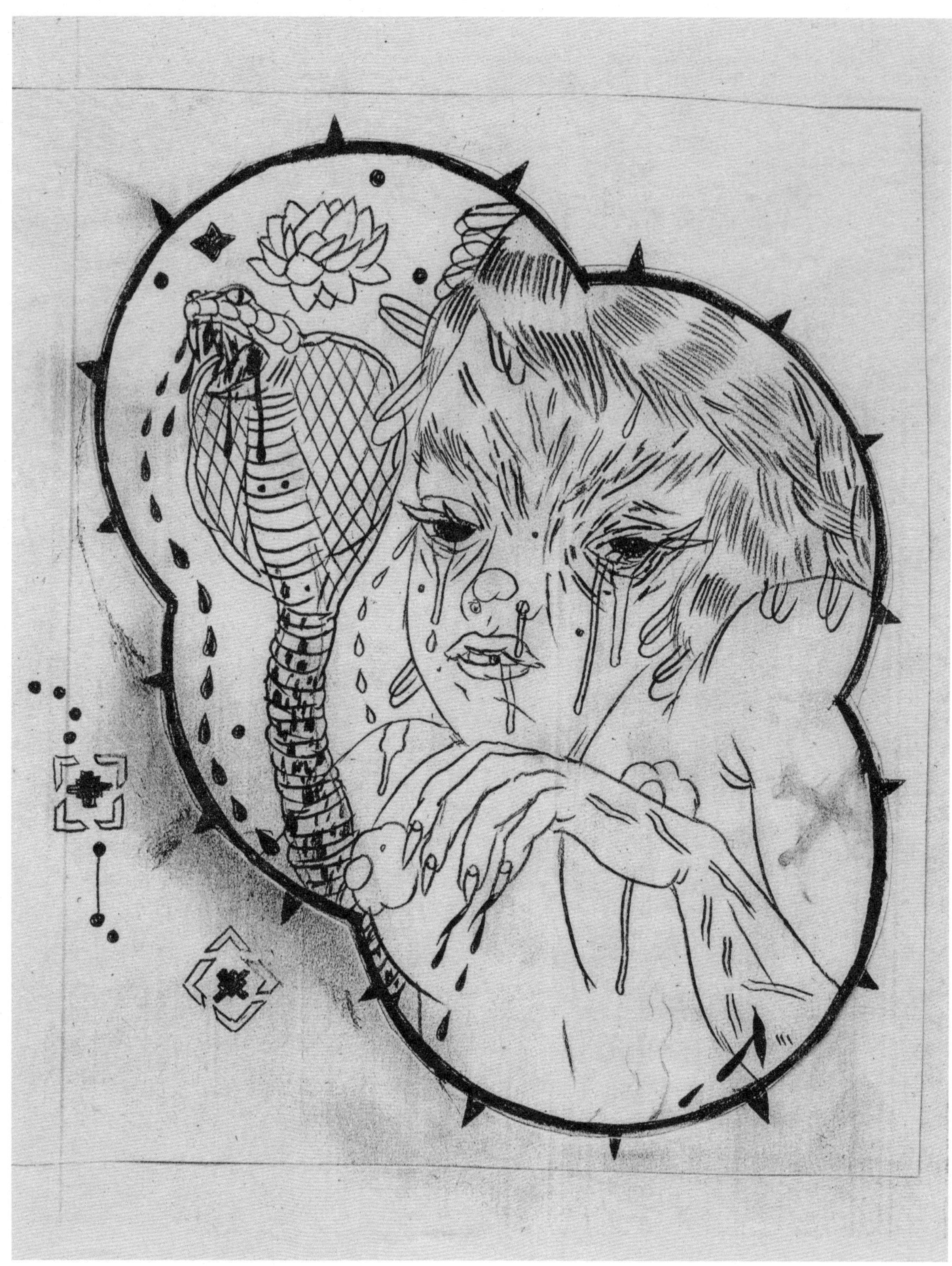

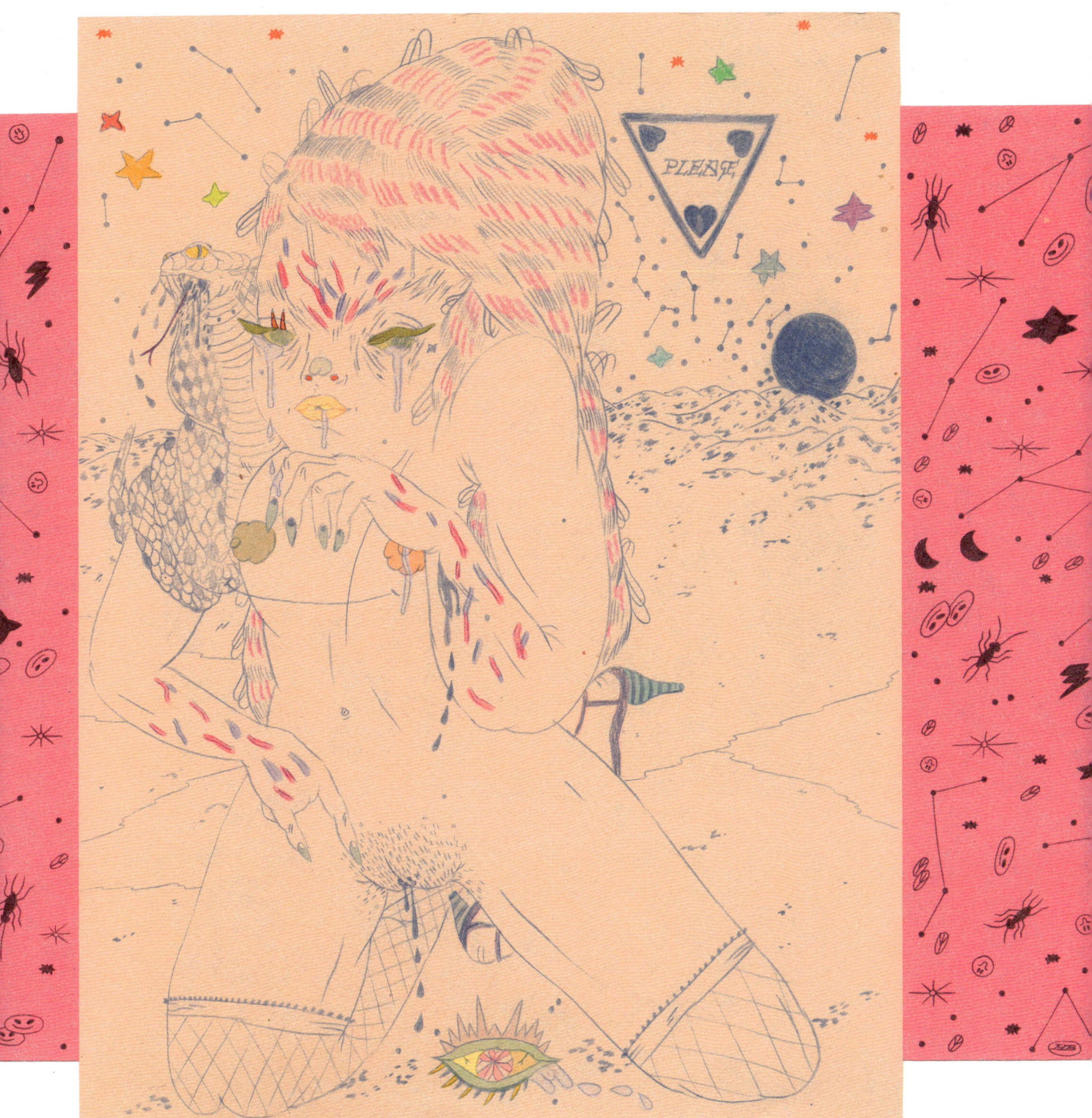
PLEASE

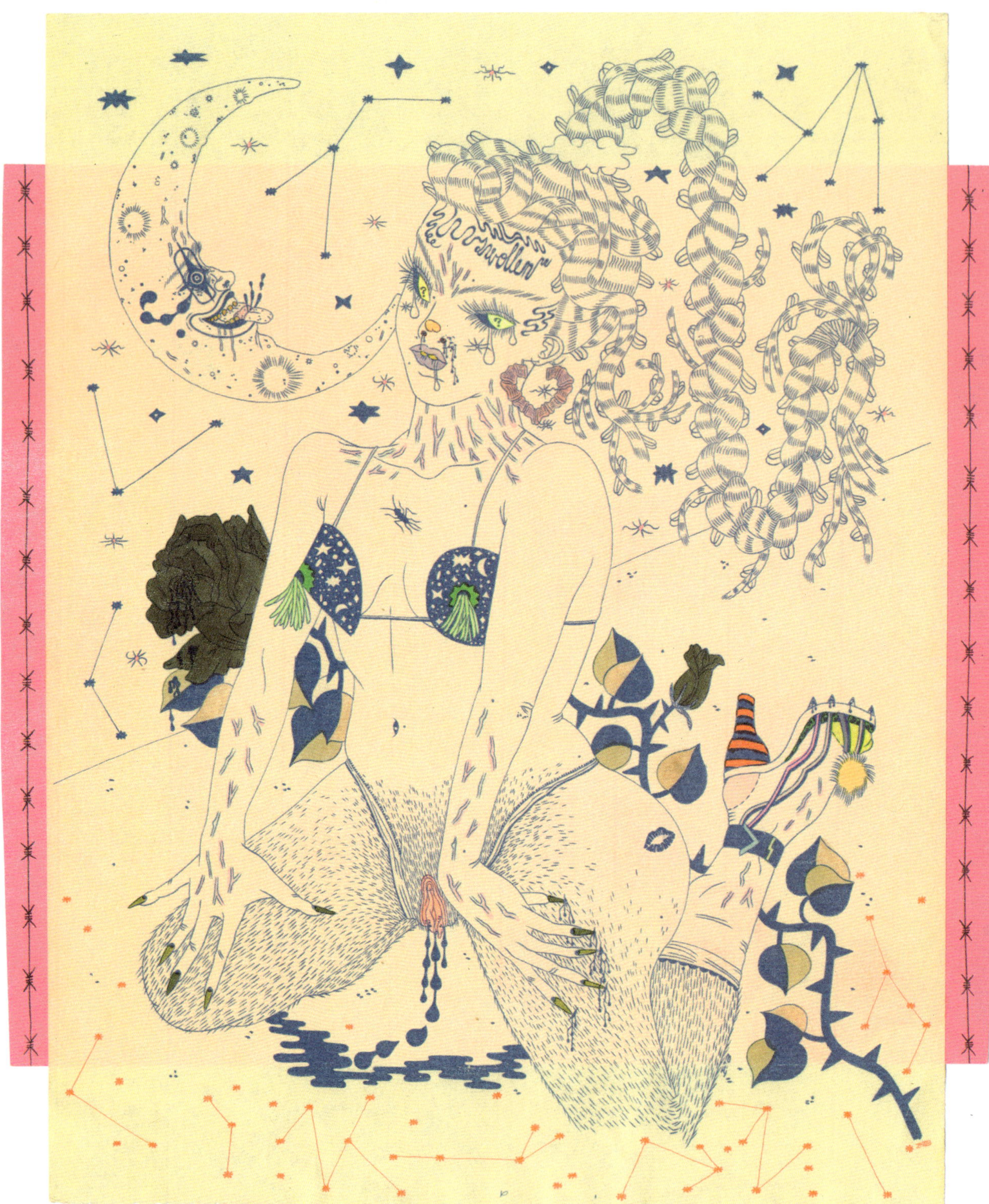

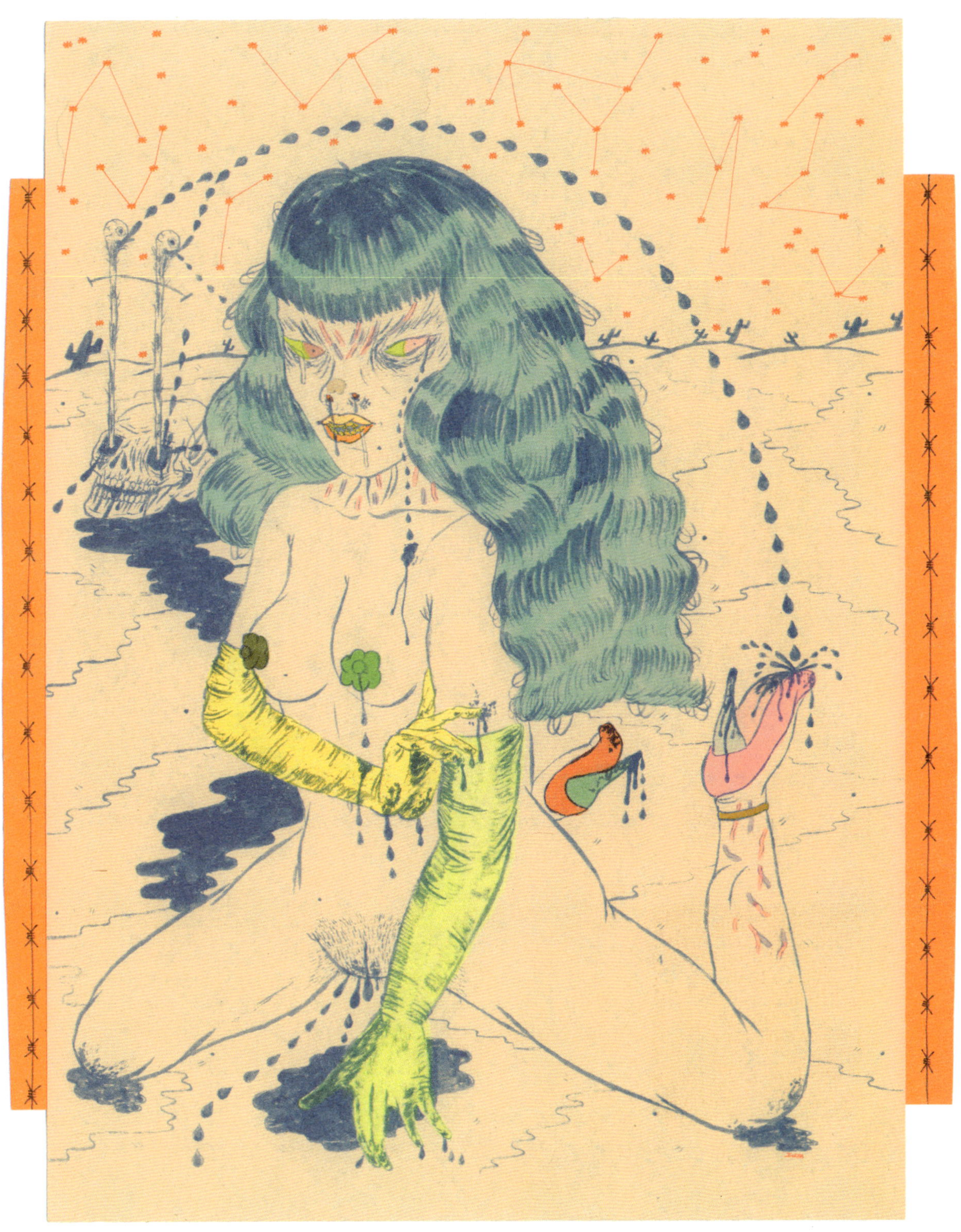

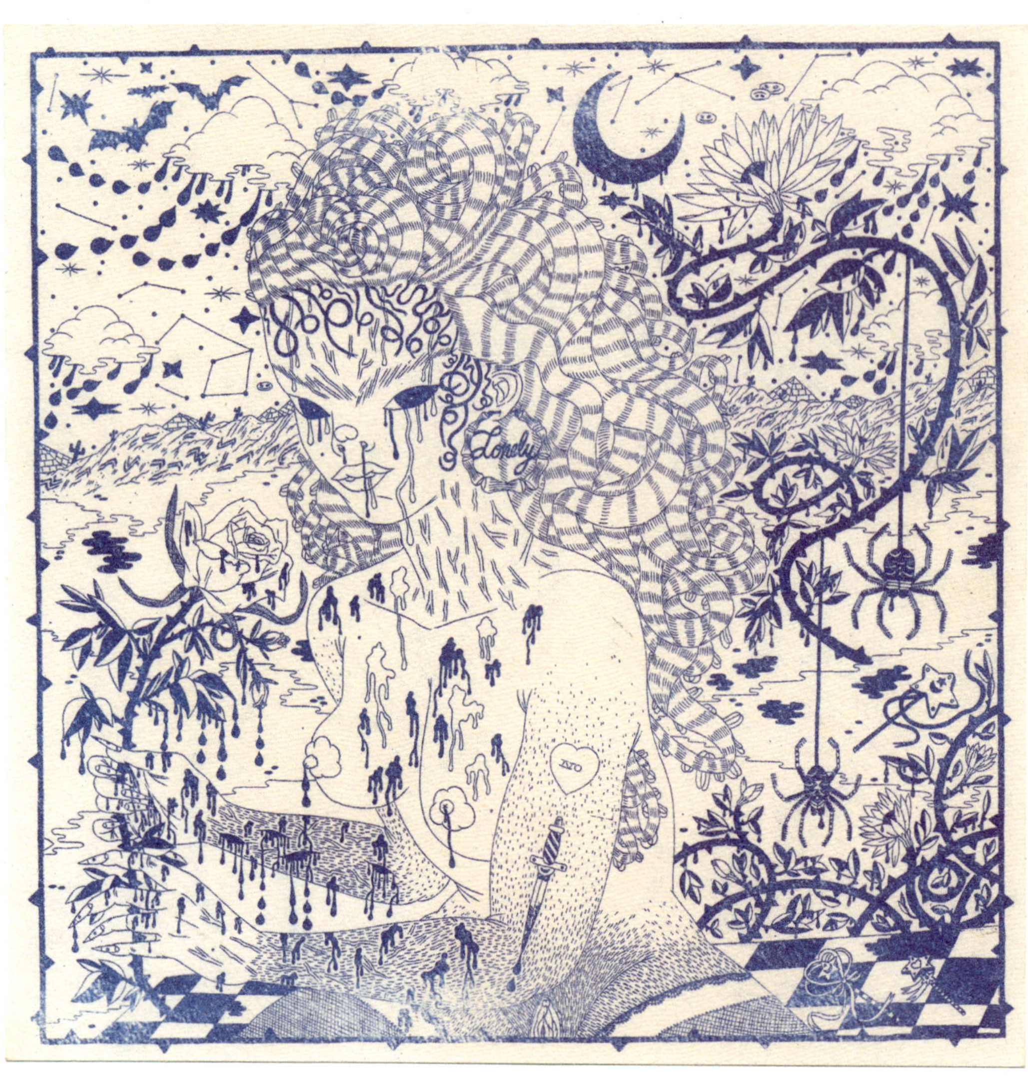

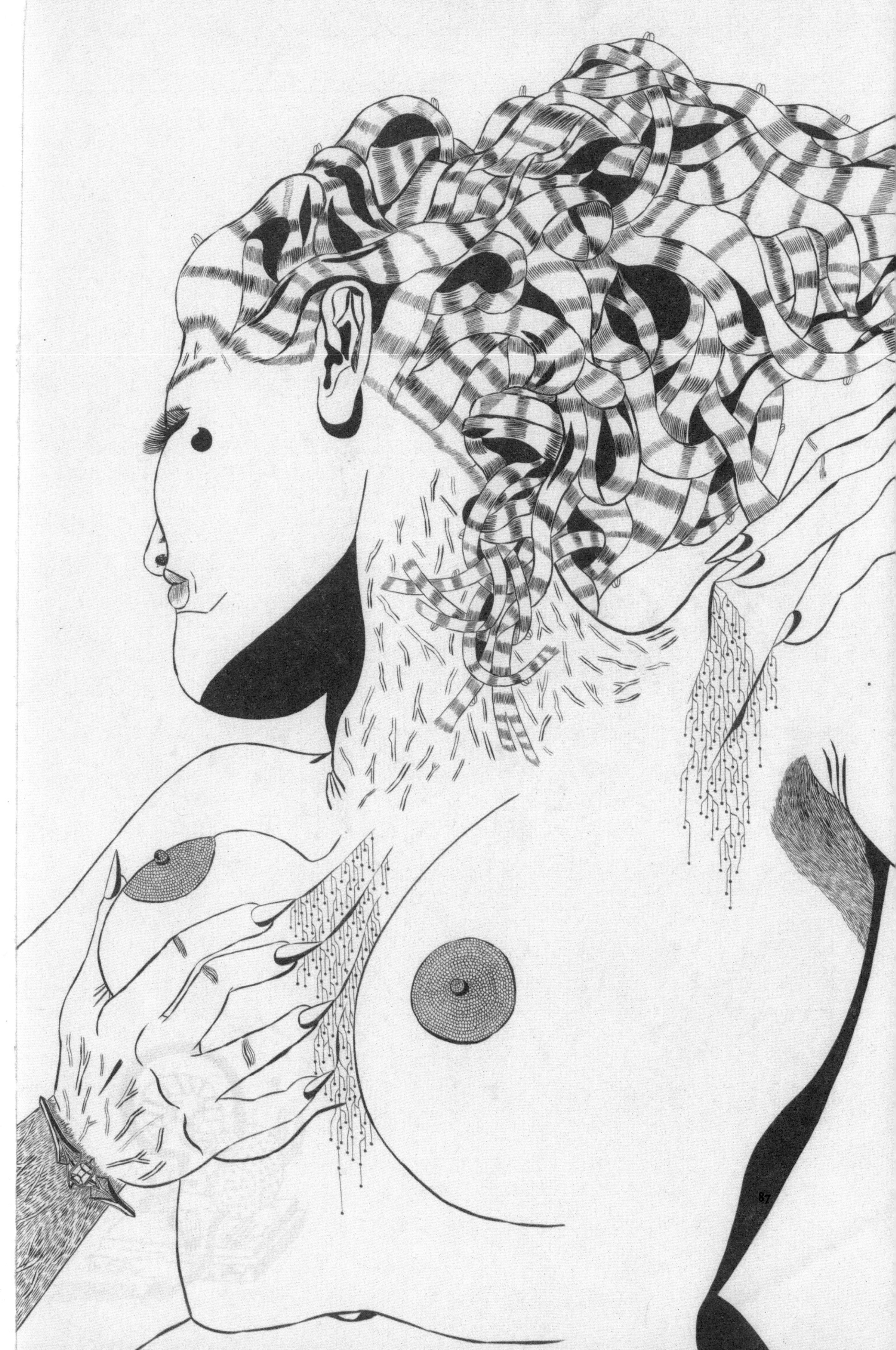

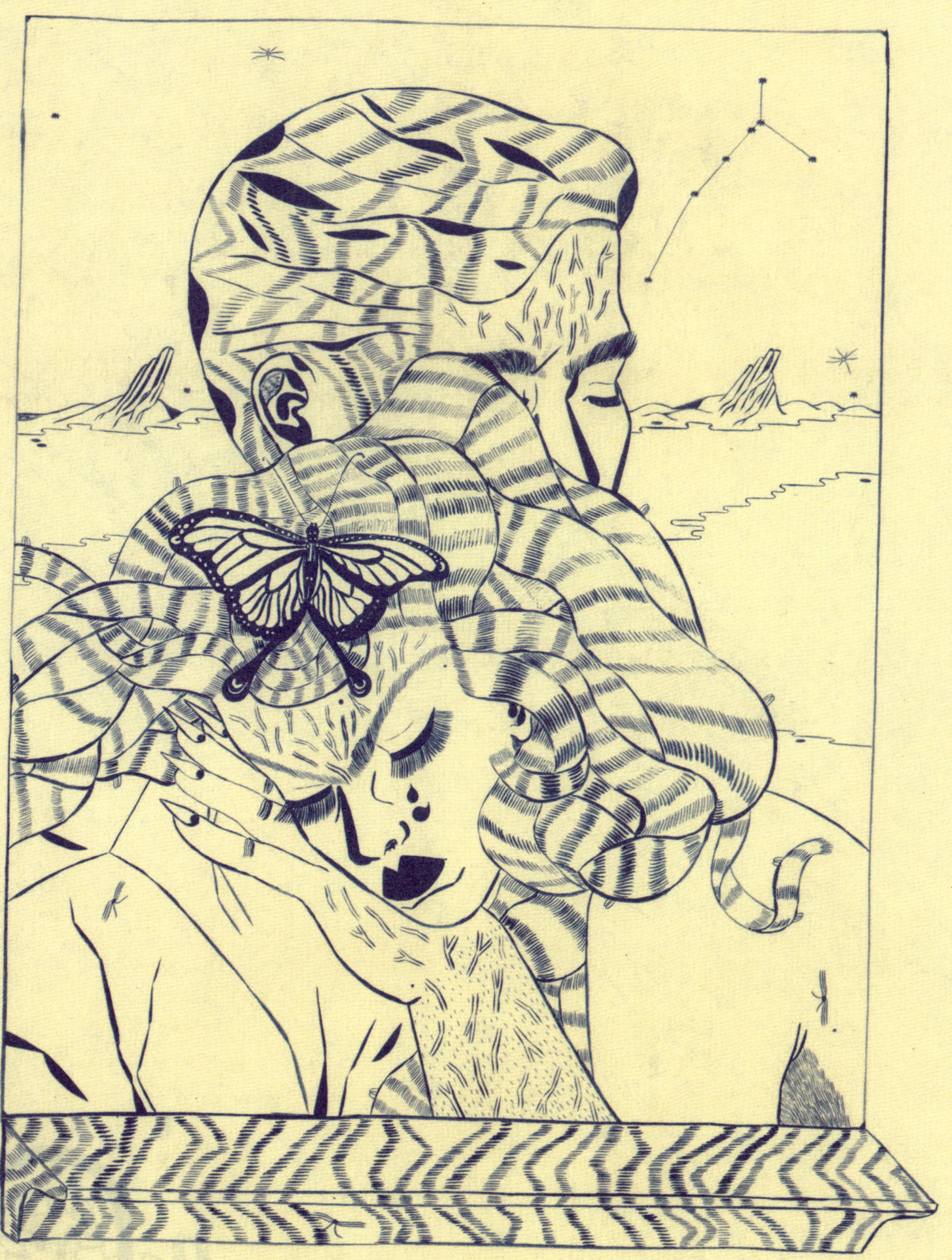

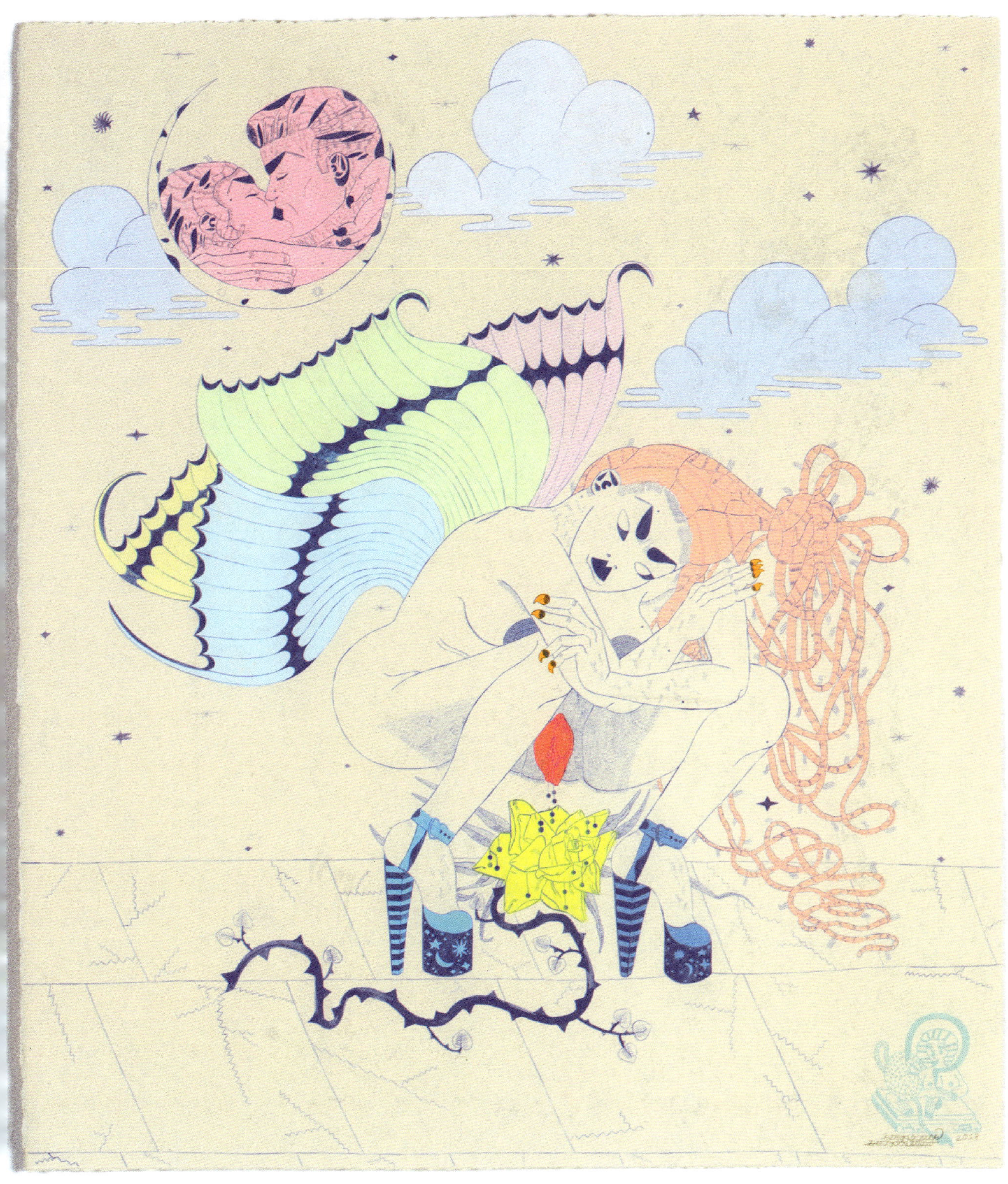

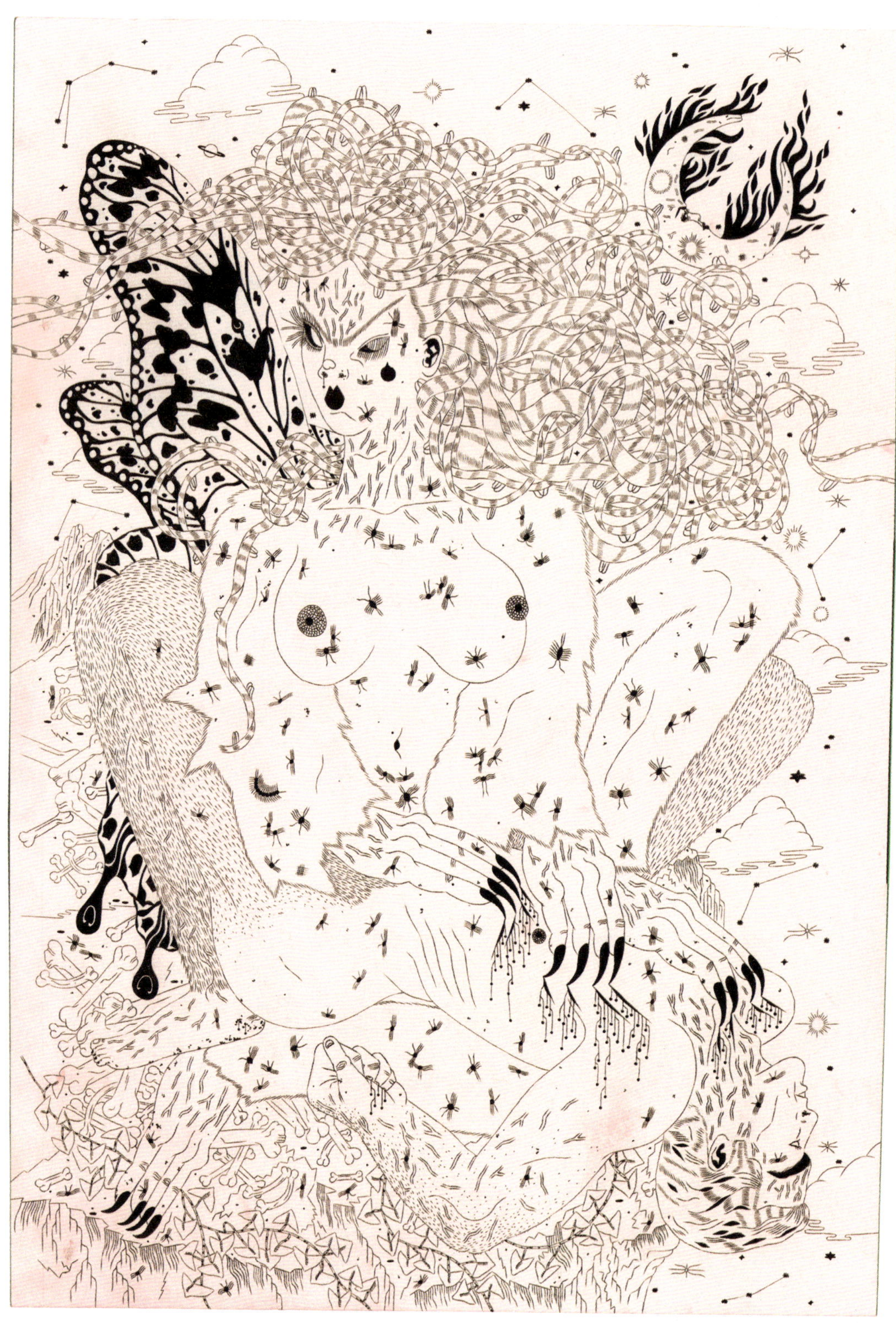

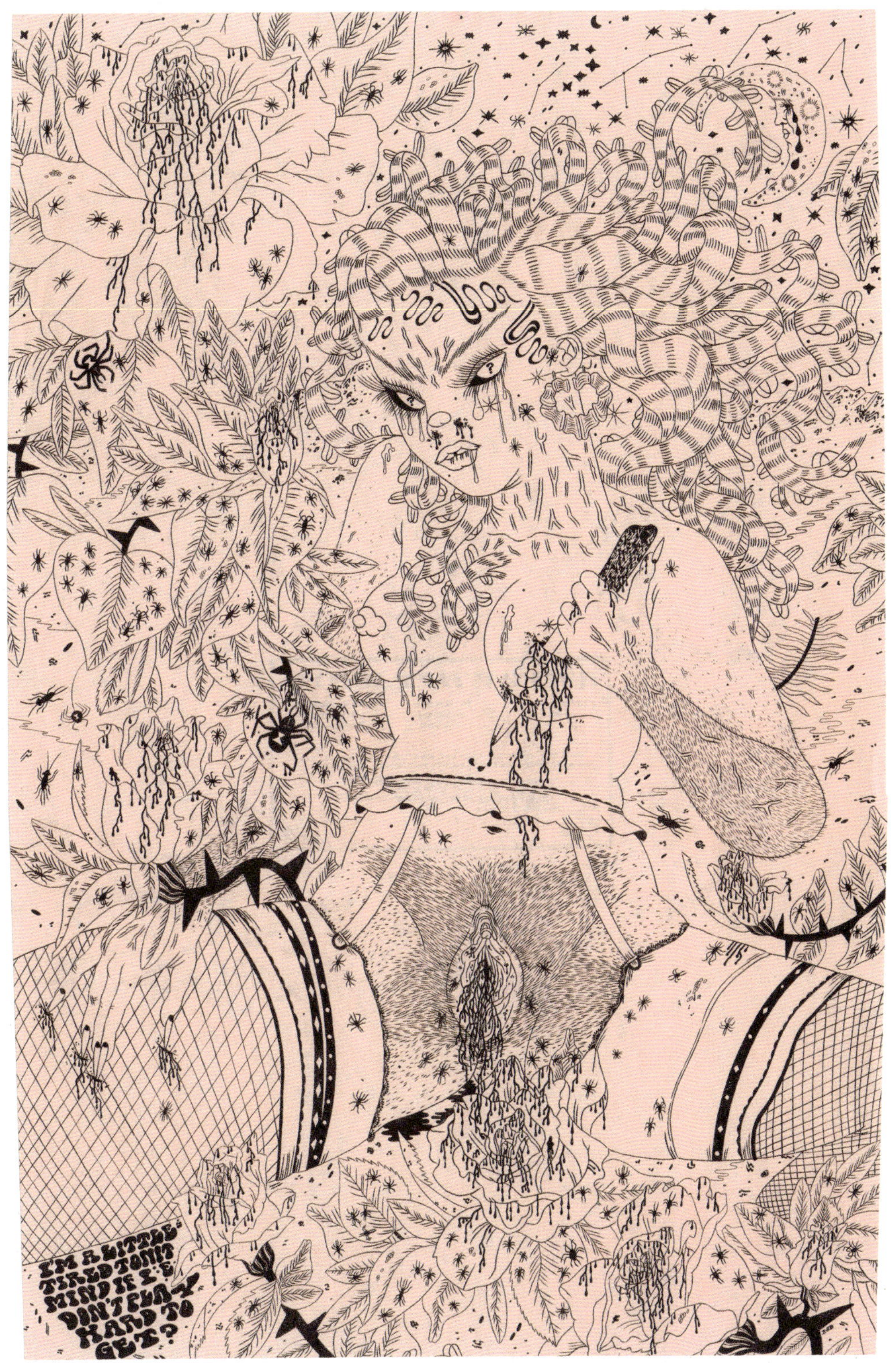

I'M A LITTLE TIRED TONIT MIND IF I DON'T PLAY HARD TO GET?

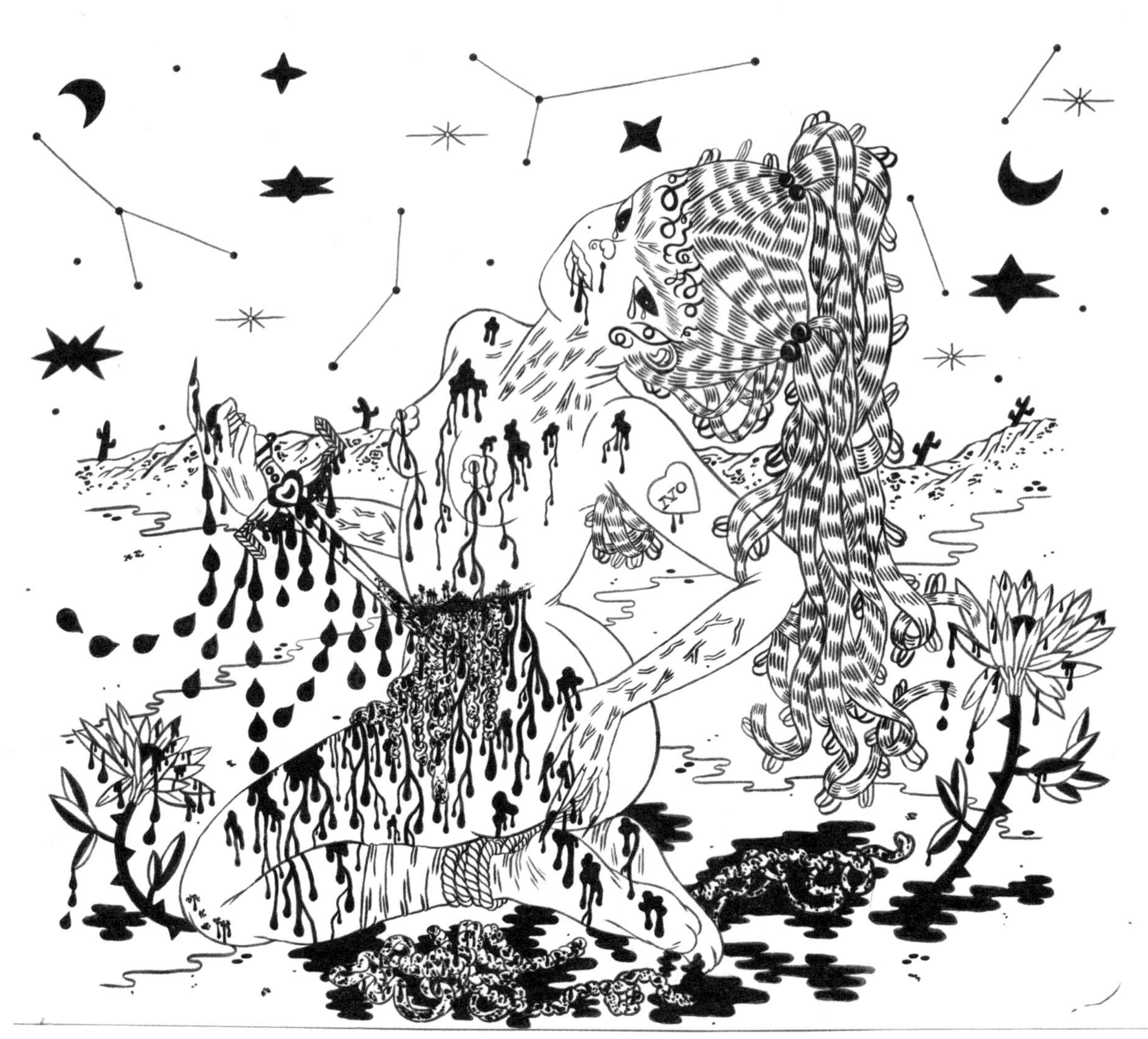

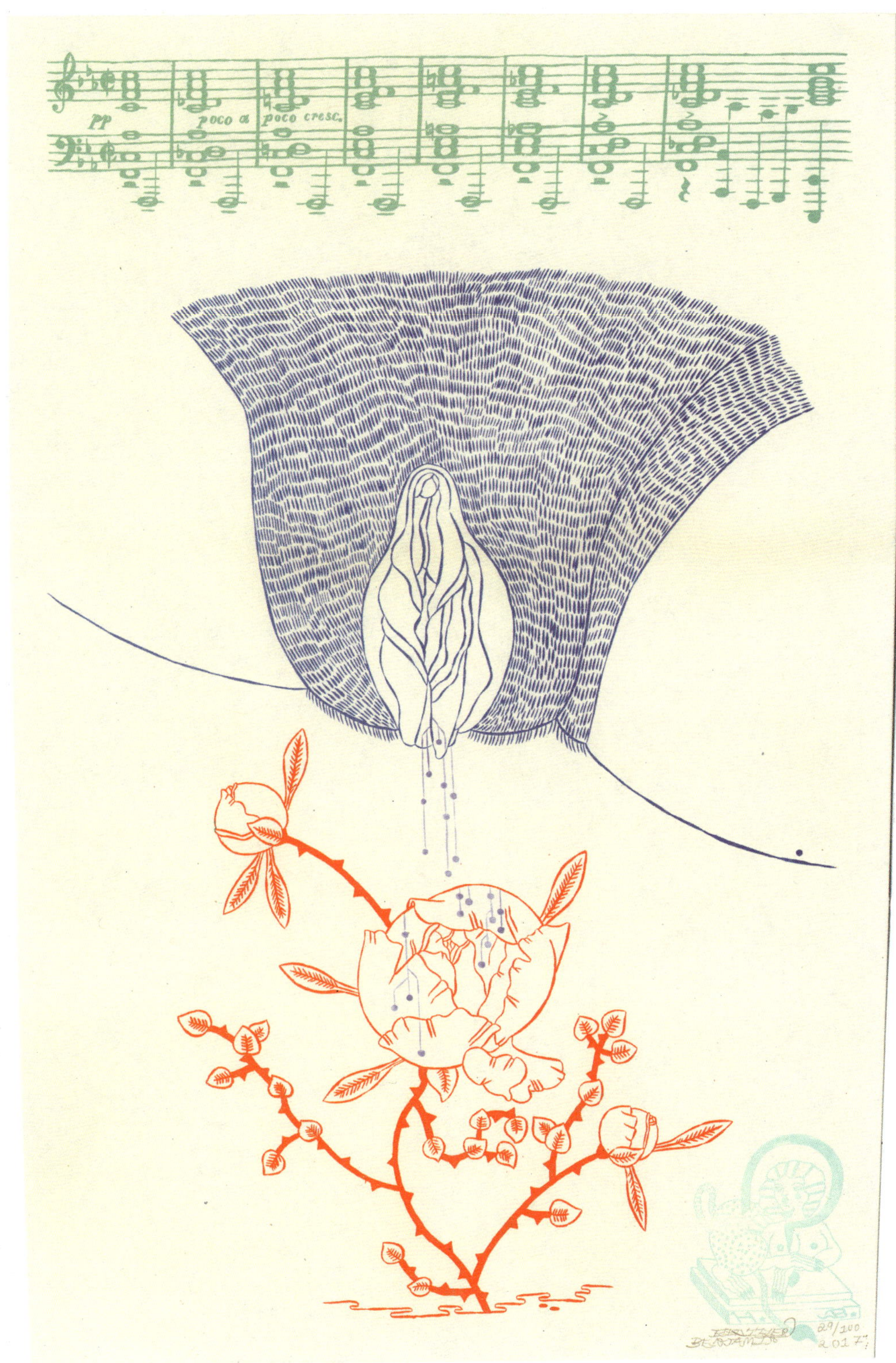

pp
poco a poco cresc.

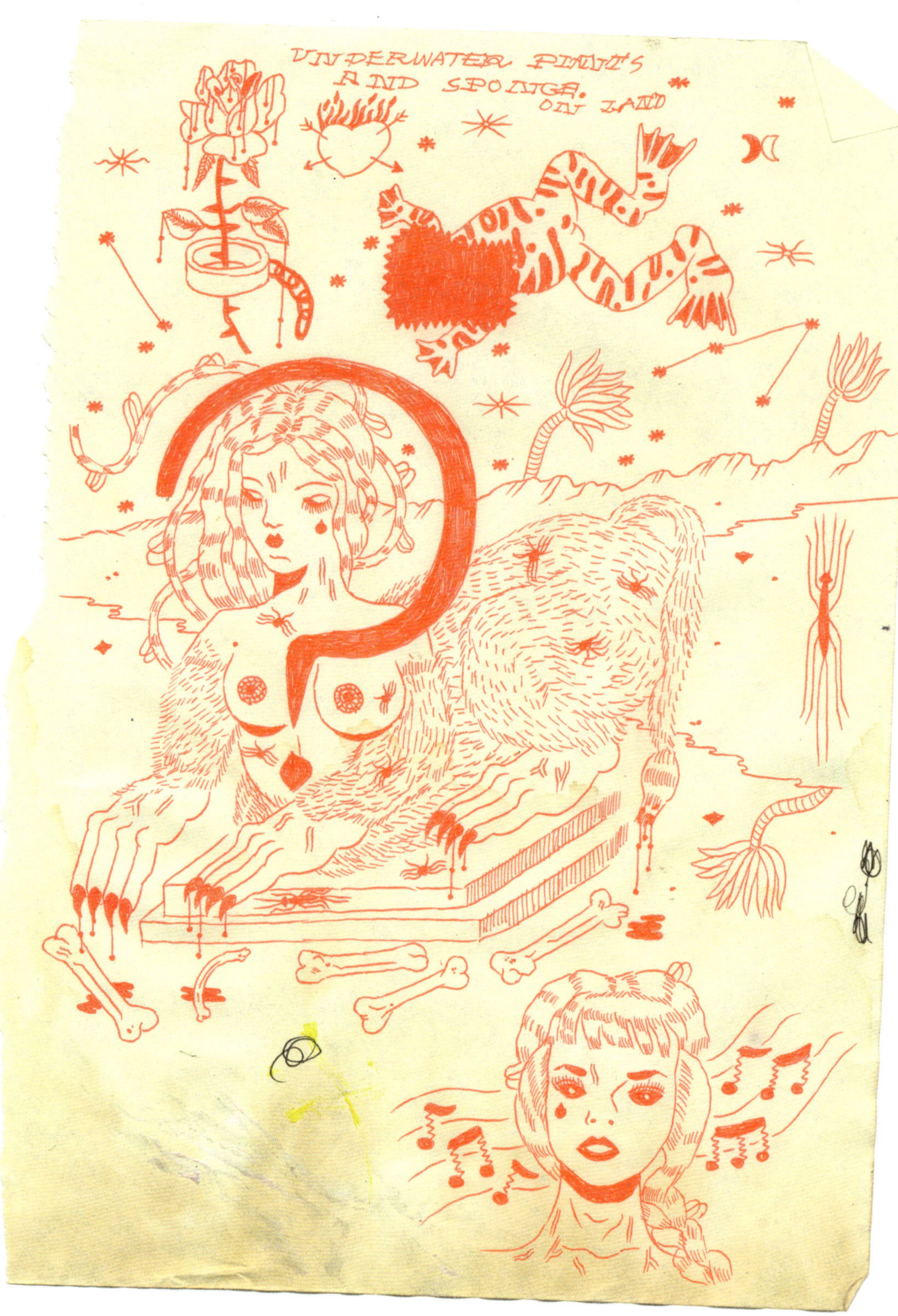
UNDERWATER PLANTS
AND SPONGE.
ON LAND

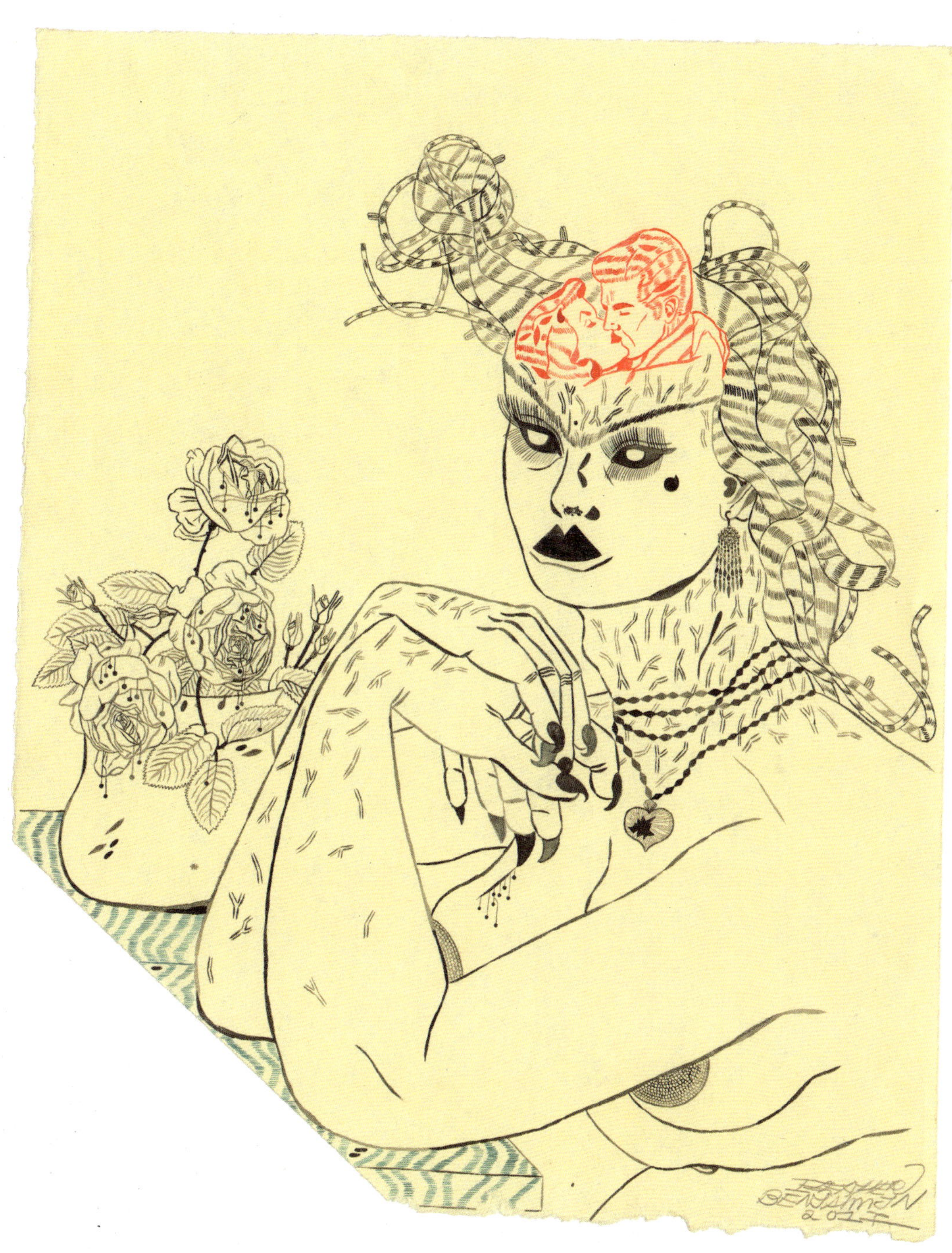

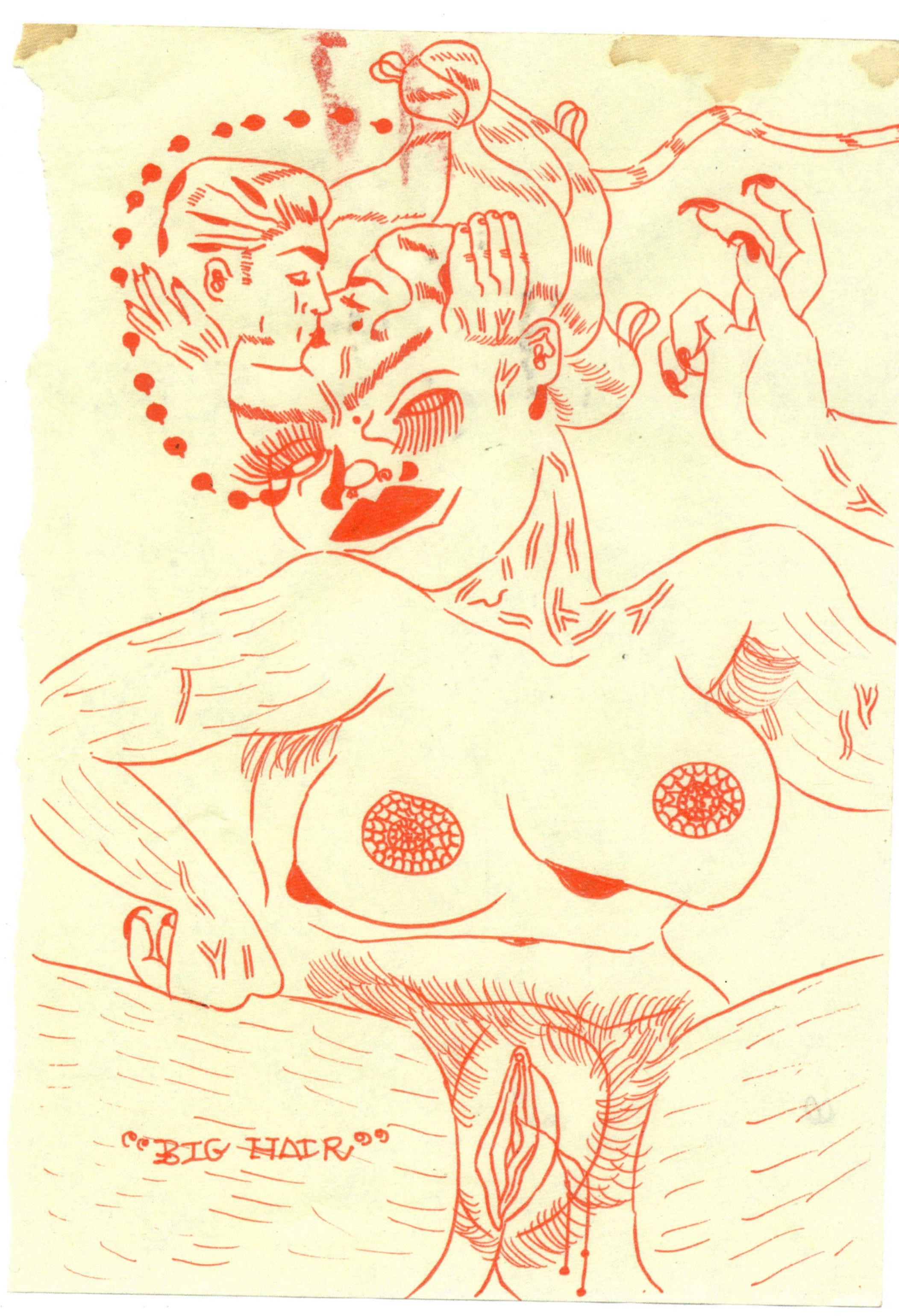
"BIG HAIR"

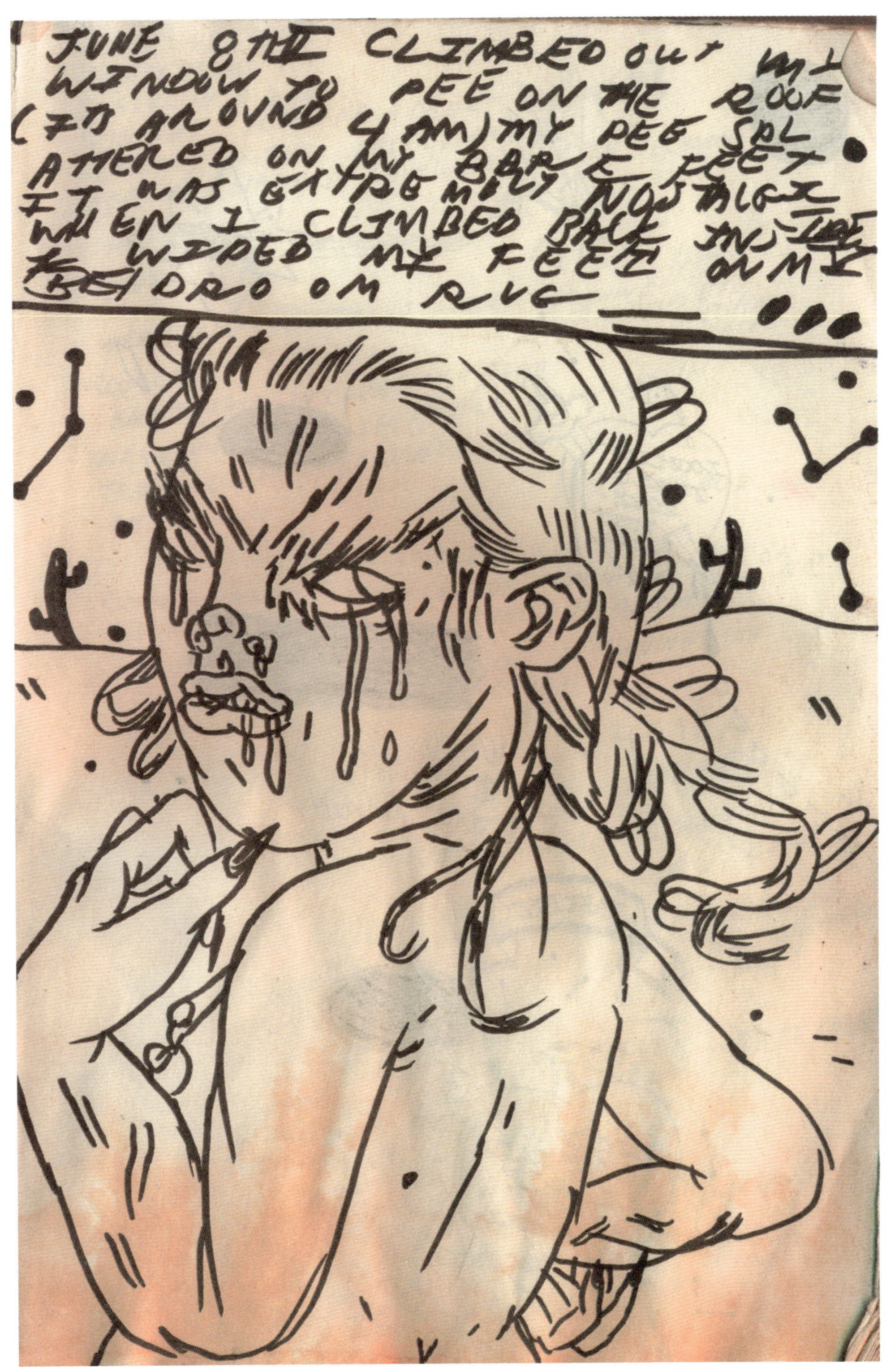

JUNE 8TH I CLIMBED OUT MY
WINDOW TO PEE ON THE ROOF
(IT'S AROUND 4 AM) MY PEE SPL
ATTERED ON MY BARE FEET.
IT WAS EXTREMELY NOSTALGIC
WHEN I CLIMBED BACK INSIDE
I WIPED MY FEET ON MY
BEDROOM RUG

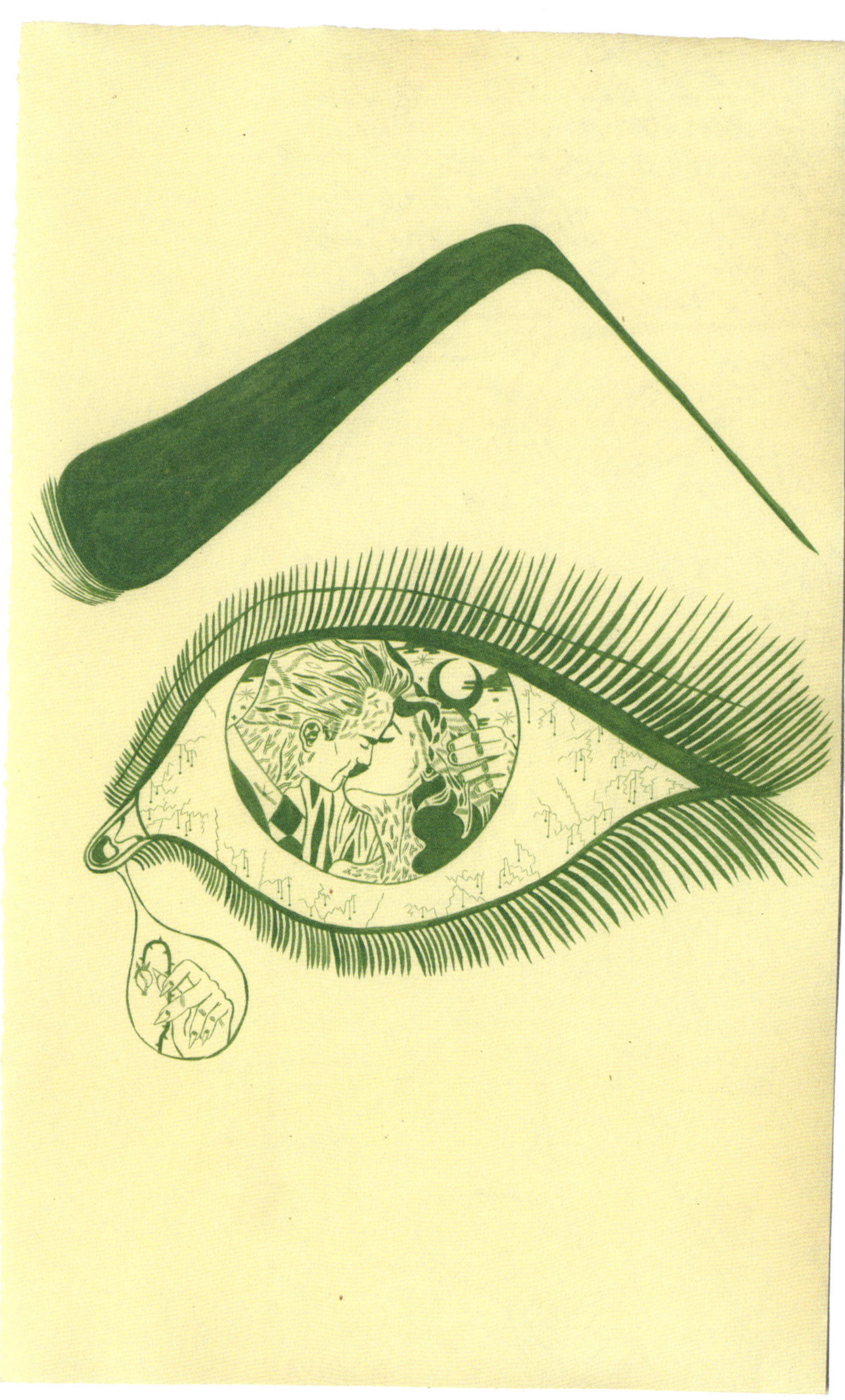

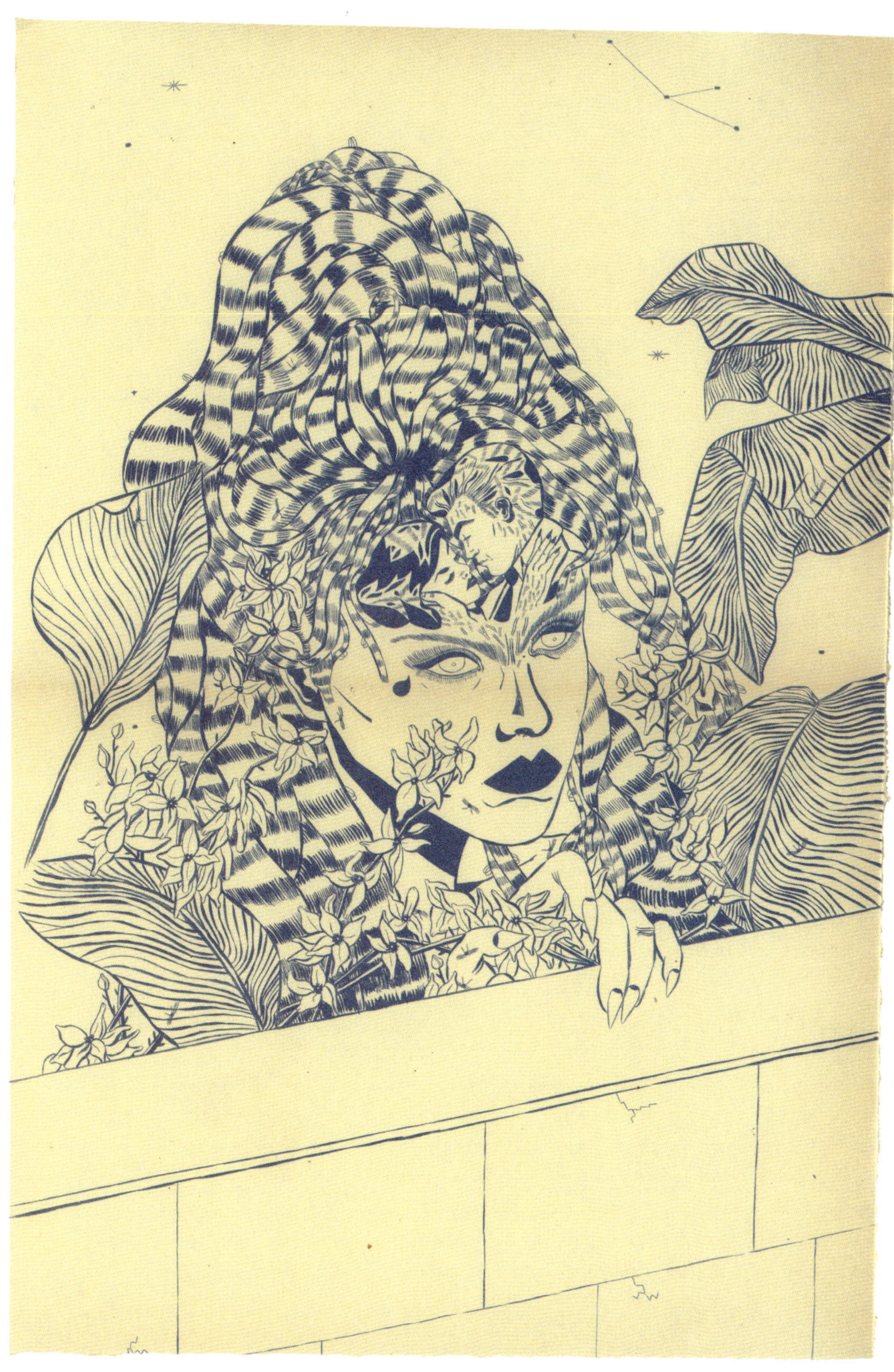

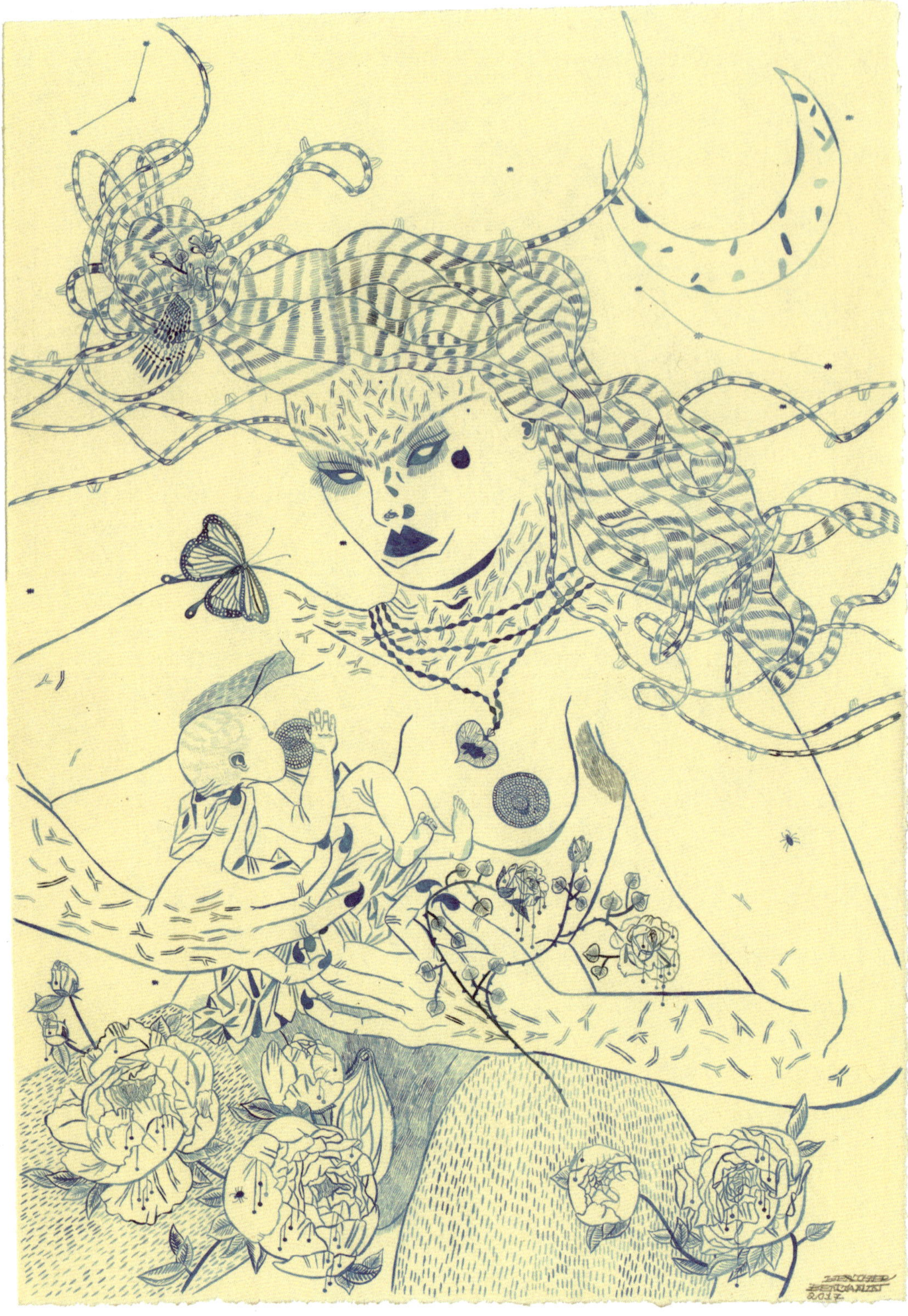

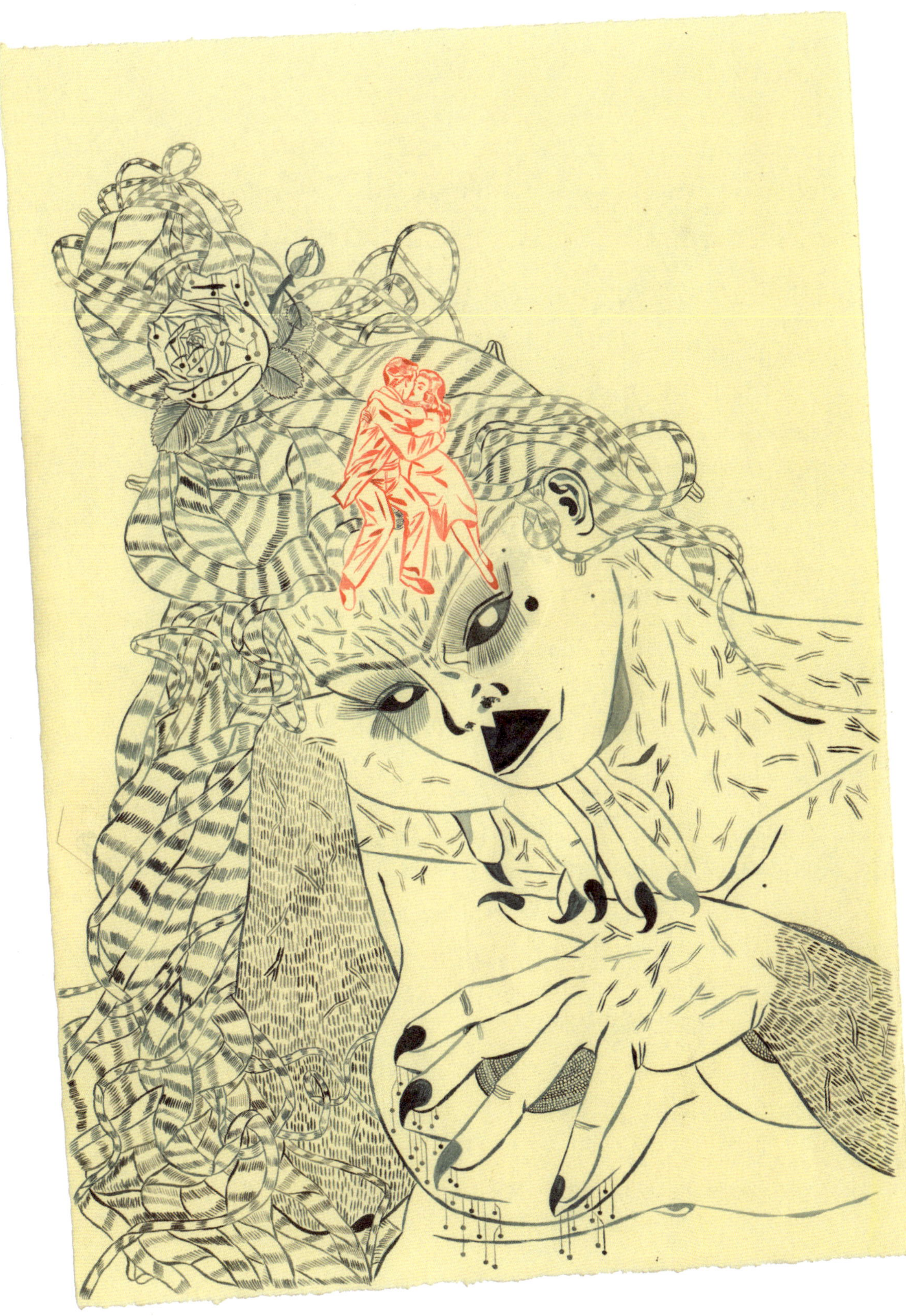

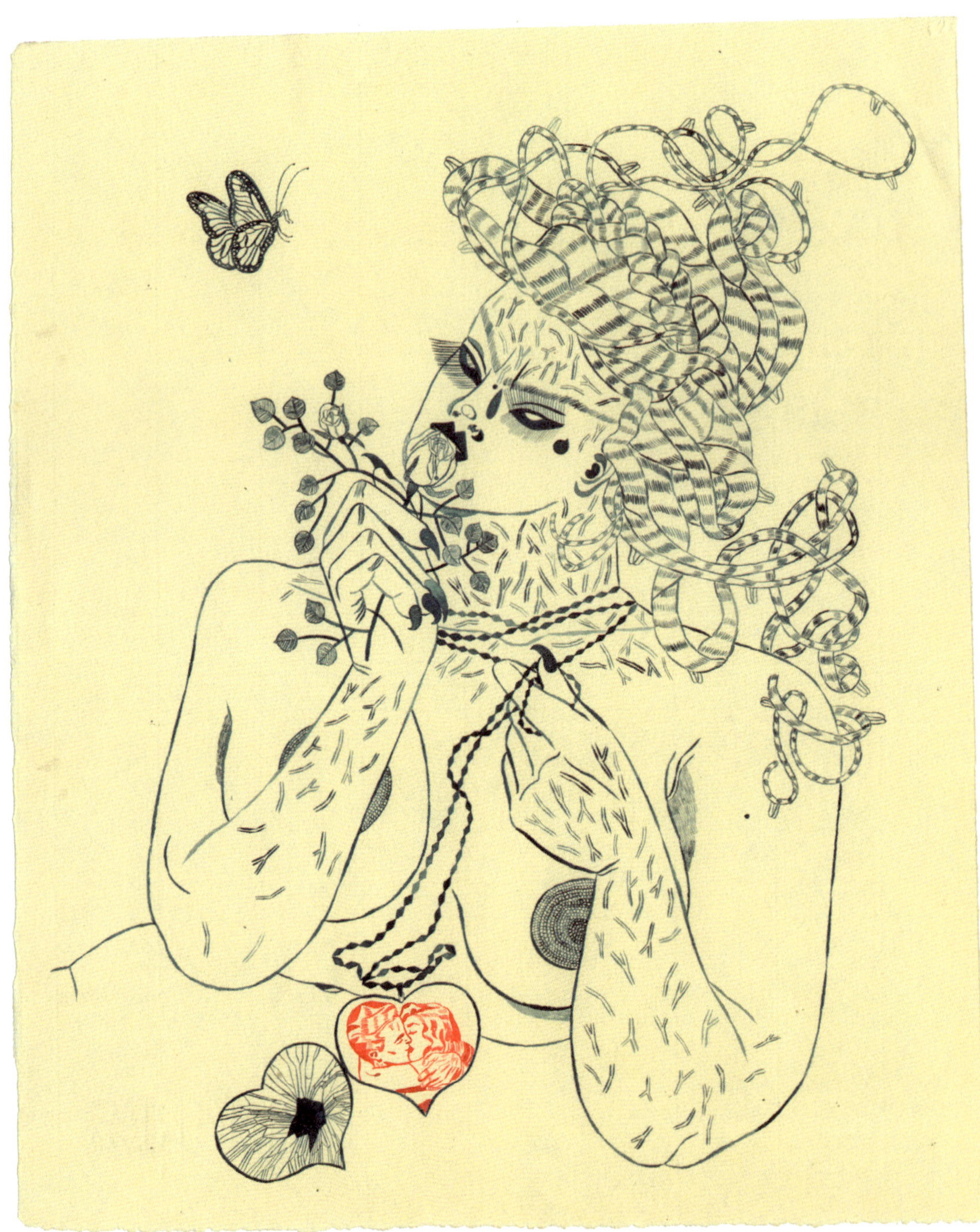

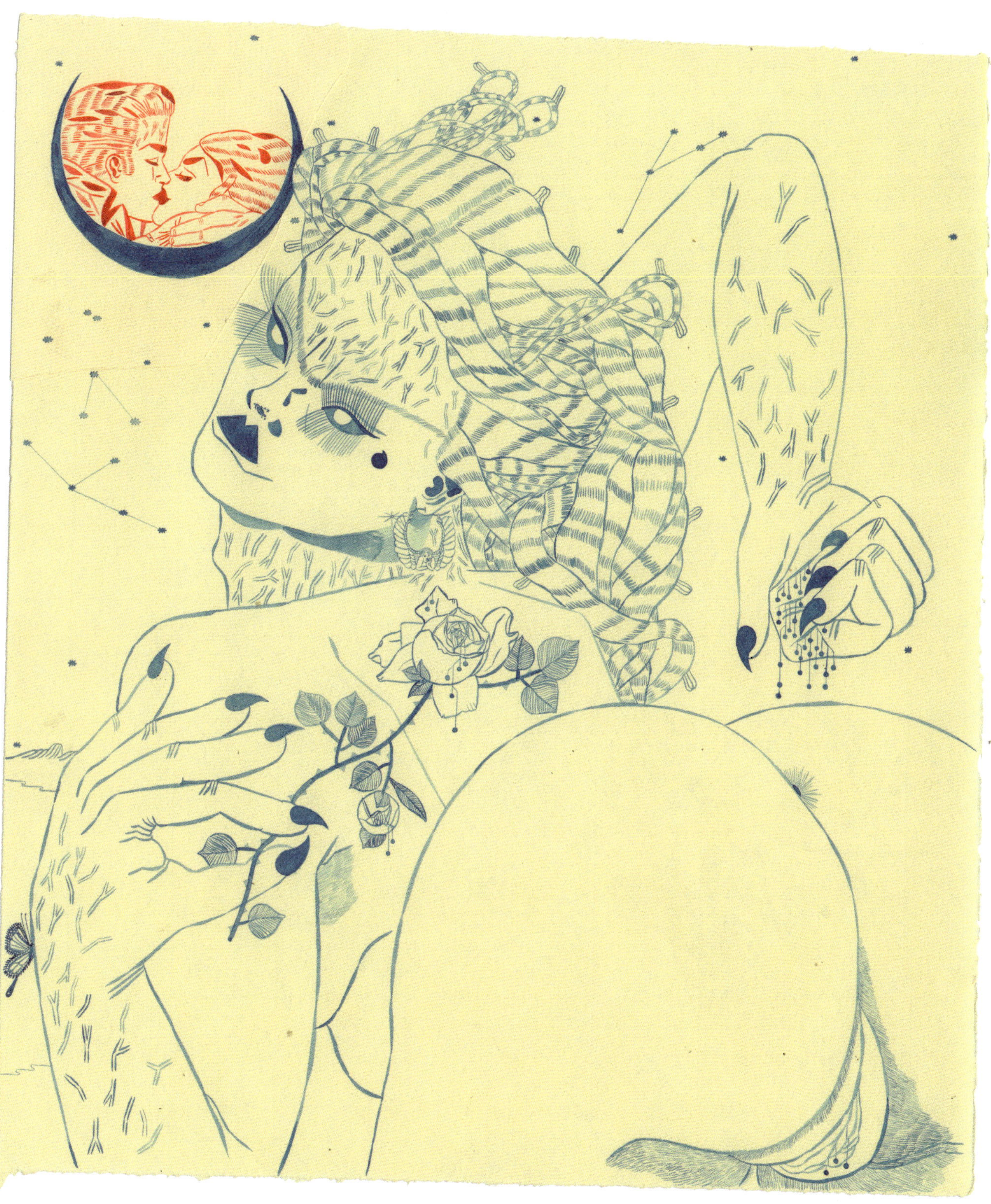

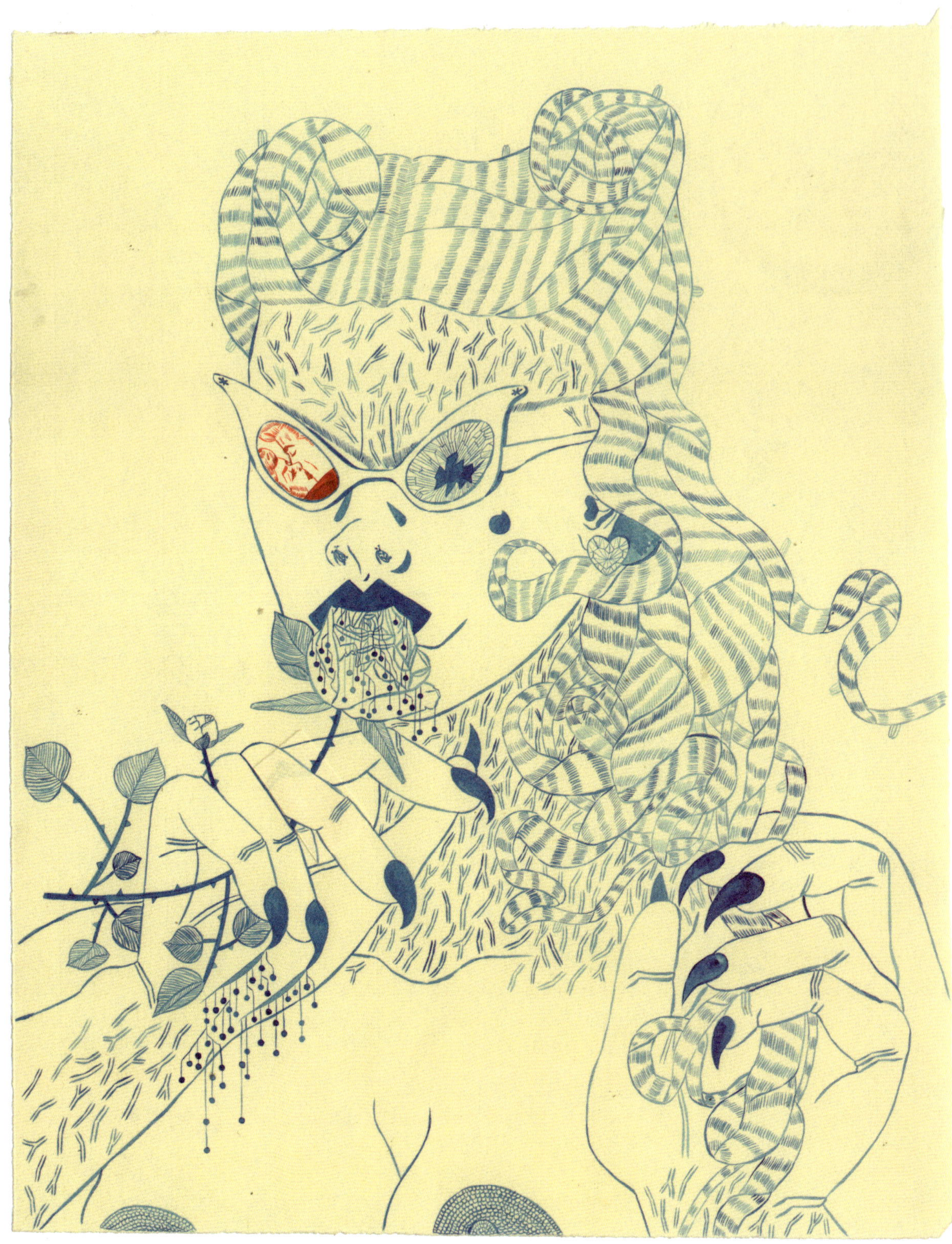

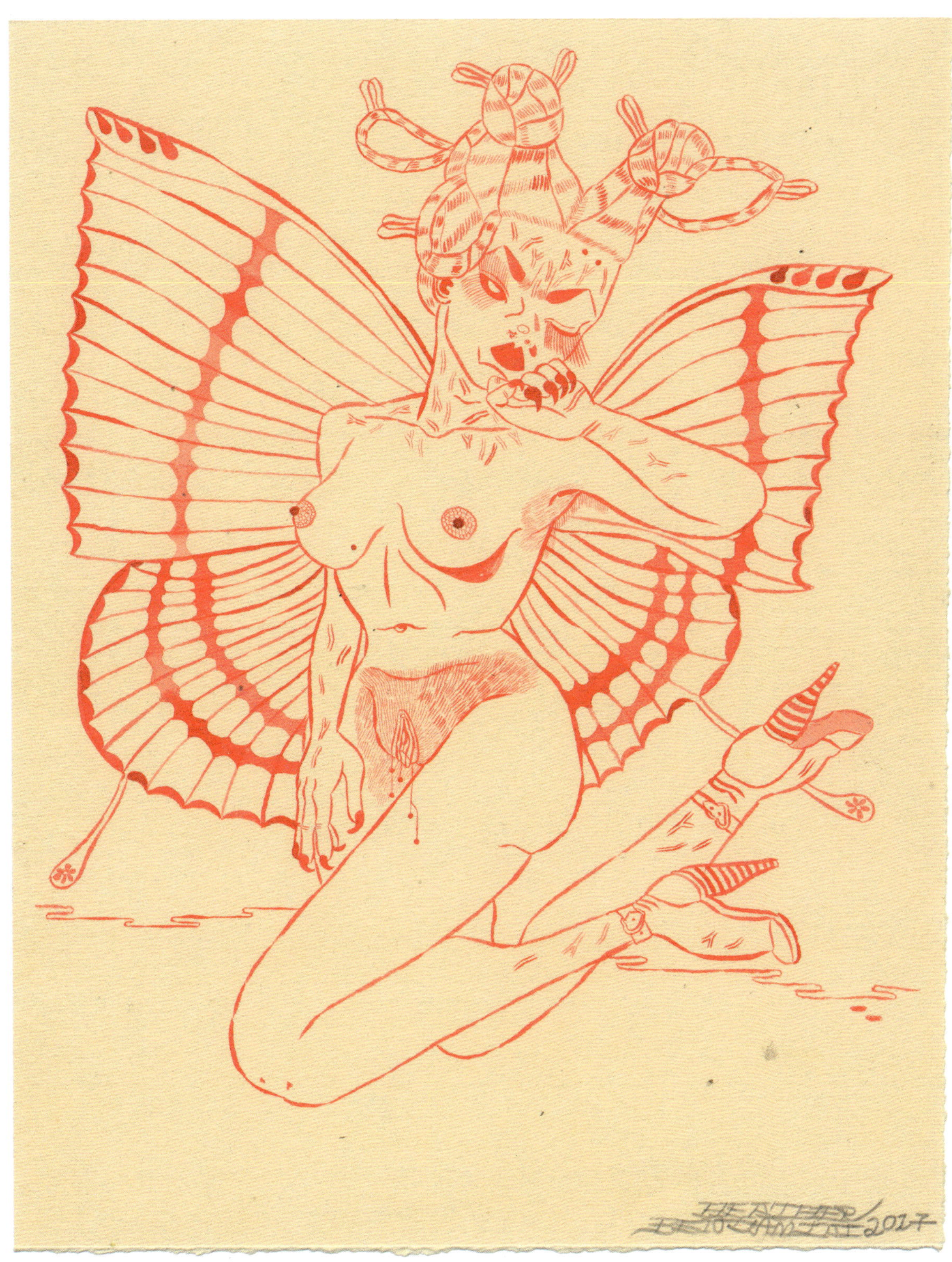

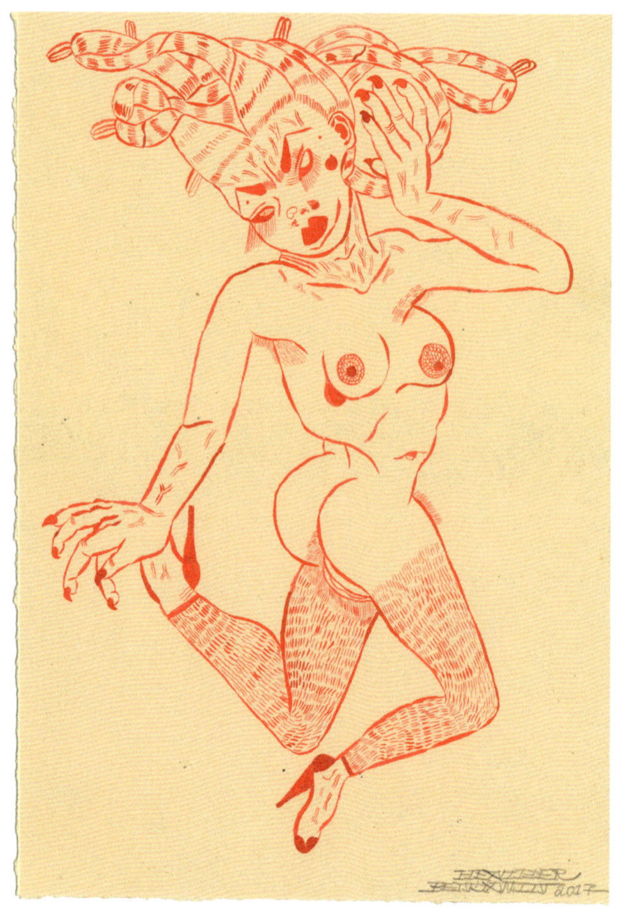 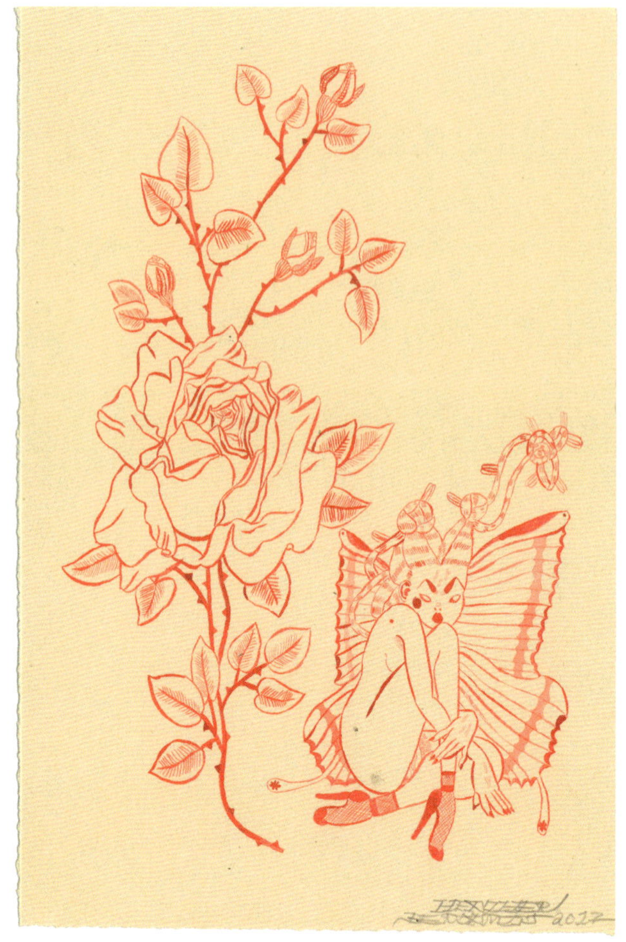

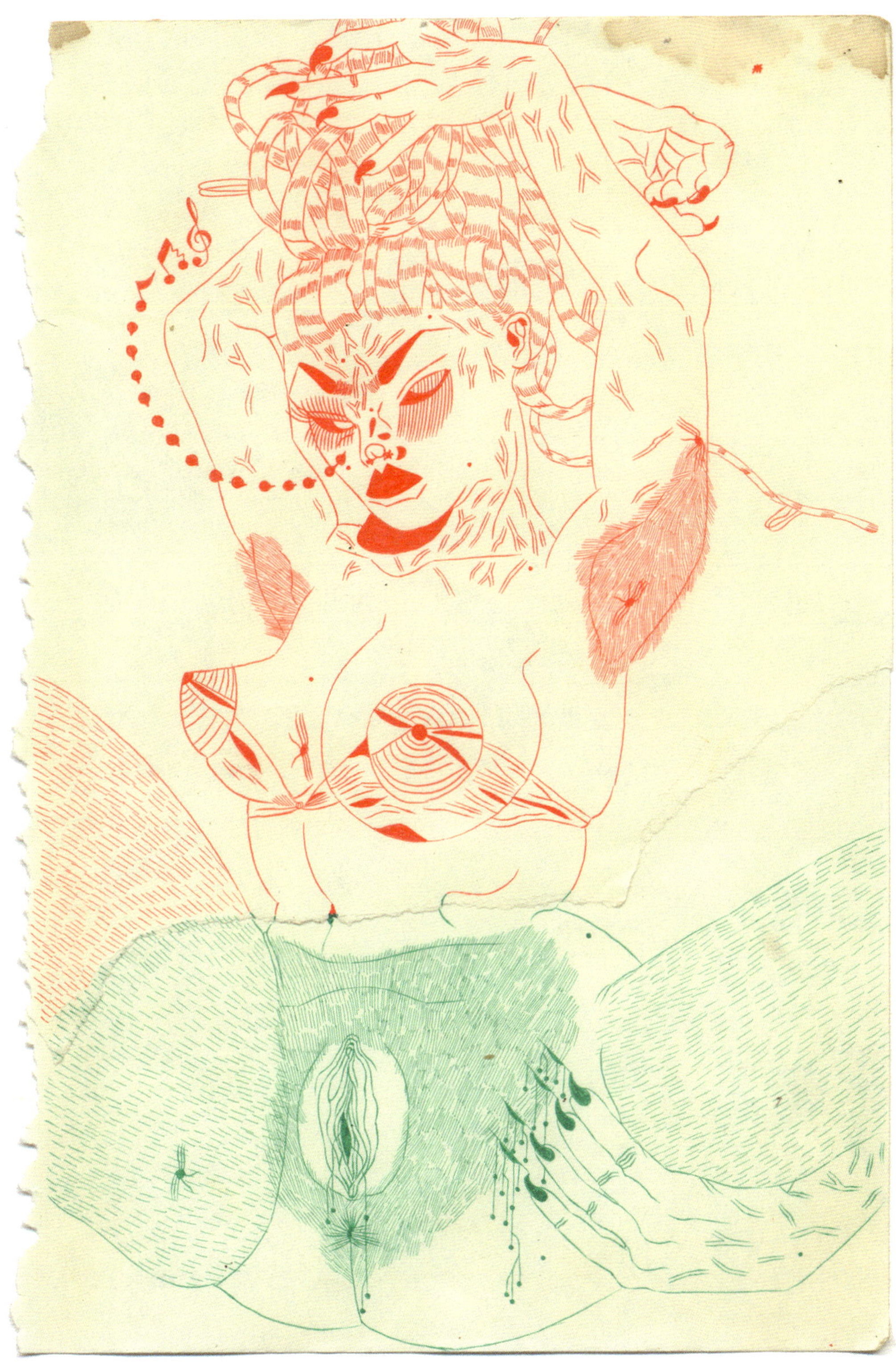

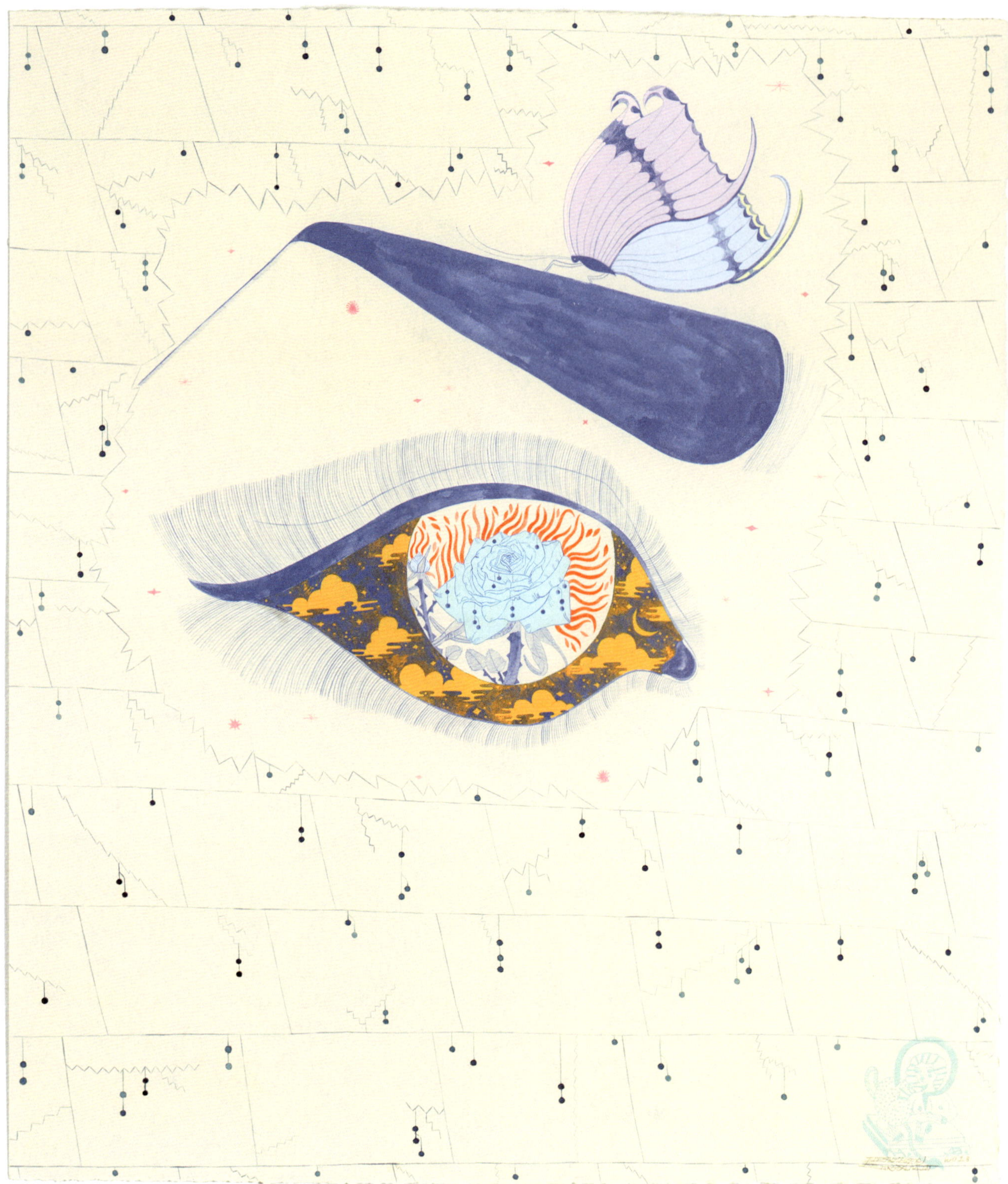

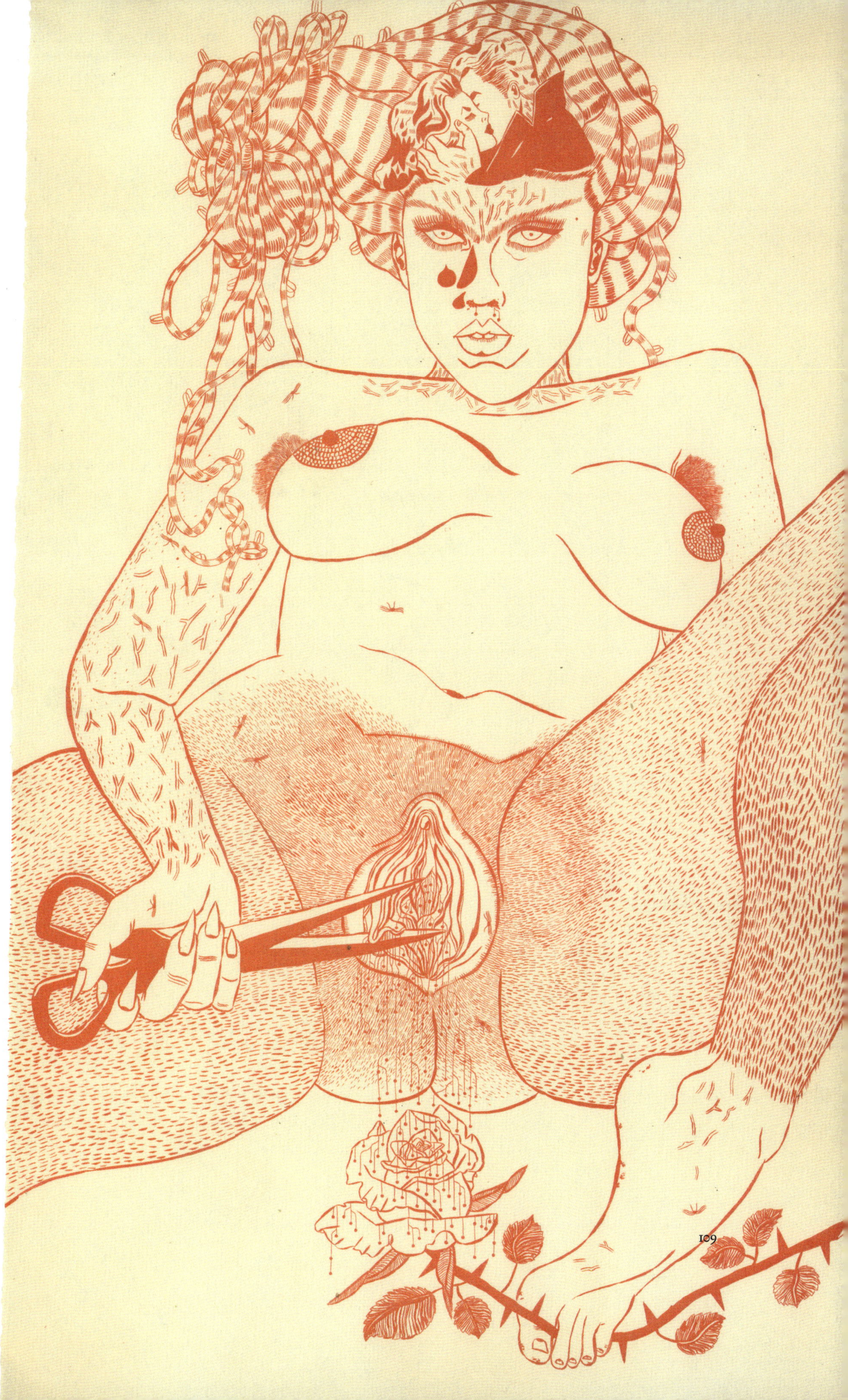

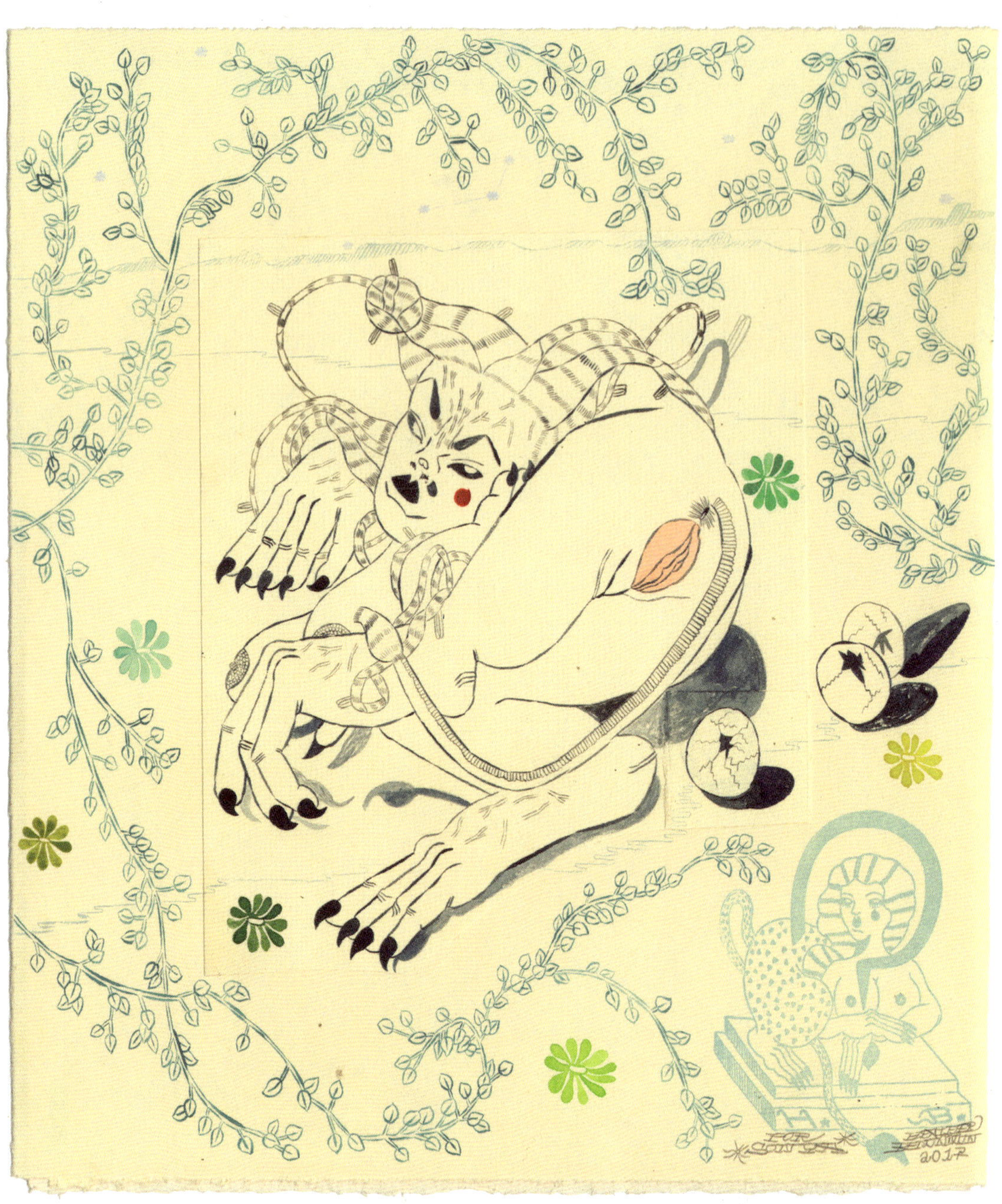

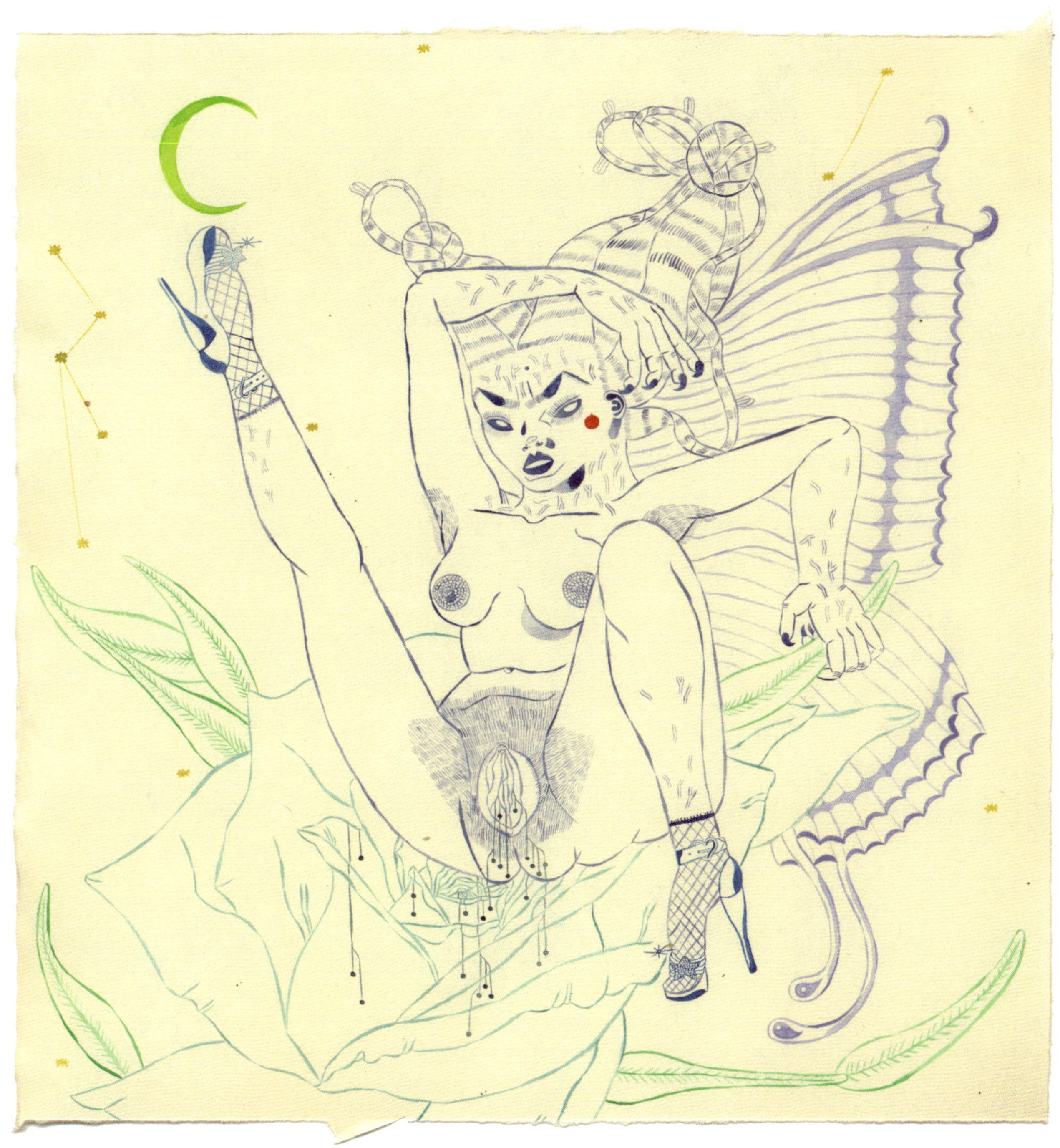

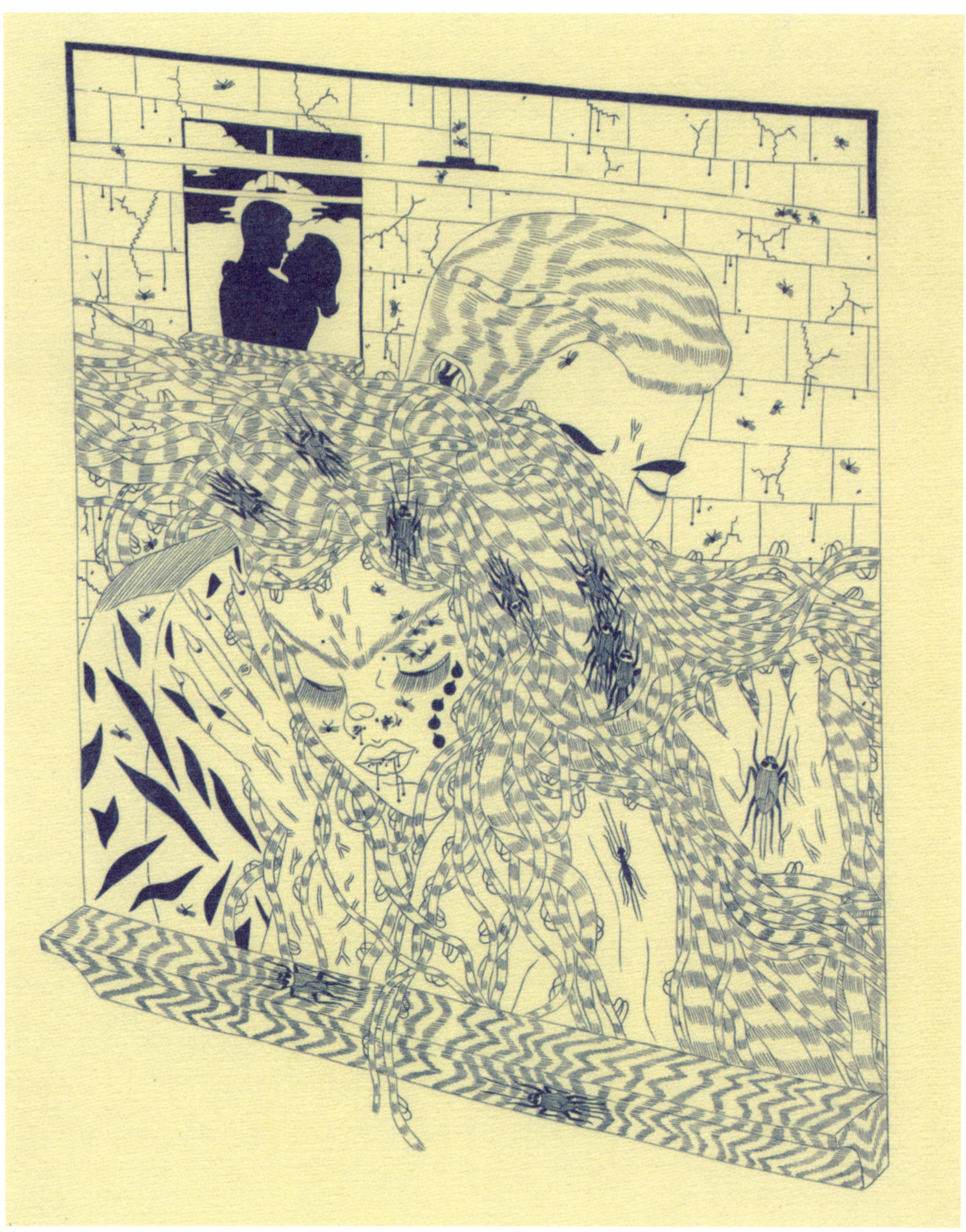

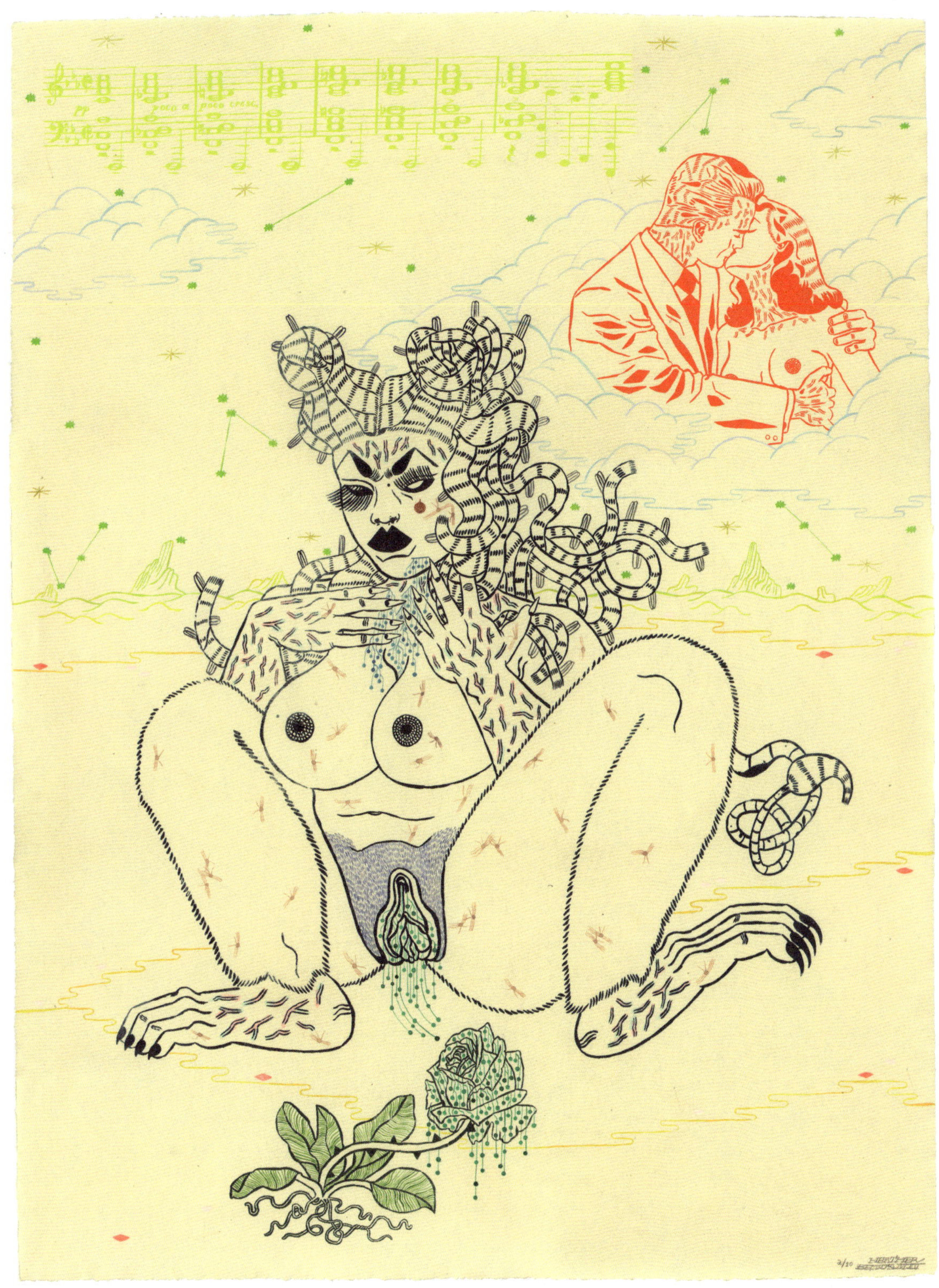

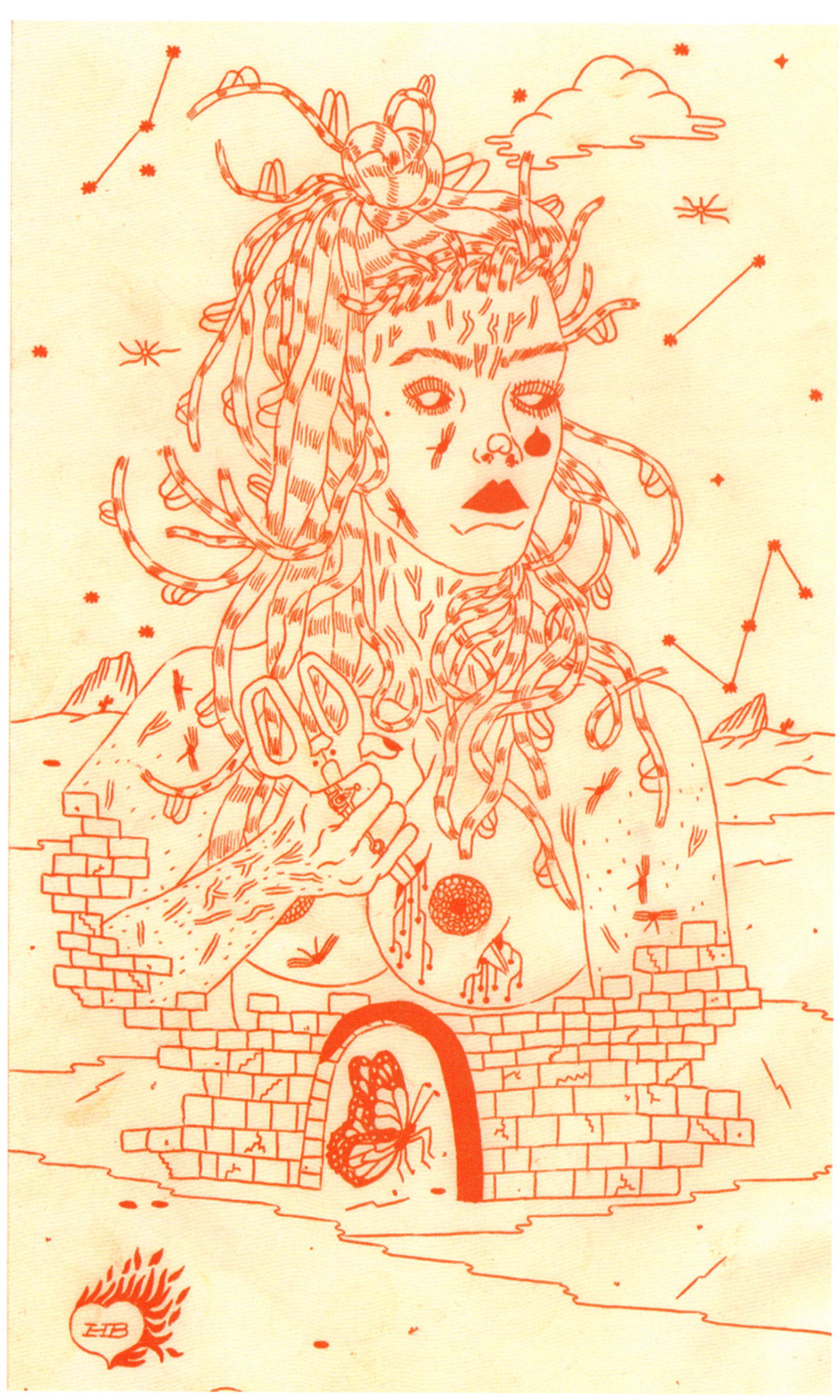

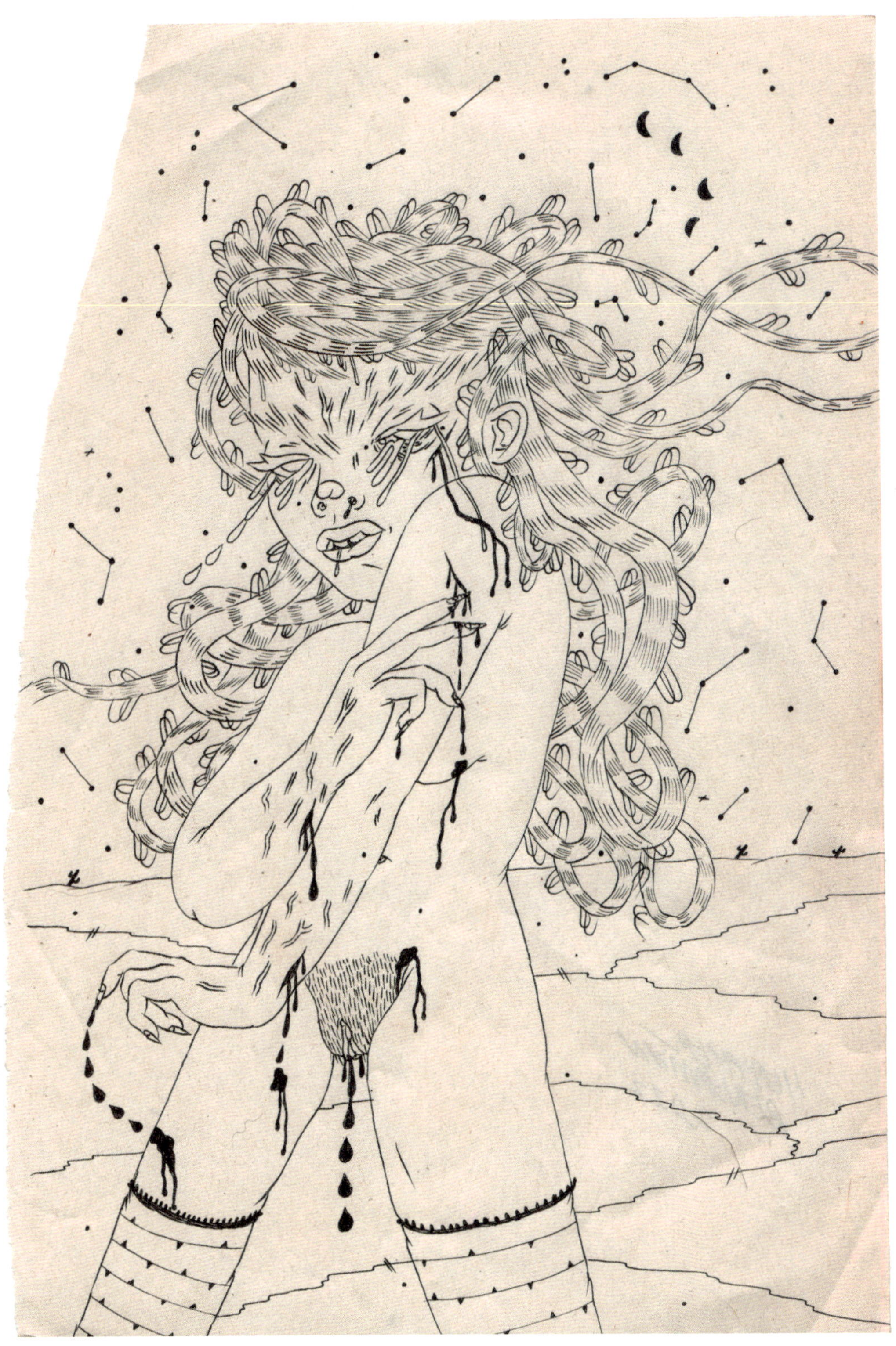

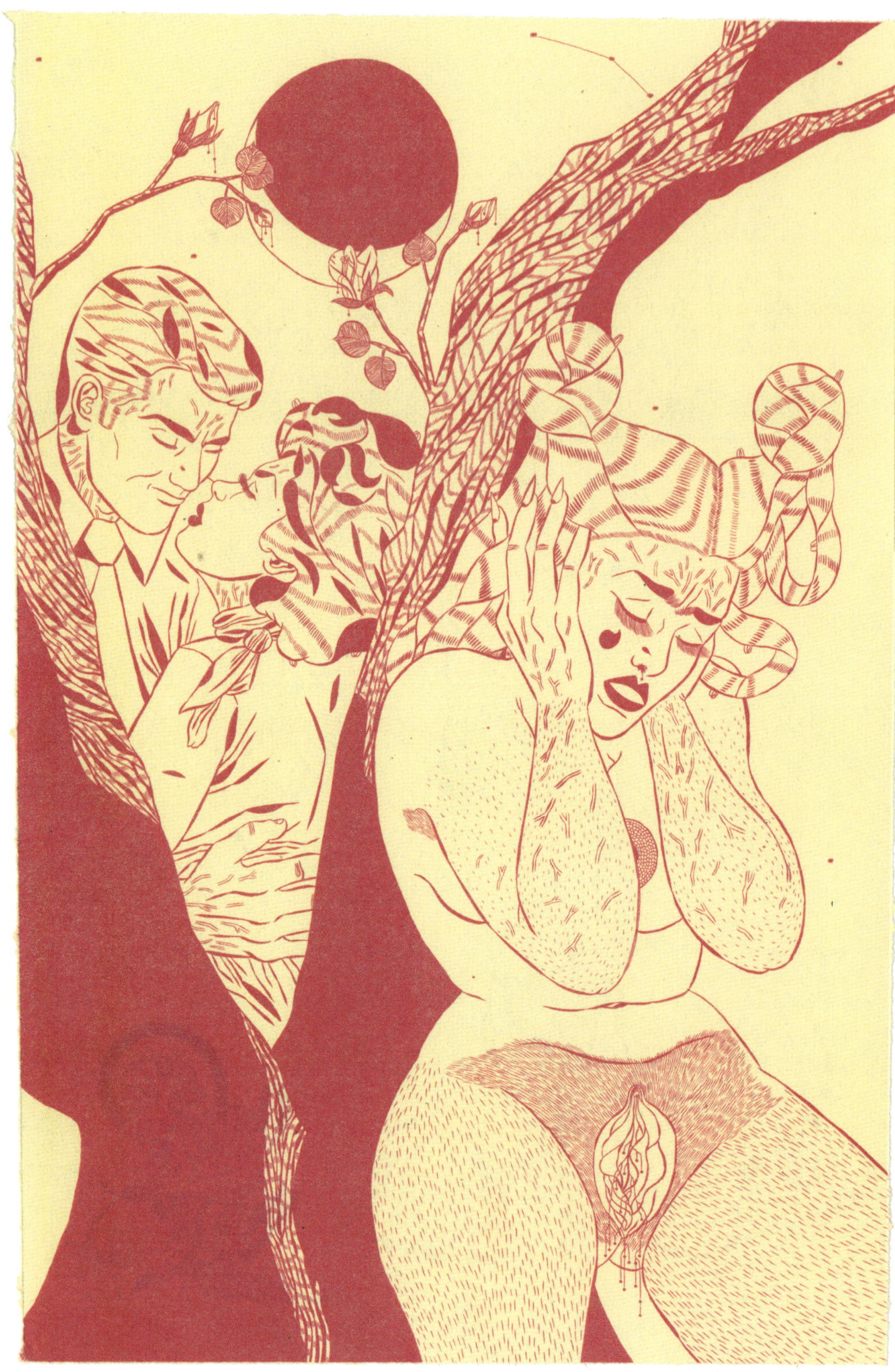

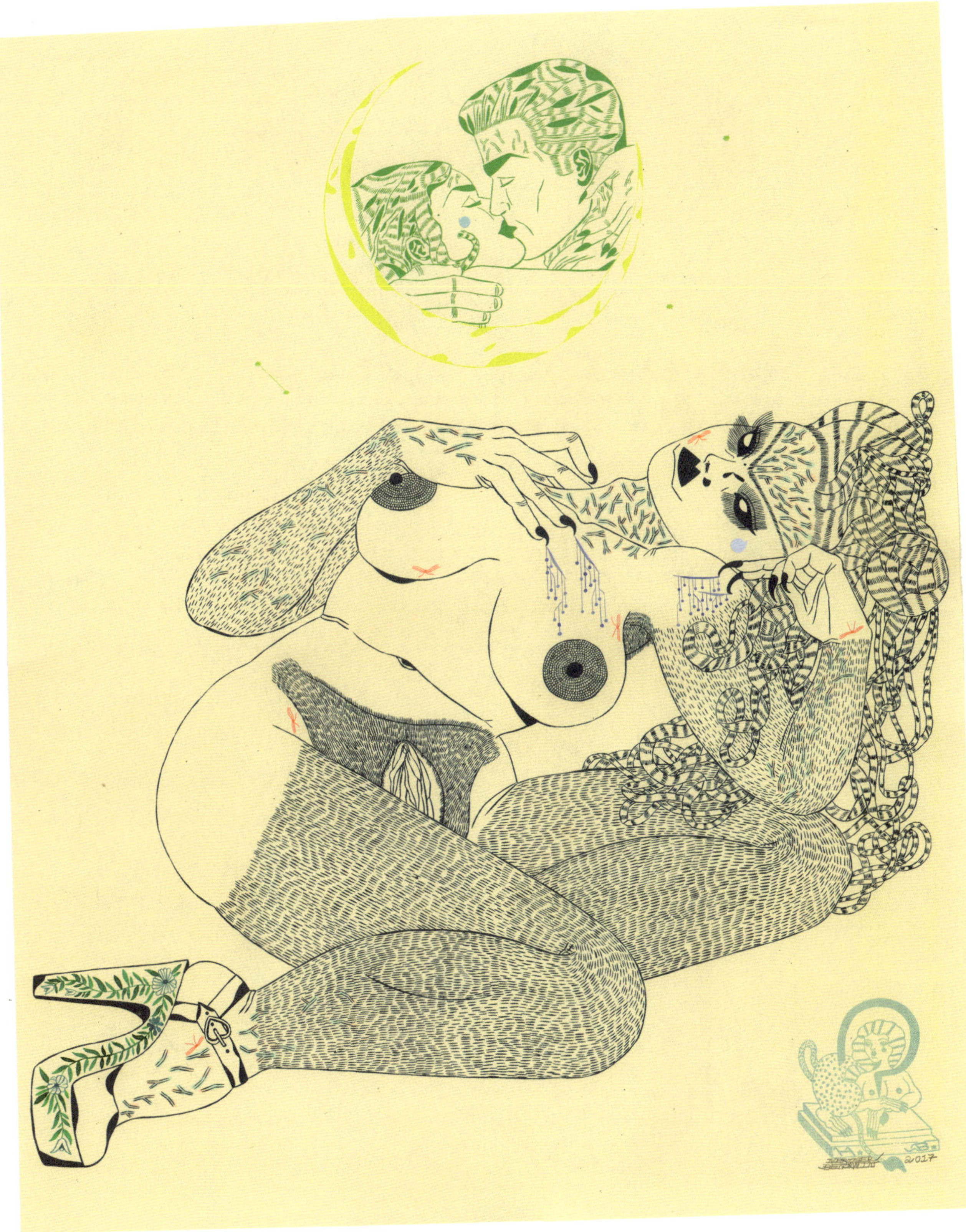

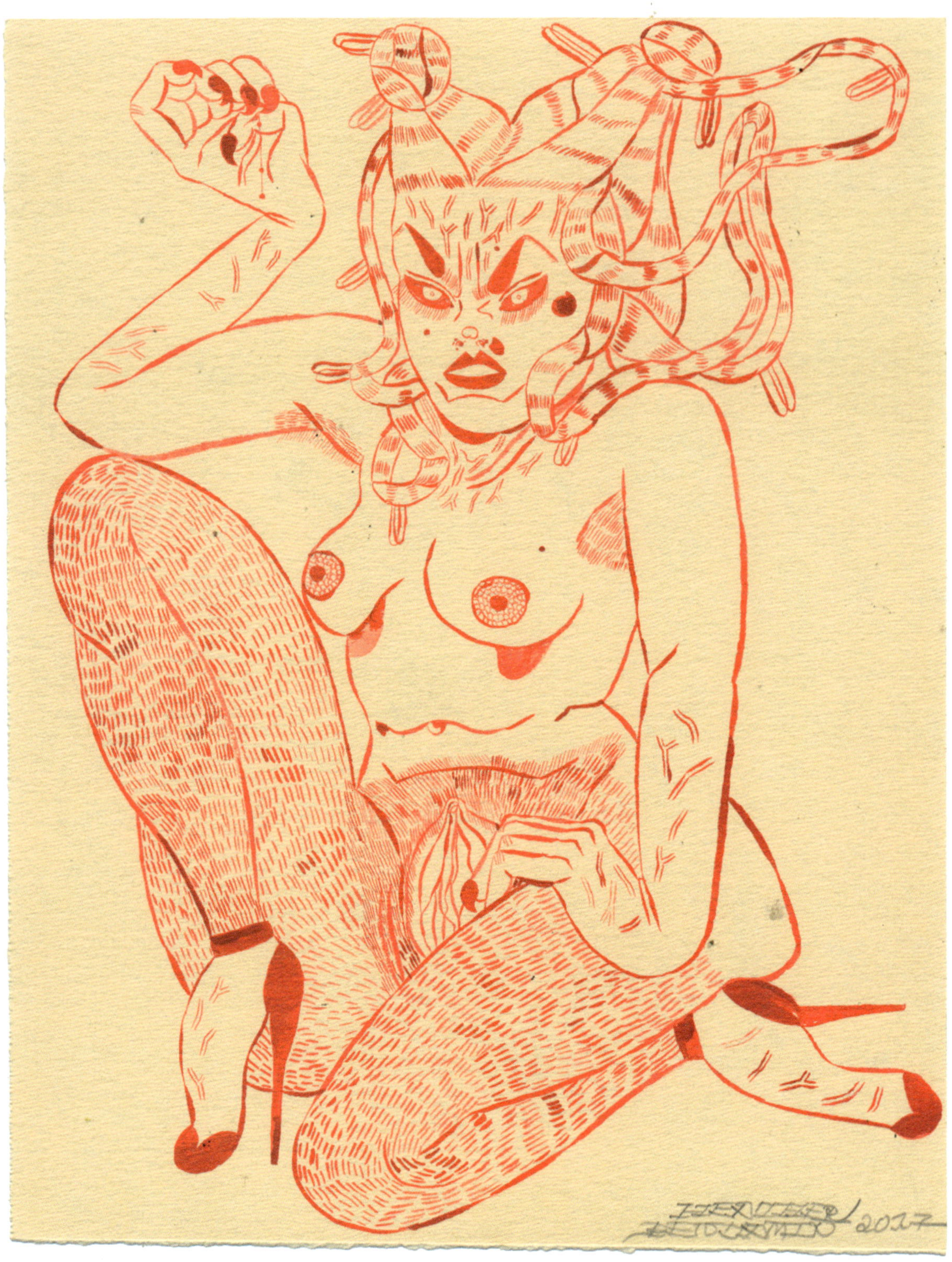

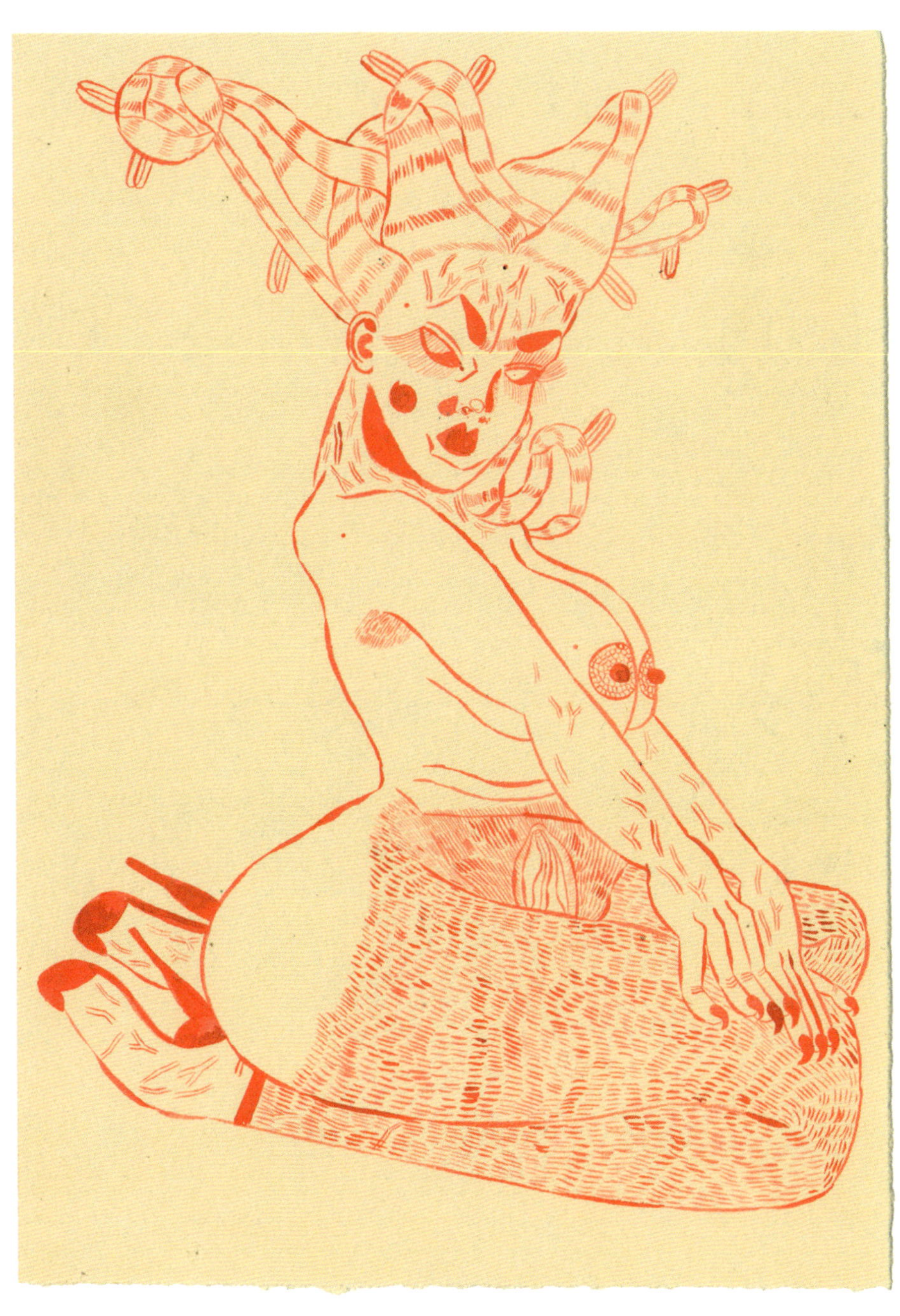

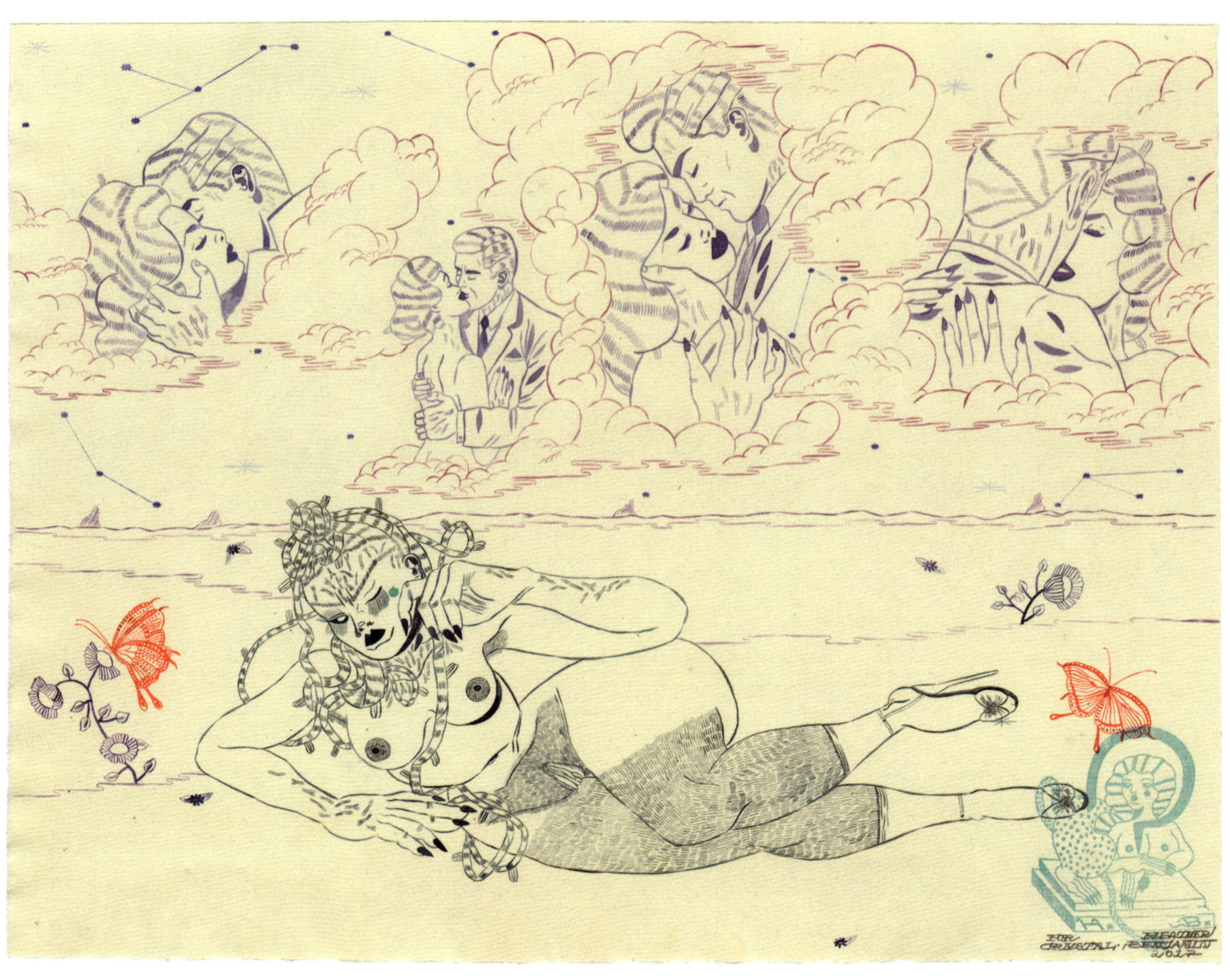

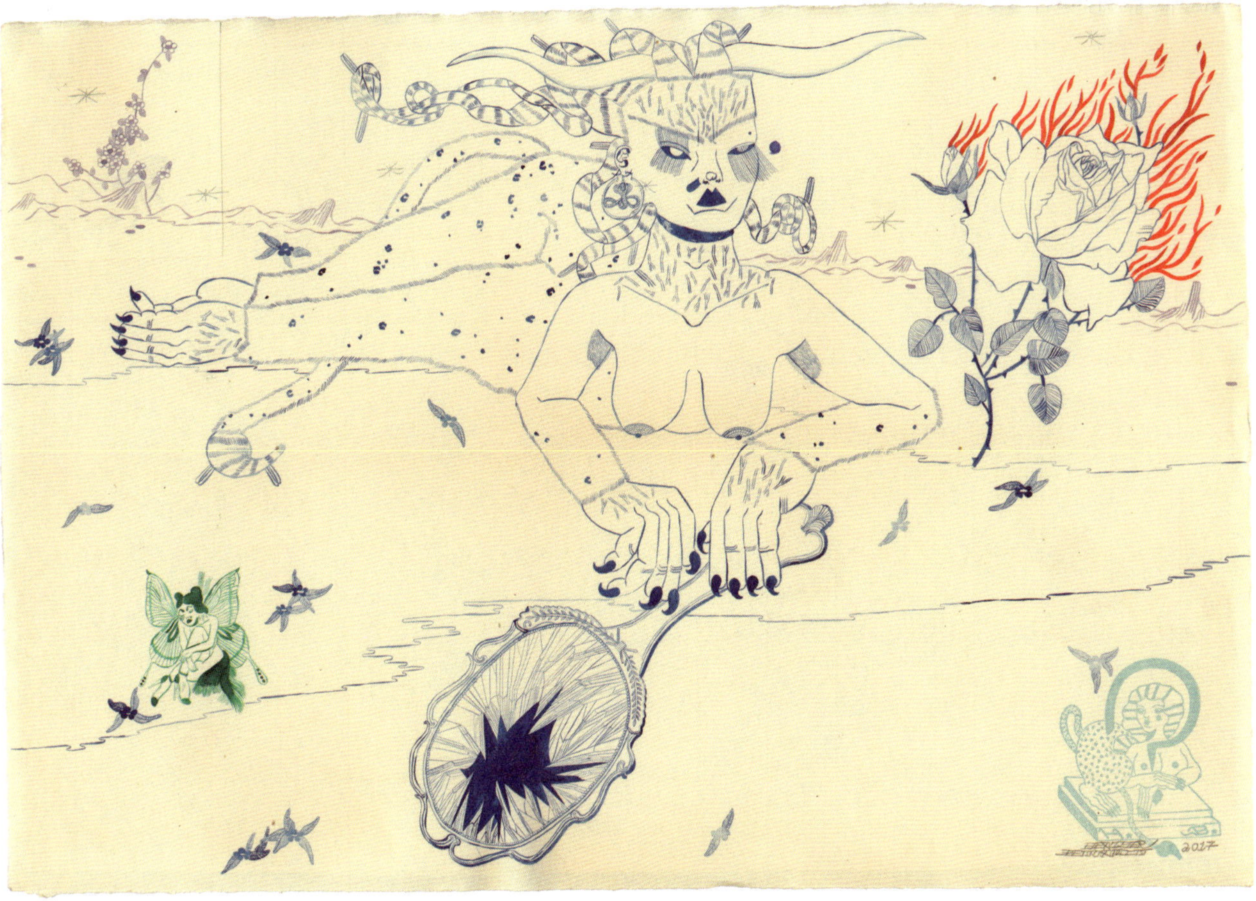

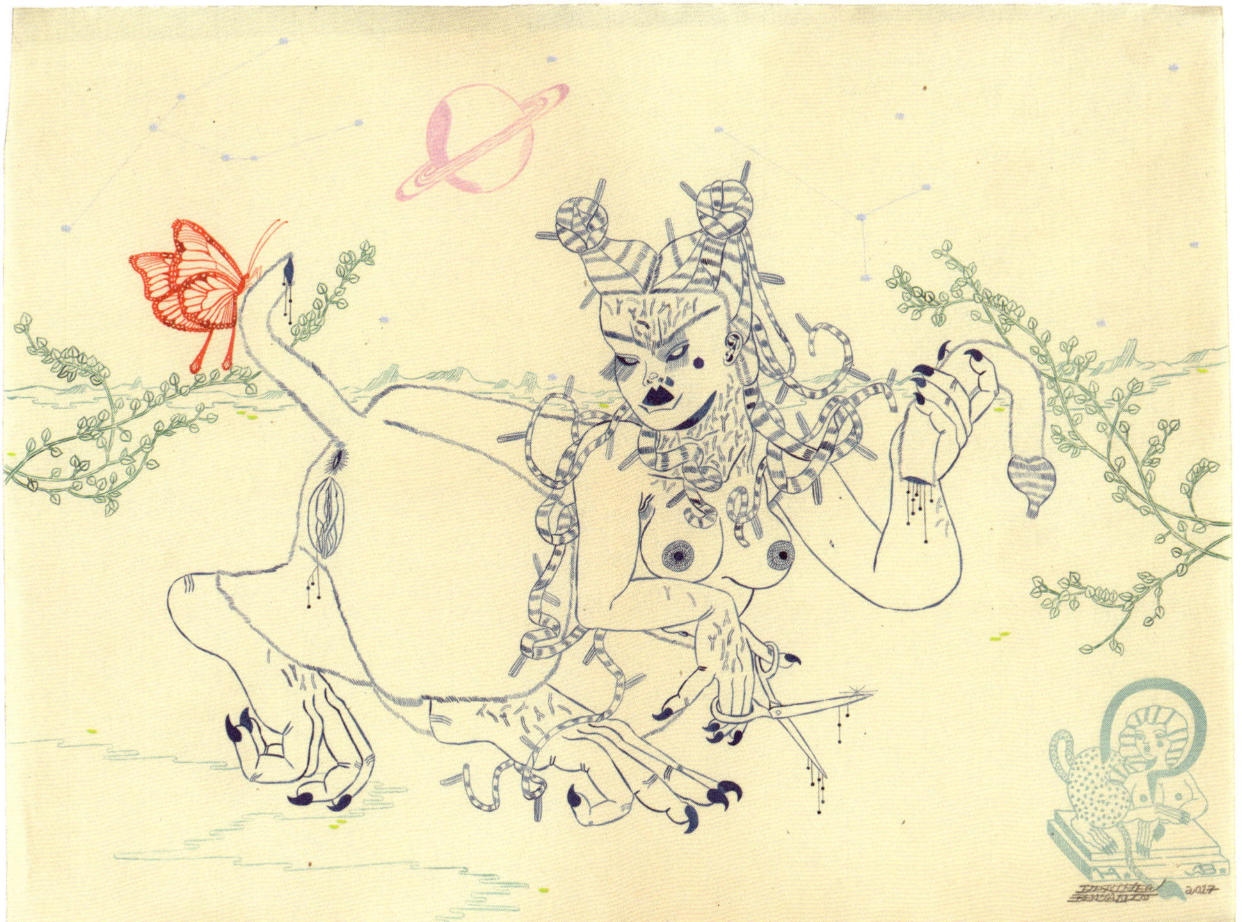

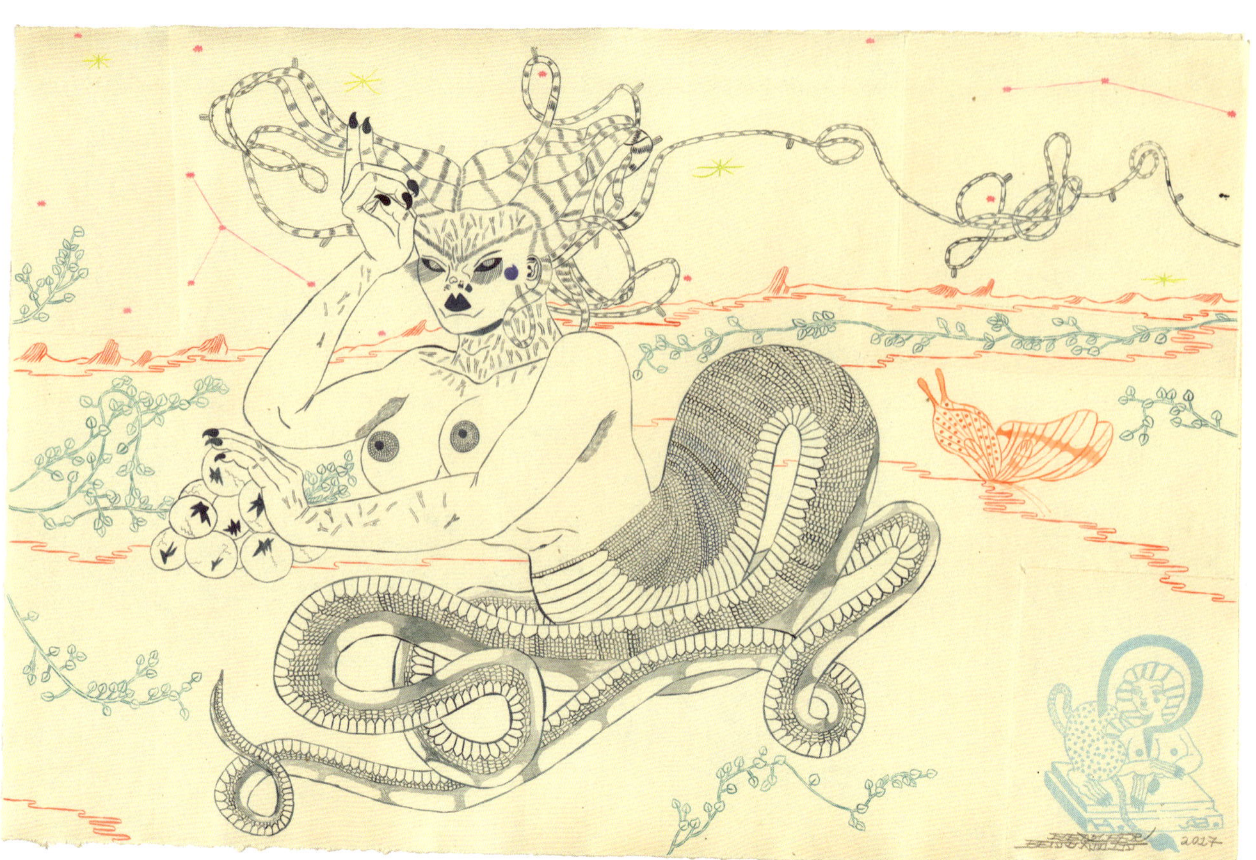

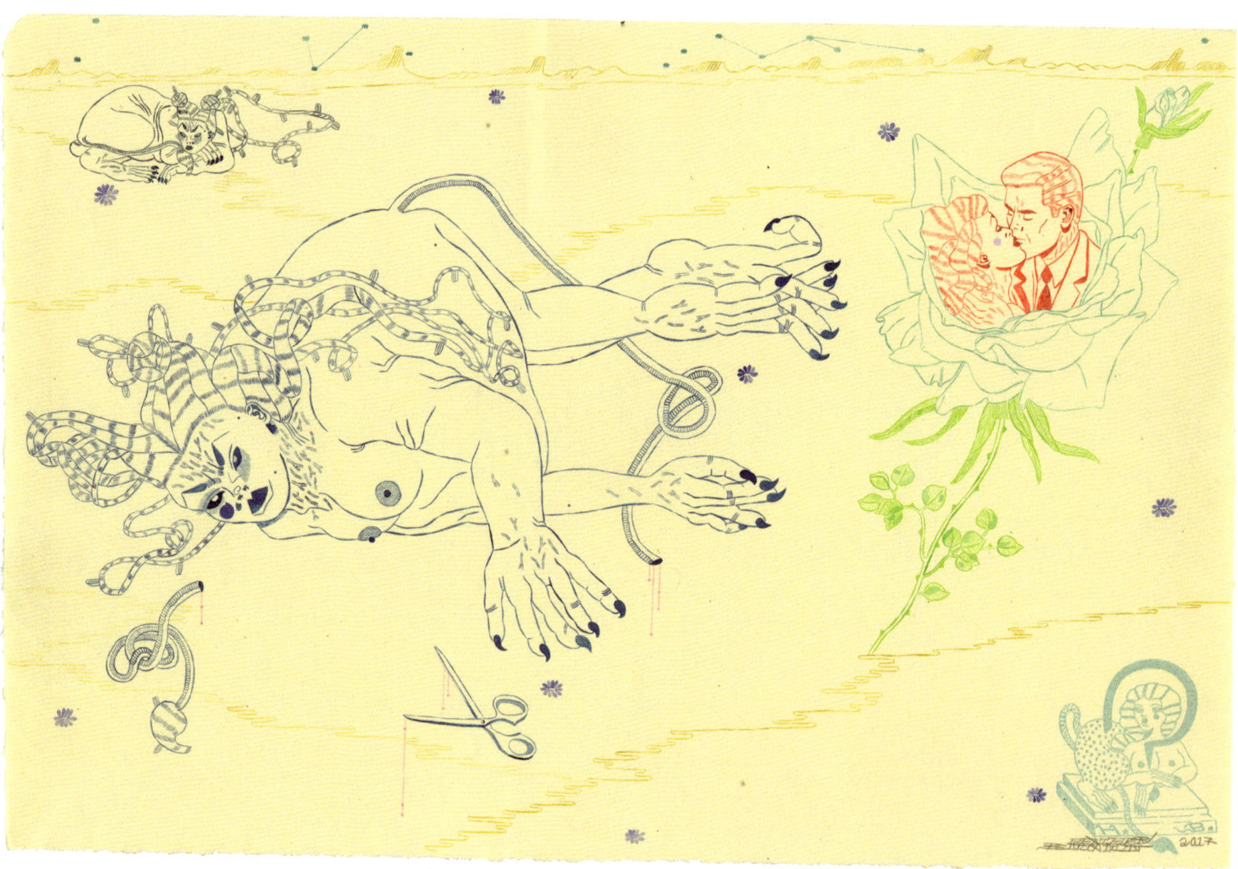

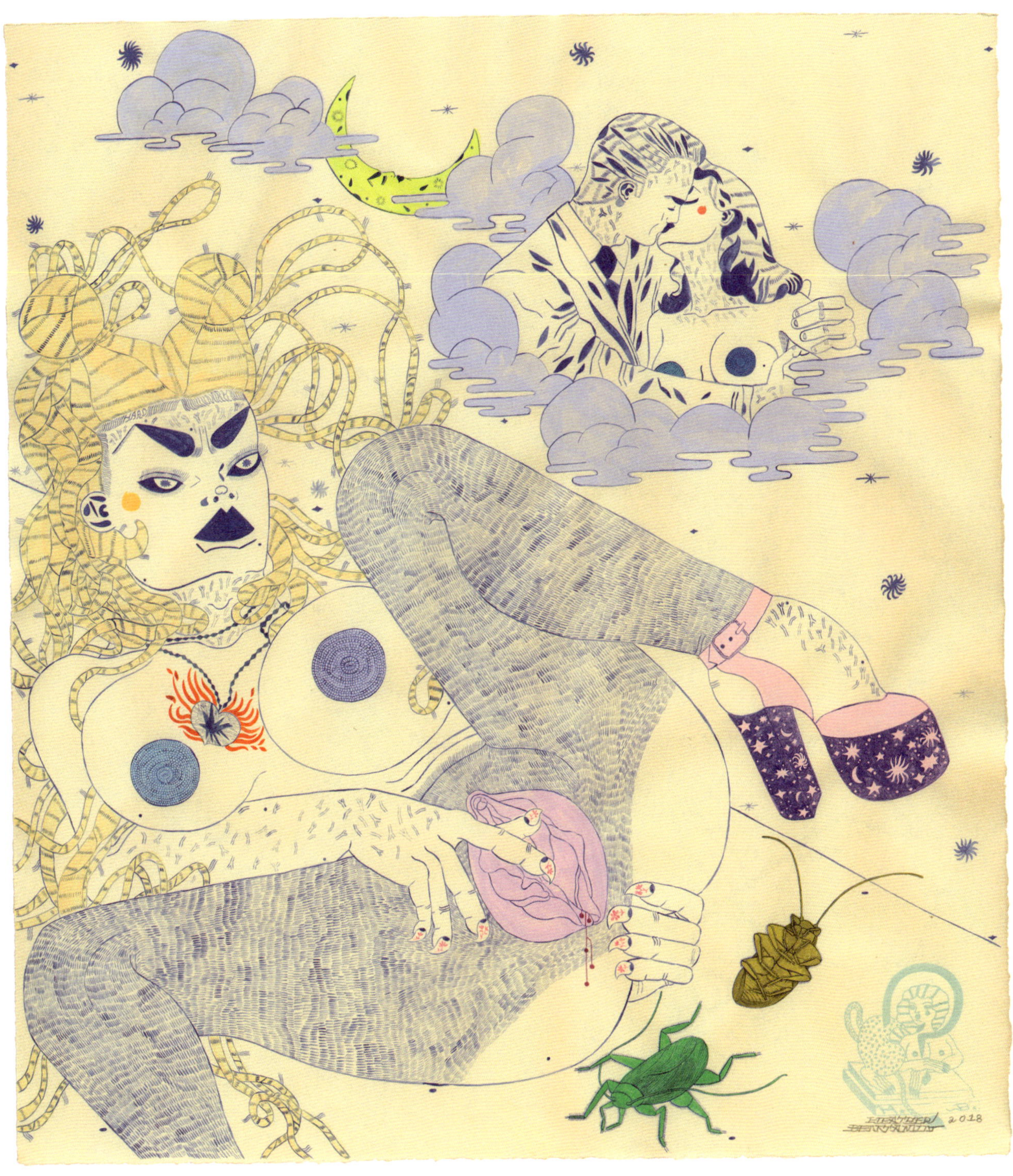

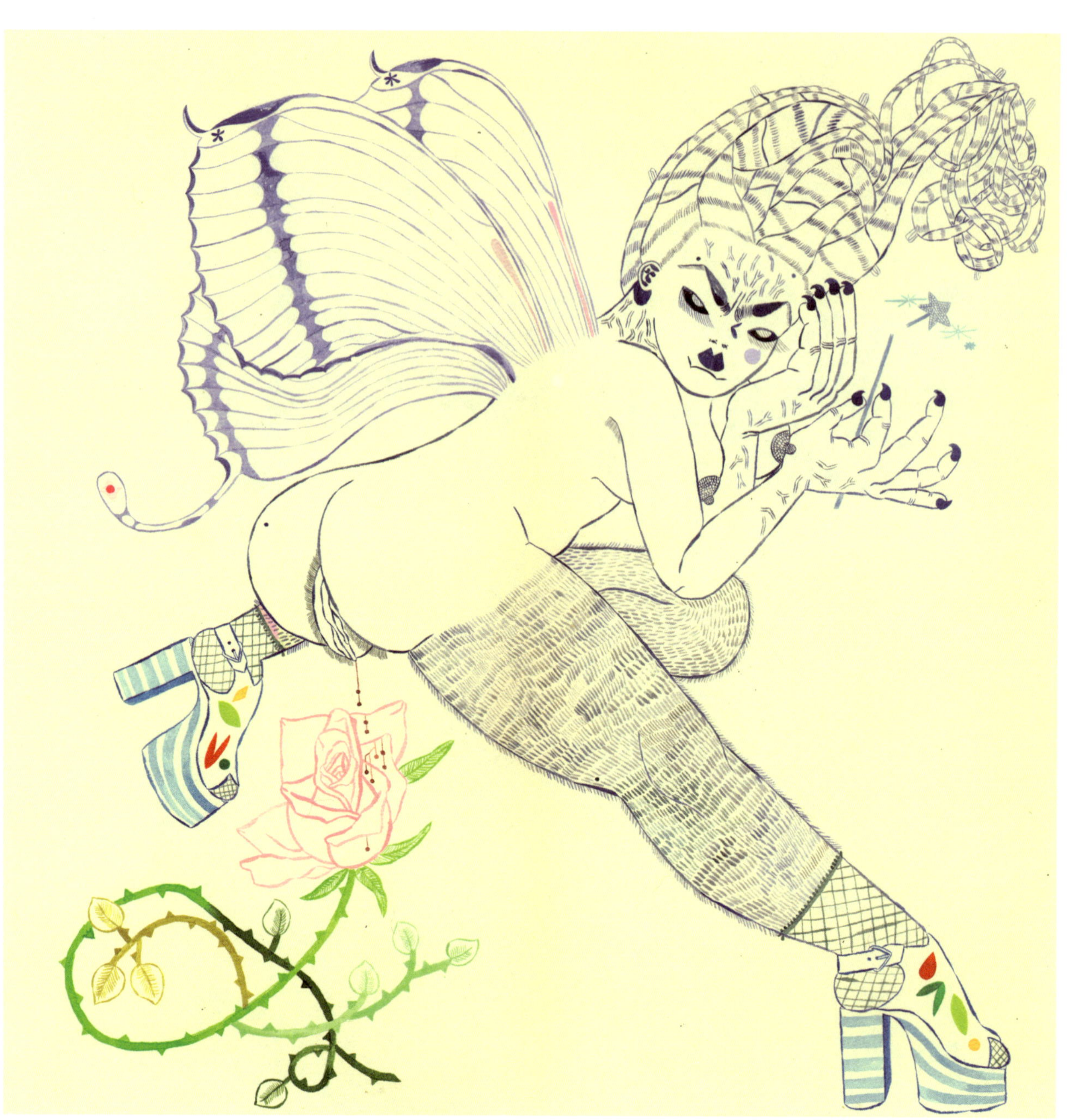

124